P9-AQX-759

WITHDRAWN

Gramley Library
Salem College
Winston-Salem, NC 27108

François Mauriac Revisited

Twayne's World Authors Series

French Literature

David O'Connell

Georgia State University

TWAS 844

François Mauriac about 1934 at his country home in Malagar.
Photo Courtesy of l'Université de Bordeaux.

François Mauriac Revisited

David O'Connell

Georgia State University

Twayne Publishers • New York
Maxwell Macmillan Canada • Toronto
Maxwell Macmillan International • New York • Oxford Singapore Sydney

Twayne's World Authors Series No. 844

François Mauriac Revisited
David O'Connell

Copyright © 1995 by Twayne Publishers
All rights reserved. No part of this book may be reproduced or transmitted in any form or by any means, electronic or mechanical, including photocopying, recording, or by any information storage and retrieval system, without permission in writing from the Publisher.

Twayne Publishers
Macmillan Publishing Company
866 Third Avenue
New York, New York 10022

Maxwell Macmillan Canada, Inc.
1200 Eglinton Avenue East
Suite 200
Don Mills, Ontario M3C 3N1

Macmillan Publishing Company is part of the Maxwell Communication Group of Companies.

Library of Congress Cataloging-in-Publication Data

O'Connell, David.
    François Mauriac revisited / by David O'Connell.
        p.   cm. — (Twayne's world authors series : TWAS 844. French literature)
    Includes bibliographical references and index.
    ISBN 0–8057–4302–2
    1. Mauriac, François, 1885–1970—Criticism and interpretation.
I. Title. II. Series.
PQ2625.A93Z688   1994
843'.912—dc20   94–27832
                                                                                                        CIP

The paper used in this publication meets the minimum requirements of American National Standard for Information Sciences—Permanence of Paper for Printed Library Materials. ANSI Z3948–1984. ⊚™

10 9 8 7 6 5 4 3 2 1 (hc)
10 9 8 7 6 5 4 3 2 1 (pb)

Printed in the United States of America

Alice Fennon O'Connell
1904–1990
in memoriam

Contents

Preface

Much has changed since Maxwell A. Smith published the original study of the life and work of François Mauriac in Twayne's World Authors Series (TWAS) in 1970. Since he had met and interviewed Mauriac shortly before the author's death, he was able to impart to his book that feeling of intimacy and understanding for his subject that can come only from such contact. But this apparent advantage can also be a double-edged sword, for the insights gleaned from personal contact are sometimes counterbalanced by a critical reluctance to see things with the same objectivity that one can apply to an author one has never met. There is also the disadvantage of time. A novelist's contributions to his culture must withstand the test of time if they are to be considered outstanding, and a quarter century ago, a sufficient amount of time had not yet elapsed to begin to measure and to fully appreciate the greatness of Mauriac's many literary achievements. Thus, time accounts for many of the differences between Maxwell Smith's study and my own. While Professor Smith had the opportunity to meet his subject, I did not begin my book until twenty years after Mauriac's death. Smith, however, did not have access to the primary source materials that Mauriac donated to the Bibliothèque Jacques Doucet in Paris, or to the other items that have surfaced and become available at the Bibliothèque Municipale de Bordeaux and the Harry Ransom Humanities Research Center at the University of Texas at Austin.

Professor Smith's natural modesty and courtliness, to which all who knew him can attest, led him to express the hope in his preface that being non-Catholic would not prevent him from giving Mauriac his due. His study, of course, succeeded in doing just that, as the thousands of students, teachers, and nonacademic readers who have benefited from his book over the years can attest.

In addition to my admiration for Smith's book, there is another reason for my alluding to him here. Although I was still a relatively young scholar when his book appeared, I would soon succeed him as the TWAS field editor for French literature. To the many books that Maxwell Smith edited in the series, I have added almost threescore. It is unusual for a monograph series to last so long and to be so successful; one of the reasons for this series' success has been that from the very beginning it benefited from Professor Smith's sure, guiding hand and good judgment. I am thus especially proud to be able to offer this revisited edition of *François Mauriac*.

David O'Connell
Georgia State University

Note on the References and Acknowledgments

There are two principal collections of Mauriac's complete works. The first was edited by Mauriac himself and published in 12 volumes by the Arthème Fayard publishing house during the years 1950–56. By this time Mauriac (b. 1885) was in his late sixties. He grouped his various works in clusters, mostly by genre, and wrote an introduction for each volume in which he expressed what he took to be their relative merits. These comments, made as he was approaching what for most people would be retirement age, are precious to a student of Mauriac's work. This edition, however, lacks a scholarly apparatus of any kind.

After Mauriac's death in 1970 the great majority of the manuscripts, typescripts, bound volumes, newspaper clippings, letters, and other memorabilia still in his possession were donated to the Bibliothèque Jacques Doucet in Paris. Serious critical and scholarly study of his work thus became possible. Gallimard then set about publishing Mauriac's *Oeuvres romanesques et théâtrales complètes* in four volumes (1978–85) in its Editions de la Pléiade series under the editorship of Professor Jacques Petit. After the untimely death of M. Petit, Professor François Durand published an edition of Mauriac's autobiographical writings in the Pléiade series under the title *Oeuvres autobiographiques* in 1990.

In addition, the Association des Amis de François Mauriac published the *Cahiers François Mauriac* for many years, while the French Department at the University of Bordeaux III has published over 30 issues of *Travaux du Centre d'Etudes et de Recherches sur François Mauriac*. The following abbreviations will be used in the text:

OC   *Oeuvres complètes*, 1950–56
ORTC   *Oeuvres romanesques et théâtrales complètes*
BN   *Bloc-Notes*
OA   *Oeuvres autobiographiques*
CFM   *Cahiers François Mauriac*
TCERFM   *Travaux du Centre d'Etudes et de Recherches sur François Mauriac*

Whenever possible, a quotation of a critical nature by Mauriac that is found in both the OC and the ORTC will be so indicated. Generally, however, citations from the works themselves are provided only for the

ORTC, which is much more readily available than the long out-of-print *OC*.

Finally, all translations provided herein are my own.

A scholar incurs many debts in carrying out an investigation like the one that lies behind the present volume. I would like to acknowledge mine.

At Georgia State University I am indebted to the friendly and hard-working staff of the Interlibrary Loan Department, especially Margie Patterson and Jane Dobson, who have tracked down so many Mauriac-related items for me over the last few years. Their patience, good cheer, and zeal are especially appreciated. I would also like to record my grati-tude to Deans Robert Arrington and Ahmed Abdelal of the College of Arts and Sciences for their support of this project in a number of ways. To my colleagues and friends who read the manuscript and offered many valuable suggestions, Professors Harold Dickerson, James Murray, and Richard Firda, I am particularly grateful. Thanks also go to Professor Gerard Pendrick. Finally, Grace Casnel, Rickie Wesbrooks, and Paul Marshall from the departmental staff made invaluable contributions in producing the final typescript.

In Paris, I am indebted to M. François Chapon, Curator of the Bibliothèque Jacques Doucet, who introduced me to its many treasures, as well as to M. Claude Mauriac and to M. and Mme Jean Mauriac, who have all been very helpful. I have also benefited from the thoughtful advice of Professor Jean Touzot of the University of Paris–Sorbonne.

In Bordeaux, Professors Jacques Monférier and Bernard Cocula of the University of Bordeaux III have opened many doors for me, not only in that great city, but also at Malagar and Saint-Symphorien. It is thanks to them that I have gained an appreciation of the physical realities of "Mauriac country." I express my gratitude to them for their help and support. I would also like to thank Linda Ashton, Assistant Curator of the Harry Ransom Humanities Research Center at the University of Texas at Austin for her help and guidance during my visit to consult the Center's interesting Mauriac collection.

Finally, special and enormous thanks must go to my ever-patient and understanding wife and children for their unfailing support, and for cre-ating such a positive work environment. Without them, this project would never have been brought to completion.

Chronology

1885	François Mauriac born in Bordeaux, October 11.
1887	Death of father, Jean-Paul Mauriac, June 11.
1892	October, enters Marianite school, the Collège Sainte-Marie, where the religious upbringing received at home from his mother and grandmother is reinforced.
1898	Enters Marianite Collège, Grand Lebrun.
1901–1902	Rhetoric class with l'Abbé Péquignot. Establishes key friendship with André Lacaze, a future priest.
1904–1905	Obtains "licence" degree, University of Bordeaux.
1907	In September, arrives in Paris to prepare for the Ecole des Chartes.
1908	In November, enrolls at the Ecole des Chartes with the intention of pursuing graduate studies to become an archivist.
1909	Withdraws from school to devote himself to literature. Publishes his first book, *Les Mains jointes,* a collection of poems.
1910	Praised in a newspaper review by the writer and intellectual Maurice Barrès, to whom he had sent a copy of his first volume of poetry.
1913	Marriage to Jeanne Lafon. First novel, *L'Enfant chargé de chaînes,* is published by Grasset.
1914	Birth of first son, Claude. Publication of second novel, *La Robe prétexte.*
1914–1917	Deferred from military service for health reasons, he volunteers for the ambulance corps and serves at the front and at Salonika. Hospitalized with fever; discharged for medical reasons.
1917	Birth of first daughter, Claire.
1919	Birth of second daughter, Luce.

1920   Third novel, *La Chair et le sang,* appears.

1921   Publication of fourth novel, *Préséances.*

1922   Great success and instant fame with the publication of
                Le Baiser au lépreux, his fifth novel.

1924   Birth of his fourth child, Jean.

1922–1927   Period of great creative activity: publication of the nov-
                els *Genitrix* (1923), *Le Fleuve de feu* (1923), *Le Désert de
                l'amour* (1925), and his first masterpiece, *Thérèse
                Desqueyroux* (1927).

1927–1930   Undergoes severe psychological and religious crisis,
                which includes a religious "conversion" in late 1928.
                Publication of the novel *Destins,* 1928.

1930   End of personal crisis. Publication of *Ce qui était perdu,*
                his first "Catholic novel."

1931   Moves in January to 19, avenue Théophile-Gautier,
                where he will live for the next 40 years.

1932   Publication of the novel *Le Noeud de vipères,* widely
                hailed as his second masterpiece and his greatest
                Catholic novel. Severe illness and throat operation.

1933   Election to the French Academy. Publication of *Le
                Mystère Frontenac,* an autobiographical novel in which
                he pays an affectionate tribute to his family. Begins to
                write regularly for the right-wing paper *L'Echo de Paris.*

1935   Publication of the novel *La Fin de la nuit.*

1936   Publication of the novel *Les Anges noirs* and the biogra-
                phy *Vie de Jésus.*

1937   Beginning of his journalistic campaign against
                Mussolini and Franco, which heralds his abandonment
                of the right and his future support of left and center-
                left political causes.

1937   Great success of *Asmodée,* his first play, at the Théâtre
                Français.

1939   Publication of the novel *Les Chemins de la mer.*

1940   *Sang d'Atys,* his major collection of poetry, is published
                in May, but barely noticed because of the war.

1941   Publication of the novel *La Pharisienne,* which reaches a

	wide public and is considered by many readers to be a "roman de l'Occupation."
1943	Publication of important Allied propaganda pamphlet, *Le Cahier noir,* by the underground press, under the pseudonym Forez, making Mauriac one of the foremost writers of the Resistance.
1944	Resumption of journalistic activity and defense of those accused of collaboration with the enemy. Personal meeting with de Gaulle.
1945–1952	Return to the theater with *Les Mal-Aimés* (1945), *Passage du Malin* (1947), and *Le Feu sur la terre* (1950). Publication of two novels, *Le Sagouin* (1951) and *Galigaï* (1952).
1952	Receives the Nobel Prize for Literature.
1954	Publication of the novel *L'Agneau.*
1955	Initiates his weekly "Bloc-Notes" column for *L'Express* from October 1955 to April 1961, after which he publishes it in *Le Figaro Littéraire* until his death
1958–1962	Journalistic support of de Gaulle's policy of independence for Algeria, France's oldest colony.
1959	Publication of *Mémoires intérieurs,* an intellectual autobiography.
1962	Publishes *Ce que je crois,* which contains his thoughts on religious matters.
1965	Eightieth birthday commemorated by the dedication of a complete issue of *Le Figaro Littéraire* to him. He is also honored by the city of Bordeaux on this occasion.
1965–1967	Continuation of his memoirs with *Nouveaux Memoires intérieurs* (1965) and *Mémoires politiques* (1967).
1969	Publication of *Un adolescent d'autrefois,* his last novel.
1970	Dies on 1 September, as a result of complications after a fall earlier in the year. State funeral at Notre Dame Cathedral.

Chapter One

The Man and the Writer

François Mauriac Today

François Mauriac's place among major French writers of the twentieth century seems secure. Since his death in 1970 at the age of 85, study of his life and work has steadily increased in both volume and quality. This is due in part to the fact that Mauriac bequeathed virtually all the private papers in his possession to the Bibliothèque Jacques Doucet in Paris. There scholars can find in one place most of his letters and, with few exceptions, the manuscripts, typescripts, and printed texts of virtually all his books and articles. In the years since Mauriac's death, a surprising number of letters and manuscripts have appeared on the auction market. The Bibliothèque Municipale de Bordeaux bids aggressively for such texts and can boast of having the second largest collection of Mauriac materials. In the United States, the Harry Ransom Humanities Research Center at the University of Texas at Austin has also shown interest in such Mauriac papers, their most important holding being the manuscript of *Thérèse Desqueyroux*.

The study of Mauriac's work is encouraged by the Mauriac Research Center at the University of Bordeaux III, which organizes colloquia devoted to his work and publishes a journal, *Les Travaux du Centre d'Etudes et de Recherches sur François Mauriac,* which is devoted exclusively to articles about Mauriac. Likewise, the Mauriac Foundation (Le Centre François Mauriac de Malagar), which is housed in his ancestral home, Malagar, about 40 miles from Bordeaux in the town of Saint-Maixant, where he wrote so many of his novels, also sponsors an annual colloquium, whose proceedings are published in an annual volume, *Les Cahiers de Malagar.* Finally, the recently established Société Internationale des Etudes Mauriaciennes is also based in Bordeaux. It publishes a journal called *Nouveaux Cahiers François Mauriac.* Paris, not to be outdone by its provincial rival, is the home of the Association Internationale des Amis de François Mauriac. This organization sponsors an annual colloquium and a journal, *Mauriac et Son Temps,* in addition to other activities. One recent success worth mentioning is the 1990 installation of a statue of Mauriac in the place Alphonse-Deville, at the intersection of rue du Cherche-Midi and boulevard Raspail. This monument is not only a fitting supplement to the commemorative plaque affixed to the outside wall of the apartment building at 19, avenue Théophile-Gautier (where Mauriac lived for the last four decades of his life), but also testimony to the widespread belief in his work's enduring value. It can be said that, in the quarter century since his death, François Mauriac has become "institutionalized," in the sense that his life and work have become fully integrated into the ongoing process that we call French culture.

It is also worth noting that Mauriac's novels continue to appeal to young people in France, who quite often become acquainted with Mauriac when they read various short novels as a part of the secondary school "programme." Interestingly, a 1989 public opinion poll taken among French secondary school teachers confirmed that Mauriac, along with Camus, Sartre, and Ionesco, still ranks among the most widely read writers in French secondary schools.[1] Le Sagouin is a particular favorite on the secondary level. Mauriac's unique style is very accessible to young readers, who also perhaps readily identify with the many teenagers and young adults presented in his novels. Further proof of Mauriac's enduring appeal to a vast reading public is provided by statistics relating to sales of his novels in the well-known Livre de Poche paperback series. According to these figures, six of his novels have sold a total of more than seven million copies, a truly remarkable figure for a serious writer.[2]

In the pages that follow I shall cover what I consider to be the successes and occasional failures of Mauriac's career as a writer and man of letters. His influence at home and abroad was enormous during his lifetime and has remained so since his death. As no "Catholic writer" of comparable stature has emerged to replace him, his achievement looms even larger.

Mauriac: A Writer with a "Différence"

When François Mauriac received the Nobel Prize for literature in 1952—when he was 67 years old—the prize committee noted that the action of Mauriac's novels is almost always set in the southwest of France, his native Aquitaine region, and that geographical setting is a major factor in his fiction. Born in Bordeaux on 11 October 1885, Mauriac grew up in that city, but made frequent visits to family properties located outside of town on either side of the Garonne River. This magnificent river winds its way in a northeasterly direction and serves as a boundary between the rolling hills covered with grapevines to the north and, not far beyond the riverbanks on the south, that vast plain called "les Landes," a seemingly endless pine forest extending for hundreds of square miles toward the Pyrenees. On the fringe of les Landes, on a property called Johanet, just outside the village of Saint-Symphorien, stands the cavernous red brick, fin de siècle chalet that Mauriac's father built in the 1890s. It is this structure that fed Mauriac's imagination once he became a writer and that became the setting for his novels. On the other side of the Garonne, just outside the small town of Saint-Maixant, on a hilltop offering a splendid view of the river below and flanked by grapevines on the gentle slopes to either side, is situated the other family property, Malagar, where Mauriac did most of his writing when not in Paris. This old house, dating back to the eighteenth century and located about 18 miles northwest of Saint-Symphorien, had originally belonged to a religious order. The upper story, one large open dormitory room, which was used as sleeping quarters for monks, testifies even to this day to its original purpose. Seized by anticlerical revolutionaries as *biens nationaux* (national property) during the French Revolution, the house was acquired in 1843 by Mauriac's paternal great-grandfather Jean. Here Mauriac spent his vacations during most of his life. The home, preserved just as it was on the day he died, has become the seat of the Mauriac Foundation.[3]

The juxtaposition of Mauriac's two family houses can be taken as a symbol of the duality that a reader may discover in many aspects of his life and work. The different worlds that the houses represent is reminiscent of Proust's titular *côtés,* or sides of life—that of Swann and that of the Guermantes—, which came to represent for him different fields of authorial experience. Although a man of intense personal piety, Mauriac tended to display in his work more than an idle interest in sins of the flesh. A son of the *grande bourgeoisie* who was able to support his wife and four children thanks mainly to his inherited wealth (although it was augmented by income from his books and newspaper columns), he was nonetheless concerned (especially after 1937) with social justice for those less well off. An intellectual disciple of Charles Maurras and the Action Française movement (which was known for its desire to see the monarchy restored and for its hostility to Republicans, Jews, and Freemasons, whom it held responsible for the French Revolution), Mauriac from the mid-1930s onward was nonetheless a devoted supporter of Jews and Jewish causes.

This duality is also found in his family, from his earliest childhood. Although Mauriac was only 20 months old when his father died at age 35, the Voltairean, freethinking, Republican, and anticlerical legacy of the Mauriac side of his family was something of which he was very much aware. This so-called Republican tradition in French life was something that the maternal side of his family, as well as their friends and acquaintances—indeed, their whole Catholic social milieu—labeled as the enemy. The traditional religious piety of his mother, Claire (née Coiffard), was reinforced by family support of the political parties of the traditional French Right. In such a family, the French Revolution, and the various forms of Republican government that it spawned in the intervening century, were usually considered to have been disastrous for France. After her husband's death, Claire was left alone with five children, François the youngest. Moving in for a time with her own mother, she sent her children to Catholic schools, where political convictions inculcated at home could be reinforced.

In the early years of the pontificate of Leo XIII (1878–1903), French Catholics had been encouraged by the Pope himself to renounce their suspicions about the parliamentary system and to give their support to the Republican form of government. A first encyclical, *Nobilissima Gallorum Gens,* was addressed to the French bishops in 1884, while a second, written in French and entitled *Au milieu des sollicitudes,* was addressed to all French Catholics. This policy of *ralliement* came to an end with the Dreyfus Affair, the great political battle of the era, which took place during Mauriac's formative years. Dreyfus, a captain of Jewish extraction in the French Army, had been accused of passing secrets to German agents in Paris. A military court found him guilty in 1894. He was imprisoned on Devil's Island in French Guyana. Catholics and Republicans generally took opposing sides in the great national debate that ensued about the guilt or innocence of Dreyfus. On the Catholic side, the Ligue de la Patrie Française argued that the guilty verdict should not be overturned since the honor of the army was at stake. Whether Dreyfus was actually guilty was beside the point—given the traditional antisemitism of the Catholic parties, Dreyfus *had* to be guilty because he was a Jew. Meanwhile, on the Republican side, the Ligue des Droits de l'Homme advocated dismissal of all charges. The daily newspaper *La Croix,* run by the Assumptionist religious order, became a strong advocate of the Catholic position, making many enemies in the process. To the *dreyfusards,* the editor/priests of this newspaper were emblematic of the power of the clergy, which they took to be unenlightened and reactionary. When the anticlerical parties assumed power in 1899, which was also the year in which Dreyfus was pardoned, revenge was one of the principal items on their political agenda. Thus, it came as no surprise that in 1901 a bill was introduced in Parliament to outlaw religious orders in France. But this was only the beginning, for by 1905, while Emile Combes was in power, Parliament would formally vote in the separation of church and state. In doing so, the anticlerical parties intended to punish the church for its political activities during the preceding decade.[4]

Discussion of these emotionally charged events was an essential part of growing up for Mauriac, and in his family support of the church was unquestioned. Enemies of the church were enemies of the family. Thus, Emile Zola, the novelist and journalist who had defended Dreyfus and who had thereby earned almost saintly status among French Republicans, was despised in Claire Mauriac's house. As a sign of this disapproval, family members routinely referred to the chamber pot in each bedroom as "le zola." Mauriac grew up as an *anti-dreyfusard* and for the rest of his life was of an essentially conservative temperament. But while he remained faithful to his origins, he was also independent-minded. Thus, later in life, he would often take political positions to which those in his social milieu took violent exception. This dichotomy between France's two great traditions, Catholic and conservative on the one hand, and anticlerical and Republican on the other, became internalized by Mauriac to such an extent that representatives of each of these traditions appear in virtually all his novels.

During these years, Louis Mauriac, the brother of Claire's deceased husband, served as a guardian for the children and took a very active interest in their well-being. His political opinions seem to have been resolutely Republican and anticlerical. Although he looked after financial matters, it was Claire Mauriac who, with her mother's help, raised the children. Prudish, pietistic, authoritarian, convinced that good could come only to the virtuous, and especially concerned about sins of the flesh, she left an indelible mark upon her youngest child. His migration to Paris as a young man was as much to escape from his mother as to set out upon a literary career. The creative tension between the freethinking Mauriac side of the family and the traditional Catholic side, represented in particular by his mother, is at the heart of Mauriac's life, and is reflected again and again in his fiction. This experience of family life as a child also led to the creation of specific characters. Louis Mauriac, his uncle, is transposed as Xavier Frontenac in Le Mystère Frontenac (1933), (*The*

Frontenacs, 1961), and his mother's example is the inspiration for Brigitte
Pian in *La Pharisienne* (1941), (*Woman of the Pharisees,* 1946), as well as
several other similar characters.

Recent scholarship indicates that Mauriac's desire to express himself
in writing was probably inherited from his father. Jean-Paul Mauriac was
actively interested in literary questions as a boy, but despite these interests he was withdrawn from the lycée by his father and groomed to take
over the family business. Jean-Paul Mauriac's diary, selected passages
from which were published in 1974, reveals a man striving to express
himself in limpid prose, a man who, like François, admired Baudelaire
and also wrote poetry.[5] Mauriac would later be tempted to wonder what
his life would have been like if it had been his mother and not his father
who had died prematurely. If he had been raised by an agnostic and anticlerical father, it is doubtful that he would have become France's fore-
most twentieth-century Catholic writer and a Nobel laureate.

Like Alain Gajac, the hero of his last novel, *Un Adolescent d'autrefois*
(1969) (*Maltaverne,* 1970), Mauriac was "différent" from other children, both at home and in school.[6] Maudlin, easily provoked to tears,
and not much given to the rough play of other boys of his age, he
remained apart, spending large amounts of time by himself, studying,
daydreaming, and reading. In fact, even in childhood, literature was
already both his personal passion and his principal means of escape and
diversion.

At the age of four he was injured while playing with his brother Jean.
A whip tipped with a sliver of steel, a pretext for a game, turned into
something else when the steel tip lodged in young François's left eyelid.
He would be deformed for the rest of his life, and, to make matters
worse, his older brothers pinned on him the nickname "Coco Bel-Oeil,"
the name of one of the lighthouses at the end of the Gironde estuary.
Mauriac's brother Pierre gives a good summary of exactly how and to
what degree François was different from the other youngsters in his
social milieu:

> He couldn't play any sport. Every attempt was a setback. I recall the
> few lessons in horseback riding that he took in keeping with a family
> tradition (they put us in the saddle at age 10): the laughter of his
> cousins got the better of his good intentions. On the tennis court he was
> as ill at ease as in horsemanship. He hated going in the ocean and I real-
> ly think he never learned how to swim. He didn't fish or hunt, never did
> more than a few meters on a bicycle and never held the wheel of a car.
> But then again, he was never pushed aside, stepped on, nor conquered,

as he had predicted. Other arms brought him the victory which, I believe, he never doubted would be his.[7]

This difference that Mauriac felt viscerally from earliest childhood would become, as his brother Pierre so clearly indicates, his principal source of strength as a writer and an intellectual.

The Early Years

Mauriac's idyllic childhood with his mother and grandmother ended rather abruptly when he was placed in a rigorous Catholic school directed by the Marianite fathers: "My awareness of unhappiness dates from the age of 7 when I entered first grade with the Marianite Fathers."[8] Enforced attendance at religious ceremonies and intense religious indoctrination would characterize his life for about the next 10 years. The teaching in Catholic schools that he attended during these years, and in fact up to the time of the Second Vatican Council, was still characterized by a strong Jansenist element. According to this view of man, which dates back to the seventeenth-century French thinker Jansenius, the exercise of the human will is insufficient to gain salvation. This school of thought also held that God has no obligation to offer divine grace to the human soul, even to someone who asks for it. The net effect of this view, which many historians of religion have likened to Calvinism, was the belief that each individual is predestined by God to either heaven or hell and that, even with grace (which in any case can only be an arbitrary gift of God and not something that the individual soul deserves to receive), the human will is seriously weakened. This doctrine had been condemned by the church in the seventeenth century,[9] but had still managed to survive over the years in a somewhat different form and was still quite powerful in the Catholic schools that Mauriac attended as a boy. Since, according to this view, all human beings, because of their sinful nature, were guilty of causing the suffering and death of Christ, and since the temptation to commit sin existed on all sides, individual conduct had to be minutely regulated.

In later years Mauriac would make negative comments about this early training, while still claiming that the good outweighed the bad. Nonetheless, the indoctrination left an indelible mark on him. He especially disliked the lugubrious aspects of his Jansenist upbringing—for instance, children meditating on Jesus' crown of thorns and the ordeal of crucifixion. He also had reservations about the taboos relating to the human body, according to which any kind of sexual pleasure, even between spouses, was to be strongly discouraged. His mother had especially strong feelings along these lines. Finally, the active practice of pharisaism, in which pious practice was regulated to within a centimeter, also upset him. For instance, since life according to the Jansenist world-view was best lived if it followed a prescibed set of formulas, any variance from the declared and official norm could be considered a serious sin. Thus, swallowing even a drop of water while brushing one's teeth in the morning could constitute the breaking of one's fast, and would thus make the reception of Holy Communion a horrible sacrilege instead of a sacramental occasion of grace. One particularly bittersweet description of these early years, in which Mauriac tries to balance the good with the bad, appeared in the memoirs published shortly before his death: "To tell the truth, if I recounted my childhood, I could easily furnish a darker or a brighter version: all I'd have to do is change the lighting" (*OA*, 679).[10] By this time it was clear that the education he had received as a boy belonged to another age and seemed terribly out-of-date. Yet it is difficult to imagine Mauriac becoming the novelist he was without this upbringing.

At the age of 12 Mauriac entered the Marianite secondary school, Collège Grand-Lebrun, located on the outskirts of Bordeaux. It was here that his first intellectual and artistic awakenings took place. He received prizes year after year for finishing at or near the top of his class in a variety of subjects, but his greatest distinction was in French composition. At Grand-Lebrun the teacher who had the most powerful effect on him was the Abbé Péquignot (in 1901–2), while his closest friend, from whom he would learn much, was André Lacaze. During the key years from the age of 10, exiting childhood, to the age of 20, on the threshold of adulthood, these two friends were inseparable. As a young man Lacaze was intent on making a synthesis of Christian faith and science. Although he became a priest and spent the rest of his life in Paris, where he remained in contact with Mauriac, it was the early years when their relationship was closest. Whereas young Mauriac's tastes tended exclusively toward literature, Lacaze shared with him his own passion: Catholic philosophy. As an avid reader of liberal Catholic thinkers like the Abbé Laberthonnière, Maurice Blondel, and the Abbé Loisy, whose works were placed on the *Index of Forbidden Books* in 1903, Lacaze introduced Mauriac to a vast world of ideas that would serve as a backdrop later on for his work as a novelist.[11] Thanks in part to the influence of André Lacaze, Mauriac began to see beyond the closed world of school and family and to become in certain respects what we would call today a "liberal" Catholic. Lacaze served as a catalyst in this transformation, for he presented new concepts to Mauriac that the future novelist probably would not have readily explored or understood on his own. Later, after Lacaze had become a priest, his claim that his vocation had been partly inspired by Mauriac's insistence that he was too physically ugly to attract a possible mate, raises questions about their relationship.[12] Mauriac would later transpose Lacaze into the character Maryan in the short story "Le Démon de la connaissance" (1929) (The demon of understanding) and, at the end of his life and four years after the death of Lacaze, he would create a portrait of his friend's intellectual quest in the character of André Donzac of *Un Adolescent d'autrefois*. This work remains a touching reminder of the importance of this pivotal friendship during the critical years of his late adolescence.

Young Mauriac failed in his first two attempts to pass the *baccalauréat* exam. An attack of pleurisy, which required that he spend several weeks in Switzerland, did not help matters. Finally, on the third try, in 1903 he passed. It was about this time that Mauriac became interested in the *Sillon* (Furrow) movement led by Marc Sangnier, a quasi-mystical lay reformer who sought, among other things, to free the church of its bureaucratic and hierarchical apparatus by introducing democratic reforms. Seeking to renew the church from within by reaching out to the poor and neglected in society and by appealing to what there was of a social conscience among bourgeois Catholics, Sangnier was doomed to fail. Yet, for a year or so, during 1905–6, Mauriac was a member of the movement, attending its local meetings and selling its newspaper in the streets.[13] When Sangnier came to Bordeaux, Mauriac opened the family house in Langon to members of the *Sillon* for meetings, and even Sangnier himself spent a night there. This episode in Mauriac's process of maturation is recounted, and only thinly transposed, in his first and somewhat flawed novel, *L'Enfant chargé de chaînes* (1913) (*Young Man in Chains,* 1963). Although his flirtation with the *Sillon* as such was short-lived, and despite the fact that the movement was condemned in a papal letter to French bishops in 1910 and disbanded shortly thereafter, we get an early glimpse here of that "différence" that would characterize Mauriac later on. He was committed to the Catholic faith, yet was alienated by certain aspects of the church as an institution. He generally accepted church doctrine, but sought a purer and more spontaneous form of Catholicism that would be somewhat more democratic in spirit and that would also limit the influence of the rich and powerful. Late in life he would claim that he had always remained faithful to this primary commitment to socially conscious Catholicism: "I established my political position early, in the days of the *Sillon* movement, and never budged after that" (*OA*, 818). While it is true that in his novels he ridiculed the selfishness and social myopia of French Catholics of the upper strata of the bourgeoisie and supported the anti-Nazi political agenda for most of the time between 1937 and 1945 (even if it meant working closely with the Communists) Mauriac was never a leftist in any true sense of the term. His admiration for the right-wing nationalist Charles Maurras, his image as an enfant terrible of the right-wing press until the middle 1930s, his courting of right-wing men of letters (without whose votes he never would have been elected to the French Academy in 1933), his cautious wait-and-see attitude about the Vichy government in 1940, and his uncritical support of de Gaulle after 1958 are just a few indications that, although Mauriac in his heart sympathized with the downtrodden and dispossessed, he always had a strong sense of order and was essentially a conservative by nature.

During the last three years that he spent in Bordeaux, 1903–6, Mauriac also took his *licence* degree at the university. When he left home in September 1906, it was to enroll in Paris at the prestigious Ecole des Chartes, the elite institution that trains France's archivists. In retrospect, we have to wonder what Mauriac's mother thought of such a career plan for her son. Did she really believe, given his sensitive, poetic temperament, that he was meant to spend the rest of his life in dusty archives? Or did she understand that this was merely a means for him to escape from Bordeaux? After failing the entrance exam on the first attempt, Mauriac was finally admitted and began taking classes in the fall of 1908. But it did not take long for him to falter as a student, for his true interests lay elsewhere. He was beginning to make important contacts in the literary world, all the while working on his first collection of poems, which would be published in November 1909 under the title *Les Mains jointes* (Joined hands). Thus it should come as no surprise to us, as it apparently was not to his mother, either, that he would drop out of the Ecole des Chartes. Seated at a table in a bar called the Palace des Champs-Elysées, hardly a place we would expect to find a bookworm destined for a career as an archivist, he wrote his letter of resignation at Easter 1909. The high life on the Right Bank was clearly more important than the less exciting scholarly attractions held out by the Left Bank. When he broke the news to his mother in a letter, she did not take all too badly his plans to embark on a career as a writer. We do not know whether Claire Mauriac was surprised by this turn of events, but in not registering any significant display of disapproval, she seems to have been giving François her blessing. She understood that she had to let him go.[14]

Nothing helps the launching of a literary career quite like the support of a powerful established writer. It is even better when one is "discovered" by such an establishment figure. Mauriac published *Les Mains jointes* in November 1909 at his own expense: 500 francs. His publisher, Charles Caillard, had barely any experience in publishing; in fact, Mauriac's book was the first one to appear under the imprint Temps Présent, an offshoot of a literary review of the same name, also edited by Caillard. As luck would have it, a copy was sent to Maurice Barrès, a prominent rightist intellectual of the day, member of Parliament, novelist, and critic. As an avowed enemy of the Freemasons and Jews—who, in his opinion, had taken control of France, separated the church from the state in the early years of the century, and in the process steered France away from the monarchy that he wanted to see restored—Barrès unabashedly used Catholicism whenever he could to achieve his nationalist political ends. In his column in the *Echo de Paris* of 21 March 1910 he hailed Mauriac's slender collection of poems and spoke in glowing terms of this new young poet, who was already a Catholic writer. To him the book possessed "a sense of balance, no lies, the sweetest and truest chamber music, clustering all its emotions around one central Catholic idea" (*ORTC*, 4:195). This sentence could be rewritten today as a general description of Mauriac's work as a whole, with perhaps only minor reservations. He went on to praise the whole book and expressed the prophetic hope that Mauriac's precocious genius would lead to greater things. Barrès's excellent connections would become the means by which Mauriac would enter new circles of friends. Already making his way into the upper spheres of French society even before he met Barrès, Mauriac was now invited to the table of Mme Alphonse Daudet, where he would meet her sons Lucien and Léon, both influential forces in the literary world of the day, as well as Jean Cocteau and Marcel Proust. As he would assert later in *Du côté de chez Proust,* (1947) (*On Reading Proust,* 1952), the reading of Balzac had had an effect on him: "Influenced by Balzac, I believed naïvely in literary 'salons' as only a boy from the provinces can" (*OA,* 275). Like Balzac's Rastignac or Rubempré, Mauriac was determined to launch his career, and contacts like these were indispensable.

Mauriac's good fortune at the very beginning of his literary career is by no means unique, but it is rare. This is especially so if we recall that

Gramley Library
Salem College
Winston-Salem, NC 27108

the work in question is virtually forgotten today and that Mauriac is hardly remembered as a poet. That Barrès himself had been discovered by Paul Bourget in much the same way a generation earlier is perhaps worth remembering. In the same manner Mauriac would discover Philippe Sollers in the 1960s. This filiation from Bourget to Barrès and from Mauriac to Sollers offers an accurate reflection of how French literature and society have evolved in the last century.

At this time Mauriac also took part in the activities of a group that called itself *spiritualiste* and that sought to initiate a rebirth of spiritual values in French literature. In 1911 they founded their review, the *Cahiers de l'Amitié de France,* (it would last only until 1914, a victim of the Great War), and in its pages Mauriac would be free to praise his favorite authors: Charles Péguy, Francis Jammes, and Paul Claudel. Their goal was to create a kind of collective *Génie du Christianisme,* as Chateaubriand had done at the beginning of the nineteenth century. They also wanted to combine literature and asceticism, a task in which Mauriac—like the fictional Jean-Paul in *L'Enfant chargé de chaînes*— found himself wanting. Claudel, the reigning Catholic writer of the day, remained distant from the group, and Lucien Daudet, who could have helped them, was not impressed by their plans. Not much would come of this early commitment of energy on the part of Mauriac other than the establishment of solid friendships with like-minded young men like Robert Vallery-Radot, the editor of the *Cahiers,* the brothers Eusèbe and Philippe de Brémond d'Ars, and André Lafon. Mauriac thus belonged to two separate worlds at this early point in his career: the "groupe catholique" of like-minded young critics and poets committed to some new form of socially active Catholicism, and the world of established French literary power and reputation.

1909–22: In Search of a "Style" and an "Atmosphere"

The years between Mauriac's arrival in Paris in 1906 and his first clear literary triumph were difficult ones. His initial success with *Les Mains jointes* in 1909 belies the fact that more than another decade of trial and error would be necessary before he would finally create what he would eventually call his own personal "style" and "atmosphère." Writing new prefaces for the 1952 edition of the *Oeuvres complètes,* he looked back upon the four novels he had published prior to *Le Baiser au lépreux* (1922) (*The Kiss to the Leper,* 1923), and noted that as a general rule "neither my style nor my atmosphere is evident" in these early works.[15] Scholars have tended to pay little attention to these early novels and in general agree with Mauriac's own assessment of their worth: they do not contain all the ingredients that are essential for his best fiction.

Although the standard literary studies of Mauriac's work usually begin about 1922 with the publication and success of *Le Baiser au lépreux,* the previous years of apprenticeship help us to understand the genesis of Mauriac's particular genius. Coming right in the middle of this period is World War I, which, at its beginning, few believed would last as long as it did or would end by sowing the seeds for yet another conflict. Although he was exempted from military service because of physical disability, Mauriac nonetheless volunteered with the French Red Cross. Sent to several garrison towns as well as to the front near Verdun, though not actually close to the action there, he finally asked for duty in Salonika, where he was sent in December 1916. Returned to France for health reasons in March of the following year, Mauriac was released from service with the Red Cross and by June he was back in Paris. By mid-1917 the war was over for him.

Since Mauriac did not later write about the war or use it in his fiction, there is a tendency to think of him as one of those French writers of the period who were not directly touched by this cataclysmic event. Mauriac's time in the medical corps seems on the surface somewhat bland in comparison to the involvement of Bernanos, Drieu La Rochelle, and Céline, for instance, all of whom were wounded and whose experience at the front influenced their later development as writers. But these are perhaps unfair comparisons.

It is informative to compare Mauriac to Hemingway, who also served as a Red Cross volunteer. Unlike Mauriac, Hemingway was famous for his bravado and, after the war, made much of his service as a medical volunteer while Mauriac denigrated his own Red Cross service. Hemingway, because of his personality as well as the fact that so few Americans actually saw service in the war, could boast of his experiences and was free to utilize and transform them in his fiction. But Mauriac, as a Frenchman, could hardly do the same thing. Millions of people had been killed in the war. His suffering, in comparison to the ultimate sacrifice made by so many others, was relatively minor, so in that sense he had little to brag about. But this does not mean that he shirked his duty to country or that the war had no effect on him. It is important to remember that when Mauriac volunteered for medical duty he was over 30 years old and the father of one child. His physical exam in early 1917 had indicated that one of his lungs was already infected, so it should come as no surprise that he fell ill shortly after arriving in Greece. Given his precarious state of health, Mauriac did all that he could to support the war effort and to share its burdens, yet 50 years later he still felt uneasy about his war record. He wrote in his *Bloc-Notes*: "I've never told the rest of the story: my attempts to serve, in spite of everything, in Champagne and in Lorraine, my departure for Salonika, where I never really got beyond the hospital room where they put me right after I got off the ship. Not that I had nothing to say about those years, but it's the time of my life that I pass over the most rapidly, with a kind of shame. However, I don't think that I could have done more than I did."[16]

Among the papers that Mauriac donated to the Bibliothèque Jacques Doucet after his death, we find traces of his experience of the war. Of particular significance are two chapters of a text that was perhaps destined to become a novel.[17] The first deals with working-class people employed in a clinic in Paris during the war and the second with their decision to leave the comparative safety of the city in order to relocate to the east, in closer proximity to the front in the Champagne region. These pages were never published, and perhaps it is a good thing that they were not, for by their style and subject matter they are alien to what we normally associate with Mauriac. They could have been written by Eugène Dabit or one of the other so-called populist writers of the interwar years. However, they do illustrate how Mauriac was searching during these years to find his own particular literary style. Later, in the 1930s, he remarked in a newspaper article that editors in the immediate postwar years had been looking for manscripts that recounted wartime experiences or transposed them into fiction. There was no concern for quality. All they wanted were books that could be "cooked up hastily and served hot."[18] This might very well have been what Mauriac was doing in these long forgotten texts written immediately after the war.

As Mauriac was gathering together the texts to be published in his *Oeuvres complètes* in the early 1950s, he went out of his way to denigrate the early years of his career.[19] Since critics later tended to follow his lead, little serious study was undertaken of the many texts that he had published prior to 1922. To remedy this problem, Jean Touzot, in his *Mauriac avant Mauriac,* tried to reconstruct the career of the young writer during this relatively obscure period of his career, from his arrival in Paris in 1906 to 1922, including the war years. This interesting collection of texts includes extracts from Mauriac's letters to his wife, a magnificent short story, "La Paroisse morte" (The dead parish), which was not published during his lifetime, and his articles for the newspaper *Le Gaulois.* Touzot correctly asserts in his introduction to this collection that the unique ingredients of Mauriac's fiction were already in place, although perhaps not in the proper balance: "in the course of the decade that interests us here, we already find an honorable equilibrium between journalism and the transposed personal diary, a double inspiration which defines in our view the very essence of Mauriac's genius."[20] Touzot's work on this period in Mauriac's life has paved the way for more detailed study of its relationship to what came later.

In 1913 Mauriac married Jeanne Lafon, the offspring of a solid bourgeois family from Talence, a suburb of Bordeaux. Despite the objections of Jeanne's father, who did not hesitate to express his concern about having his daughter marry a poet, even a gifted one, the marriage took place on 3 June, in Talence. After a honeymoon trip to Italy and Switzerland, where the young couple found a copy of the recently published *L'Enfant chargé de chaînes* prominently displayed in a bookstore window, they returned to France and took up residence in Paris in the traditionally bourgeois sixteenth arrondissement at 89, rue de la Pompe. In April 1914 their first child, Claude, was born. Despite his military exemption, Mauriac still tried to serve his country. His second child, Claire, was born in August 1917 after his return from Salonika, and Luce, two years later, in April 1919. The fourth and last Mauriac child, Jean, would be born in August 1924. These increasing family responsibilities form an important background element during the crucial years when Mauriac was searching for the formula that would bring together his personal style.

His first two novels had been written and published before the war. *L'Enfant chargé de chaînes* appeared in 1913, when Mauriac was 27 years old. The autobiographical dimensions of the novel are readily apparent. Its hero, Jean-Paul Johanet, is transparently autobiographical: Mauriac's father's name was Jean-Paul and one of his most beloved places in the Bordeaux region is Johanet. Jean-Paul is living the lonely life of a student in Paris. Through a friend he is introduced to a group of young Catholics interested in social action. Their leader, Jérôme Servet, is a thinly veiled transposition of Marc Sangnier, and their movement, *Amour et Foi,* is clearly Sangnier's *Sillon* movement. The hero will attempt to cross the social gulf and interact with working-class people, but to no avail. He is "chained," as the title hints, by both his class upbringing and his Jansenist background.

Mauriac took a somewhat different tack in his second prewar novel, *La Robe Prétexte* (1914) (*The Stuff of Youth,* 1960), a poorly structured work that patches together five different novellas. The young protagonist, Jacques, reminds us of Jean-Paul of *L'Enfant chargé de chaînes*. He is an orphan, for his mother is dead and his father is absent. In the first part of the novel he competes against Philippe, his cousin from Paris, for the affections of Camille, while in the second part it is against another young man, José Ximenès, that he must measure himself. As in the earlier novel, the autobiographical elements are not difficult to discern. Mauriac the critic would write later in life that fledgling novelists usually give us "the direct depiction of their sensitive soul and its sentimental and metaphysical adventures" (*OC*, 8:288). In other words, since they have not lived long enough to accumulate all that much "experience," they simply write about themselves. This is precisely what Mauriac did in this work.

   La Chair et le sang (Flesh and Blood, 1954), Mauriac's third novel, was begun as early as 1914 but abandoned during the war years. It was finally published in 1920. Here we find the young author attempting to enlarge his work's area of investigation beyond the limits of the young hero's desires and intentions. Upper-class society becomes a factor in the novel, and Mauriac is clearly out to draw blood. His hero, Claude Favereau, a former seminarian, is torn between his Christian upbringing and his pagan instincts, and the title of the novel underlines the attraction that carnal desire has for him. The fourth novel, *Préséances (Questions of Precedence*, 1958), appeared in 1921. Here Mauriac enlarges still further the social dimension only barely adumbrated in *La Chair et le sang* and writes a Balzacian novel that satirizes the upper bourgeoisie in Bordeaux. He attacks this group as a closed world where it takes years to learn all the essential social behavior mechanisms, of which the most important is perhaps knowing one's place in society and then remaining in it. Through his hero Augustin, who is in love with Florence, a daughter of one of the wealthy Bordeaux families, Mauriac sets an outsider against the establishment.

   As Mauriac aptly observed in the preface to the volume of the *Oeuvres complètes* containing these four novels, "if there is such a thing as a small planet, the Mauriac planet, it only exists in this volume in a confused way, although its essential elements are already there, but mixed with borrowed accessories" (*OC*, 10:ii–iii). He was still searching for the right mix. Everything that was based on childhood memories, his lived experience, and the atmosphere of his native region could be kept. What he had to eliminate was the social protest element, the caustic and satirical dimension of his work that gave the mistaken impression that he was more interested in class conflict than in the human condition. Once this focus was achieved, his novels would be able to attain universal heights.

1922–27: The Great Novels

In *Le Baiser au lépreux* (1922) (*The Kiss to the Leper,* 1923) Mauriac finally put his childhood to rest, for the weak and sickly protagonist of the novel, Jean Péloueyre, is not a direct transposition of autobiographical elements. It is here, finally, that Mauriac succeeds in combining his style and his atmosphere. The success of this novel changed Mauriac's life dramatically. The novel sold 18,000 copies in its first four months, and has since sold many hundreds of thousands more. This was the first of Mauriac's books to be translated into English, with both London and New York editions. Being both a *succès d'estime* among the critics and a popular success, it enabled the Mauriacs to take a long vacation and to go somewhere other than their family home in the Landes. Accompanied by their maid, Catherine Bechler, who would remain with them for the next 50 years, they spent some of their new wealth by taking a luxurious vacation on the Riviera.

Mauriac was conscious of his success and relished each stage of it. After all, how could the creator of so many self-conscious characters fail to be conscious of his own development? His voluminous autobiographical writings as well as his correspondence with other literary luminaries of the day attest to his developing self-confidence. By now he was in regular contact with major literary figures like Gide and Barrès, while younger writers, like Jacques-Emile Blanche and Jean Cocteau also expressed their esteem for him. In retrospect, we are probably safe in saying that Mauriac's great success with *Le Baiser au lépreux* was an event that was waiting to happen, given the reputation he had already earned among a small but important coterie prior to the publication of this novel. His newspaper articles, his early critical essays, and his contacts in two important literary salons, those of Mme Mühlfeld and Mme Alphonse Daudet, had already bestowed a certain kind of celebrity on him among Parisian literati. On 3 February 1918 Mauriac made the acquaintance of Marcel Proust. Between then and Proust's death in November 1922 (he had lived long enough to witness the success of *Le Baiser au lépreux),* they corresponded and came to admire each other's work. At the same time Jacques Rivière, editor of the prestigious *Nouvelle Revue Française (NRF),* the leading literary monthly of the day, counted for something in helping Mauriac find an audience. Converted to Catholicism by Claudel, Rivière remained open to religious questions and admired Mauriac's work in part for that very reason.[21]

Mauriac continued to tap the same vein exploited in *Le Baiser au lépreux* while working each day in his "cagibi", the small maid's room set aside for him in the family apartment. In addition to his novels, there were essays, theater criticism, and newspaper articles to make demands on him. At the same time, Mauriac explored Parisian nightlife in more depth. There were the endless soirees with Mme Mühlfeld, events at the nightclub *Boeuf sur le toit*, and of course the theater. Through the 1920s Mauriac would be a theater critic for both the *Revue Hebdomadaire* and the *NRF*. Several nights each week, he and his wife could be seen in the front rows of the Gymnase and Vieux-Colombier theaters. Mauriac's life was hectic and, as his son Jean Mauriac once related to me, it would remain so, with book reviews and newspaper columns to be delivered, incessant phone calls and interruptions of all kinds competing for time with the novels. During this frenetic period Mauriac lived the Parisian literary life to the fullest. Yet, in the midst of all this activity, he was able to write his important early masterpieces.

Le Fleuve de feu (1923) (*River of Fire*, 1954) is the last novel written before *Le Baiser au lépreux,* although it was published a year after it. Written first as a novella that Mauriac considered unpublishable, it was put away in a drawer while the young writer went to work on *Baiser.* It should thus be considered the last of what I call Mauriac's early novels. The fact that *Le Fleuve de feu* did not sell as well as *Le Baiser au lépreux* or receive the same kind of critical acclaim did not slow down the Mauriac bandwagon. His publisher, Bernard Grasset, perhaps afraid that Mauriac might defect to Gallimard (which also published the *NRF),* offered him what was for the time a fabulous contract: an advance of 10,000 francs for each of his next three novels. Mauriac was ecstatic, for he suspected that he was on the threshold of even greater success. Things were falling into place for him. Thus, he kept working as hard as ever. *Genitrix* (1923) (*Genitrix,* 1924), *Le Désert de l'amour* (1925) (*The Desert of Love,* 1926, 1947), and *Thérèse Desqueyroux* (1927), (*Thérèse,* 1929, 1948), three of his greatest novels, followed in short order. He was at the pinnacle of success when disaster struck.

1927–30: Spiritual and Emotional Crisis

After the success of *Thérèse Desqueyroux* in 1927, Mauriac began to wonder whether the Catholic critics who found fault with his novels might be right: how could he claim to be a "Catholic novelist," or to use the term that he preferred, "a Catholic who writes novels," when his seemingly pessimistic novels portrayed greed, incest, murder and adultery? The Catholic daily *La Croix* routinely pilloried Mauriac. Their reasoning was simple: if the fruit of Mauriac's imagination was impure, then the source of his work must also be tainted. In his earliest novels, Mauriac had, in the manner of Balzac, paid perhaps excessive attention to the stresses and strains caused by the interaction of characters from different social milieus. Abandoning this tack from *Le Baiser au lépreux* onward, he took an enormous risk when his work became concerned primarily with deep psychological analysis of character, including strong attention to sexual desire—and especially its suppression. Such subject matter went against the basic *bon sens* (common sense) of his upper-class, Catholic, and conservative caste, which relegated these concerns to social misfits, who, in addition, were afflicted with a serious case of bad taste.

A typical example of the consternation, even disgust, that Mauriac's novels caused among Catholic clergy of the day can be gauged by the reaction of Jean Calvet to his work. In his study *Le Renouveau catholique dans la littérature contemporaine* (1927), the Abbé Calvet excluded Mauriac's novels from consideration, claiming that they could not be called "Catholic novels." While he was willing to concede that Mauriac belonged to a group that he referred to as "catholiques écrivains," or Catholics who also happened to be writers, he refused to concede that Mauriac was an "écrivain catholique" or Catholic writer.[22] By the late 1920s, Mauriac had become a "Catholic novelist" by writing novels that were routinely pilloried and vilified by the pious "bien-pensant" Catholic press. Within the Catholic upper class, he was truly "différent," and this difference created enormous problems for him.

By 1928 Mauriac was plunged into a horrible state of depression, though only a few close friends were aware of it at the time. His situation was probably akin to what we would call today a midlife crisis; it resulted in part from the contradiction between the nature of his success as a writer and the simple piety that had characterized his upbringing. Another cause, about which details are in short supply, was that Mauriac seems to have experienced a sentimental attachment to a younger person at this time. We do not know who the person was, but the individual's identity is of little interest at this point. Married and by now the father of four children, known in France and throughout Europe as a Catholic writer, Mauriac struggled to deal with this situation. The 1920s were a perilous time. In the wake of World War I, standards of moral behavior that had prevailed in the prewar years were severely shaken. Likening the end of the war to the experience of coming out of a tunnel, Mauriac wrote:

"And right away, at the end of the tunnel [there was] this frenzy, which to a limited extent took hold of me. But this limited influence was actually a lot, in fact too much, because for me eternal life was at stake. What appeared to others as simply a permissible dalliance afflicted the most secret part of my spiritual being, the source of true life" (*OA*, 745). Addressing more specifically the problem that led to his need for "conversion" in 1928, he tells us: "For two or three years I was like a madman. Almost nothing appeared on the outside. The particular reasons for this madness were caused by deeply hidden drives at the intersection of the body and soul, at the age of forty in the middle of the road of life. . . . I wandered about Paris like a lost dog, like a dog without a collar"(*OA*, 616).

One attempt to solve the problem took the form of a book on his literary idol, the seventeenth-century classical playwright Jean Racine, who had experienced similar problems. In writing about Racine, Mauriac was really, and to a large extent, talking about himself. This essay, *Vie de Jean Racine*,[23] appeared in 1928. André Gide (1869–1951), the reigning pontiff of French letters at that time, read the work and wrote a letter to Mauriac to express his concern about what he took to be a certain hypocrisy in Mauriac's position. Accusing him of wanting to have it both ways—that is, of being able, as a writer, to explore in depth the subject of carnal desire without as a Christian having to disavow it—Gide called this hypocrisy a "reassuring compromise which allows [you] to love God without losing sight of Mammon."[24] In reaction to Gide's letter, which in reality was less an attack upon his art than an honest appraisal of it, Mauriac attempted to explain his predicament and justify his position by writing the essay *Dieu et Mammon*. At this time he also wrote *Souffrances et bonheur du chrétien* (Suffering and happiness of the Christian; translated as *Anguish and Joy of the Christian Life*, 1964). These two texts are published in a single volume today, but they were written separately and should be read this way.

Souffrances du chrétien was supposed to be an essay on the *Traité de la concupiscence* (*Treatise on Concupiscence*) by the seventeenth-century moralist Bossuet, but it turned out to be a rather direct response to Gide's observations. Perhaps without realizing it, Mauriac revealed to his reader a good deal of the frustration that he felt in his life for both artistic and personal reasons. The general theme of the work, announced in the opening sentence, is that Christianity makes no room for the needs of the flesh, and in fact suppresses them. When Charles Du Bos read *Souffrances* after its publication in October 1928, he saw that his friend was in a serious state of depression.[25] He thus acted quickly to put Mauriac in contact with his own confessor, the Abbé Jean-Marie

Altermann. The priest's spirited direction would have a tonic effect on Mauriac, just as it had had on Du Bos himself. By December, during a retreat at Solesmes, Mauriac was already at work on *Bonheur du chrétien*, which he would write hastily and publish in the April 1929 issue of the *NRF*. This second essay contradicts the first in that it gives serious consideration to the human and consoling aspects of Christianity, thereby balancing and in fact rejecting many of the statements made earlier in *Souffrances*. Mauriac also seems more at peace with himself in this work, perhaps because his sentimental involvement had by this time run its course; the worst of the storm was over. But as we look in retrospect at Mauriac's life, it is obvious that although the "conversion" of 1928 represents the most crucial phase in his midlife crisis, he did not settle down completely until after his mother's death in June 1929. That event marked the final episode in this dark period. The whole experience of these years would have a decisive effect on the rest of his life and work. In succeeding chapters, I will show how this crisis is reflected in several novels, his poetry, and especially his short stories.

1930–45: The Great Catholic Novels and the War Years

As he was coming out of the crisis, Mauriac wrote *Destins* (1928) (*Lines of Life*, 1957) and *Ce qui était perdu* (1929) (*That Which was Lost*, 1950). In the first novel he depicts a middle-aged person hopelessly in love with a younger one, and in the second he attempts to write what is generally considered his first truly Catholic novel—i.e., a novel of conversion in which grace acts in the soul of one of the principal characters. He was still very much under the influence of his confessor, the Abbé Altermann, when he wrote this work. After these morally uplifting novels—which he intended to be seen as such—he published his second great masterpiece, *Noeud de vipères* (1932) (*Vipers' Tangle*, 1933). This was followed by *Le Mystère Frontenac* (1933) (*The Frontenac Mystery*, 1952), which he wrote in part to thank his family for the love and care they had expressed to him before and after his operation for throat cancer in 1932.

In 1933 Mauriac was elected to the Académie française, thereby becoming one of the 40 cultural "immortals" of the day, and for the rest of the decade he wrote novels that reflected his desire to suffuse his work with a decidedly Catholic content while also experimenting with the novel form. This highly creative period culminates with what I consider his third great novel, *La Pharisienne* (*Woman of the Pharisees,* 1946), written in 1940 after the fall of France, and published in 1941.

In the 1930s, as the years of this crucial decade went by, his most implacable critics continued to be certain right-of-center Catholics who disapproved both of what he said and of his political allies. The concern about his novels expressed by the Abbé Jean Calvet was by no means an isolated example. The campaign mounted against him in 1930 by *La Croix,* and the attacks aginst him by the Abbé Bethléem, are other salient examples of this opposition.[26] Of course there were liberal Catholics who hailed Mauriac in these years as a "Catholic writer," but their opinions were more than compensated for by those of the traditional Catholic Right. Furthermore, many of those who approved of Mauriac's politically and socially conservative positions as a journalist still took a dim view of his seeming obsession with sex as a novelist. The small coterie of left-of-center Catholics in France who sympathized with and understood Mauriac as an artist would not come to the fore until after 1945.

The turning point came politically for Mauriac in 1937, when he supported the Spanish Republicans despite their Communist element and virulent anticlericalism. With the neo-Thomist philosopher Jacques Maritain and fellow Catholic novelist Georges Bernanos, he attacked General Franco and took the position that Catholicism could not be allied with fascism. Mauriac suddenly condemned the Spanish generals (whom he had supported for the first eight months of the war) because of the killing of Basque priests who sympathized with the Republicans. Turning a blind eye to the fact that the Republicans themselves had already executed thousands of priests and systematically destroyed church property, he objected to the fact that the Spanish generals were presenting their cause as a moral crusade of Catholics against Communists and, in so doing, had accepted military support from Mussolini and Hitler, who were also fervent anti-Communists. Thus, from 1937 to 1940, Mauriac turned his back on his innate sense of hierarchy and order, which he had expressed until then in his political journalism, and gave his full support to the Spanish Republicans and their Marxist allies, whom he had earlier opposed. His support of the Left in these crucial prewar years was no doubt genuine, and in retrospect it was the politically correct position to take. Most Catholics at the time, however, including the Vatican, supported Franco against what they saw as a Communist threat. Once again Mauriac was clearly politically "différent."

After his rather sudden move to the left during the Spanish Civil War, Mauriac also began speaking out on behalf of Jews and Jewish causes.

He lamented that Jews, deprived of their civil rights in Germany, were being encouraged to emigrate. Thus, he wrote in February 1938, "if there is one problem that requires our intervention, it is the one that, on a worldwide scale, creates such a wave of hatred against Israel." He continued: "Against this hatred, I have always opposed the admiration that I feel for certain Jews, living or dead, and the affection that more than one of them inspires in me. There is no better antidote for racial hatred than to think upon certain people who are dear to us. There is no better response to anti-Semitic doctrines than to take stock of what French culture and German culture owe to their Jewish element—and of what, in return, Israel's genius owes to Western civilizations."[27] Mauriac's expressions of sympathy for the Jews were no doubt sincere, but like his protestations of support for the Spanish Republicans, these not only were new political positions for Mauriac, they also were not in keeping with the views generally held in his social milieu. Mauriac's sincerity in what Elie Wiesel would later call in a letter to me, "son attachement au peuple juif" (his attachment to the Jewish people), became apparent during these years. Beginning in the 1930s, before anyone had ever heard of ecumenism, Mauriac's hand was already outstretched to the Jewish people as a whole.

When war came in 1940, Mauriac adopted a wait-and-see attitude. Like everyone else, he could not be sure what was going to happen. He seemed during these months to be sympathetic to Marshall Pétain who was named head of state when the Parliament of the Third Republic voted itself out of existence after the fall of France in the summer of 1940. He spent that first fall and winter with his family at Malagar, with several German soldiers billeted upstairs in his house. In these most unusual circumstances he wrote and published *La Pharisienne*. It would be his last novel for many years.

By 1941 Mauriac had swung wholeheartedly to the Allied side. His great admiration for de Gaulle—who, despite being only a one-star general in 1940 managed to convince Churchill and Roosevelt that he represented not only "the free French" outside the country, but also an abstract idea that he called "France"—was instrumental in this shift. During 1941 the alliance between Catholics and Jews, Rightists and Communists in what came to be called the Resistance, became one of the major political developments in twentieth-century French politics. Although this alliance lasted barely four years and needed the threat of Nazi power to make it work, it created new alliances and lines of communication between previously hostile groups. Mauriac emerged as one of the living symbols of the Resistance movement inside France. Since so many other intellectuals who shared his political convictions had fled the country, he stood out for his refusal to leave. His name was evoked regularly in BBC propaganda broadcasts to France, further heightening his stature as a patriot. When his pamphlet in support of the Allied cause, *Le Cahier noir,* appeared in 1943 under the pseudonym Forez, it attracted further attention and was translated immediately in London as *The Black Notebook.*[28] For this reason, Mauriac decided to leave Paris, where he had been living for the last year or so, since he felt he would be safer outside the city. Thus, he moved to his wife's family house at Vémars some 20 miles north of Paris for the last months of the Occupation.

1945–70: New Directions in the Postwar Years

At the Liberation, Mauriac finally met de Gaulle personally and his oldest son, Claude, became de Gaulle's personal secretary. A new relationship was being built. When the creation of the Fourth Republic in the late 1940s was marked by the return to power of the politicians and the parliamentary system that had played such an important role in the downfall of the Third Republic, de Gaulle withdrew to his country estate to write his memoirs while Mauriac, remaining in Paris, returned to his former allegiance with the anti-Communist center-right political formations.

In 1948 Mauriac was instrumental in helping to found the literary review *La Table ronde,* which in theory would represent all points of view in those first years after the war when Catholics and Communists still entertained fond and fresh memories of having worked together against a common enemy. Since the prestigious *NRF* had compromised itself during the Occupation, having continued to publish under Nazi auspices, Mauriac at the beginning hoped to replace it with this new review. Circumstances changed in 1953 when the *NRF* was allowed to resume publication under the name *La Nouvelle Nouvelle Revue Française.* Nonetheless, *La Table ronde* survived well into the 1960s, even though Mauriac resigned from its editorial board in 1954.

Most of Mauriac's energies were devoted to political journalism during the postwar years. In 1952 he began to publish his now famous newspaper column *Bloc-Notes.* It first appeared in the pages of *La Table ronde* and then moved to *L'Express* (1954–1961) and finally to *Le Figaro* (1961–1970). It ranged over a wide array of subjects and was generally recognized by contemporaries as first-class journalism. It is still considered important enough that a new, critical edition of the five lengthy volumes of *Bloc-Notes* has recently been published by Professor Jean Touzot of the Sorbonne. In the *Bloc-Notes*, no one was immune to Mauriac's barbs, whether it be Sartre and the left-wing existentialists on one side, or right-wing figures on the other. While so many former friends and allies in the struggle against fascism now overlooked or made excuses for the excesses of the emerging Communist regimes, Mauriac attacked the Communists and their apologists with the same vigor and virulence he had displayed in his earlier antifascist writings.[29]

During the early 1950s, at the height of the Cold War, Mauriac's political enemies, despite his continued success as a journalist (or perhaps in part because of it), painted him as an old man whose career was over and who would do well to simply disappear from view. They responded to his anticommunist invective as those who have no rational reply usually do—with ad hominem arguments. Matters were not helped any by the failure of Mauriac's play *Le Feu sur la terre* (1951). The theatrical vocation that he thought might have been his late in life seemed doomed to failure, and he was deeply hurt by this setback. But then the unexpected happened. To the surprise of just about everyone, Mauriac was awarded the Nobel Prize for literature in 1952. This recognition stoked the old creative fires within his breast and gave him new life.

In these last years Mauriac returned to the novel. *Le Sagouin* (1951), (*The Little Misery*, 1952), *Galigaï* (1952), (*The Loved and the Unloved*, 1953), *L'Agneau* (1954), (*The Lamb*, 1955), *Un Adolescent d'autrefois* (1969), (*Maltaverne*, 1970) and the posthumous fragment of a novel called *Maltaverne* (1972) revealed that in fact he had not lost control of his "style" and "atmosphère." He also published truly important Catholic essays during these years: *La Pierre d'achoppement* (1951), (*The Stumbling Block*, 1952), *Le Fils de l'homme* (1958) (*The Son of Man*, 1960) and *Ce que je crois* (1962), (*What I Believe*, 1963). His international fame abroad as a Catholic writer reached its apogee between 1952 and 1966, as the number and quality of the translations of his books attest. Finally, two endearing and no doubt enduring works of note also appeared during these closing years of his life. *Mémoires intérieurs* (1959), (*Mémoires Intérieurs*, 1960), a kind of intellectual autobiography in which he talks of the books that had influenced him most as a writer, was complemented in 1965 by *Nouveaux Mémoires intérieurs* (*The Inner Presence: Recollections of My Spiritual Life*, 1968), which might be characterized as an affective autobiography, for it provides a chronicle of his inner feelings and offers important insights into his relationship with family and friends, as well as his professional development.

In the last decade of his life, Mauriac at first embraced the Second
Vatican Council and generally supported the many changes that it
brought to traditional Catholic devotional practice. But he finally concluded that conciliar reform had gone too far and had made too many
compromises with worldly values. He expressed these reservations openly in his *Bloc-Notes*. In April 1969 he wrote: "God knows that I suffered
from the resistance to change of the old Church in my youth. But much
less than to see today the very rock on which it is built being shaken"
(*BN,* 5:45). He had welcomed the liturgical reforms that did not threat-
en the essential deposit of faith, but by the time he died he had become
concerned that those essential doctrines might be in danger.

These years also coincide with General de Gaulle's exercise of power,
from the beginning of the Fifth Republic in 1958 until 1969. During
this decade Mauriac backed him strongly, and his essay *De Gaulle* (1964)
(*De Gaulle,* 1966) was the most formal and organized expression of this
support. Mauriac was the object of many jokes for this faithfulness to an
old soldier's vision, but in the end it was because he continued to see de
Gaulle as a symbol of unity.[30] The close collaboration of Catholics and
Communists that had characterized the war years (and which had been
concretely symbolized both by de Gaulle the person and by his flag, the
Republican tricolor with a Christian cross—the so-called Cross of
Lorraine—attached to it) remained vivid for Mauriac until the end. The
antipathy between Catholics and anticlerical Republicans was something
he had known from birth and depicted again and again in his novels.
Since Mauriac considered this to be a divisive force in French life, he
looked to de Gaulle, as he had to the Second Vatican Council for a time,
as a principle of unity that might be capable of creating a new fusion of
different philosophical viewpoints. As a patriot who wanted to include
all Frenchmen in the seamless garment of the national family no matter
what their background, Mauriac always saw de Gaulle as the politician
capable of making this inclusion take place. The values that they shared
were tolerance, concern for others, and a respect for a power greater than
ourselves as we seek self-knowledge.

Mauriac was not only one of the most important French men of letters
of the twentieth century, he was also one of the most outspoken public
figures of his age, and he paid the price for it. He could boast of bitter
enemies on both the Left and the Right. Mauriac's biographer, Jean
Lacouture, does not exaggerate when he acknowledges that Mauriac,
except for Clemenceau, Blum, and de Gaulle, "was the most widely
attacked and vilified Frenchman of the 20th century" (Lacouture, 617).

On 1 September 1970 Mauriac died at the age of 85. His funeral at Notre Dame Cathedral in Paris was a national event that was complemented by other, nonreligious, ceremonies. De Gaulle, in his letter of condolence to Mme Mauriac, put his finger on Mauriac's special gift when he wrote that "through his writings, his magnificent talent was able to touch and to move people in the depth of their souls" (Lacouture, 590). De Gaulle was quite correct in this assessment; he might only have added that there are very few writers who deserve such praise. Those words are still true today, for Mauriac's multifaceted work lives on.

Chapter Two

The Early Fiction and the Short Stories

The Early Fiction

Mauriac's first four novels, of which two were published before World War I and two after it, should be studied together. They represent attempts by a young, aspiring author to develop a mature style capable of communicating what he wants to express. During the nineteenth century, the French ecclesiastical hierarchy had maintained its conservative stance and was often opposed to the legitimate aspirations of working people. Fair wages, decent housing, paid vacations, health care, and the other benefits that we take for granted today were nonexistent. Clerics like Lacordaire and Lamennais preached a social gospel through the middle of the century, but their opponents, Joseph de Maistre and his intellectual offspring, the pessimistic supporters of the status quo (for whom the French Revolution had been a disaster that unrealistically raised the hopes and aspirations of the working class), carried the day with the hierarchy. Then, at the end of the nineteenth century, Pope Leo XIII's famous encyclical *De Rerum Novarum* (1891) expressed strong support for the concept of social justice. Such an idea, coming from Rome of all places, sent a shudder down the spines of many people in Mauriac's social milieu, the landowning, monied classes of the city of Bordeaux and its surrounding area. "The poor you will always have with you," the Gospel says, and this verse, taken at face value, was read as a justification of the status quo. Thus, the bourgeoisie and the army stood shoulder to shoulder with the church against social change. Mauriac's first four novels should be read with this historical background in mind.

L'Enfant chargé de chaînes (1913)

Mauriac's first novel (*Young Man in Chains*, 1963) is a highly autobiographical satire in which he attacks the adolescent he had been, as well as the *Sillon* movement of which he had been briefly a part. Based on his diary from his late teens, the novel tells the story of a young man trying to find his proper place in the world. Like Mauriac's father, who also had literary ambitions, he is also named Jean-Paul. His surname, Johanet, evokes Mauriac's roots in the Landes. Through a friend he is introduced to a group of young Catholics interested in social action. Their leader, Jérôme Servet, is a thinly disguised transposition of Marc Sangnier, and their movement, *Amour et Foi,* is clearly Sangnier's *Sillon.* Jean-Paul attempts to cross the social gulf and interact with working-class people, but to no avail. The novel scandalized Sangnier's followers, who read it as a roman à clef. They were upset because their leader was satirized mercilessly. But why did Mauriac, here at the very beginning of his career, attack a man whose spiritual dedication and commitment he really never questioned? An entry in his *Bloc-Notes,* published many years later, mentions a falling-out between Mauriac and Sangnier and his followers, who looked upon him more as an "intellectual" than as a "militant." Mauriac emphasizes that Sangnier had not called him personally by name, presumably the way Jesus had called each of his disciples personally: "If he had called me by name, if he had selected me, maybe I would have followed him, and perhaps my life would have been different" (*BN,* 3:37–38).

Told in the third person, the novel recounts Jean-Paul's experiences as a dilettante who flits from one issue to another. If anything, the portrait of Jean-Paul (here an orphan like Mauriac himself) is even more mocking than that of Jérôme Servet, for the young man is often aware of his own contradictions, and the novel's narrative voice does not hesitate to point them out. For instance, he preaches to his friends that they should try to revive the great mystical tradition of the Middle Ages and presumably adopt an ascetic lifestyle. Having said this, he leads a small group of followers over to the Right Bank, where they spend the rest of the evening in a nightclub. Today we might be tempted to smile at such inconsistency in an adolescent's intention and achievement, but Mauriac is deadly serious. In fact, one of the most significant and unforgettable relationships in the novel is that between Jean-Paul and the worker Georges Elie, who is let down by the difference between Jean-Paul's words and actions.

At the heart of the novel we also find two young women. After an amorous adventure with Liette, whom he keeps in an apartment for a while, Jean-Paul finally returns to Marthe, a symbol of piety and stability. This return is also a return to religion. He begins to pray regularly, and in one of his prayers he asks God why he has remained "the child bound in chains" (*ORTC,* 1:77) of the title—that is, the young man so terribly self-conscious and absorbed with himself that he is unable to form successful relationships with others. Finally he realizes that through his love for Marthe he will be freed from his problems. "The day," he tells himself, "when my thoughts were turned to Marthe in a tender and sustained way, that's when I began to free myself from my self-centeredness" (*ORTC,* 1:78).

L'Enfant chargé de chaînes is a novel of apprenticeship in a double sense. Written by a young man who had already been moderately successful as a poet but who now wanted to try his hand seriously at fiction, it took as its subject matter a young man struggling to establish his identity, taking those first perilous steps along the road to adulthood. Although the brooding atmosphere of the later novels is absent, Mauriac's psychological insight into character is already present here, as is the magnificently classical and transparent writing style. Set in Paris, this first fictional effort is squarely in the Balzacian tradition that portrays the young provincial trying to make it in the great city. It would be unfair to call this novel a failure, as some readers have been tempted to do. It is actually a solid first step forward for an apprentice novelist trying to transform personal experience into art.

La Robe prétexte (1914)

La Robe prétexte (*The Stuff of Youth,* 1960) occupies a special place among the Mauriac's early novels. This special consideration on the part of Mauriac himself is illustrated by the fact that when he was editing his *Oeuvres complètes* in the 1950s, he retained *La Robe prétexte* in the first volume—at the beginning, where he felt it belonged—while banishing *L'Enfant chargé de chaînes, La Chair et le sang,* and *Préséances* to the purgatory of volume 10. He kept it in its chronological place because "there again I painted myself; I partially succeeded in the portrait of the adolescent that I was, a frontispiece which deserved its place, it seemed to me, at the beginning of the 12 volumes" (OC, 10:ii; ORTC, 1:988). But despite this autobiographical accuracy, he still had no illusions about the novel as a work of art. When it finally did appear in the collected works a year or two later, he found it to be an embarrassment and wished that he had placed it in volume 10 with the other *oeuvres de jeunesse.*

The title of the novel, referring to the Roman *toga praetexta,* which was worn by young Romans of the senatorial class before they reached their majority at age 18, when they could don the *toga virilis,* helps to situate the social class and the age of the hero. The novel's action is told in the first person and the hero, Jacques, is like Jean-Paul of *L'Enfant chargé de chaînes,* in that he too is an orphan. His mother is deceased, and his father has mysteriously disappeared to Tahiti, à la Gauguin, to devote his life to painting. Jacques is raised in a stifling atmosphere, surrounded by four women—an old grandmother, an aunt, a nun who waits on the grandmother, and an unmarried and poor cousin of the grandmother. This portrait bears a strong resemblance to Mauriac's own childhood.

Mauriac patched this novel together from five different short stories and novellas published between 1911 and 1914. In order to make the book function as a novel, several other sections had to be worked into the overall structure. The result is a novel that shows its seams, that creaks along at a slow pace and seems a good deal more amateurish than its predecessor. The work can be divided into two principal parts, in each of which the narrator must measure himself against an outsider. In the first, the intruder is the prestigious cousin from Paris; in the second, a certain José Ximenès. Camille is the female who attracts Jacques's attention and whom he idolizes. But Camille's role in Jacques's life is just the opposite of Marthe's role in Jean-Paul's. In fact the reversal of the hero's experiences in the two novels is striking. In the first novel Jean-Paul seduces Liette, lives with her, and then comes back to Marthe, who is faithfully waiting for him. But Jacques, after turning his back on his first lover, is unable to come back to the idealized Camille. She is a realist and wants a man with a practical turn of mind, not someone like Jacques, who, in her opinion, belongs in a seminary. Mauriac was right when he wrote that the hero of this novel was still a choirboy who was afraid of life and full of himself. Ironically, however, this is precisely the type of temperament and sensibility from which good novelists are sometimes made.[1]

La Chair et le sang (1920)

Mauriac struck out in a new direction with *La Chair et le sang (Flesh and Blood,* 1955), begun in 1914 but not completed until after the war in late 1918 or early 1919. Thus, instead of a novel of formation and development, which is essentially what the first two novels had been, he tries to write a novel that depicts bourgeois society in Paris and Bordeaux. Also, instead of centering his attention on the inner development of his self-centered protagonist, he gives equal emphasis here to the social interplay between the various characters. The process of experimentation continues in this novel, and the search for the proper "style" and "atmosphère" goes forward.

The first two novels had been based on Mauriac's personal experiences as reflected and preserved in his diary and imbedded in his temperament and personality. Breaking with this autobiographical type of inspiration, he now selected a historical event as his point of departure: the suicide of Charles Demange, Maurice Barrès's nephew, who took his life in 1909 in despair over a woman. Like Demange, Mauriac's hero shoots himself in the head in a hotel room and dies several hours later. Around this event Mauriac builds his story. If we recall that he had published *Les Mains jointes* in 1909 and that Barrès's positive reaction to it had helped more than anything else to launch his literary career, we can understand why Mauriac was tempted to select this particular historical event as the basis for his novel. It has been said that when Barrès read Mauriac's poems a few months after this tragedy, he could not help but think of his deceased nephew, who had died by his own hand in the name of love. The young novelist from Bordeaux was thus setting his imagination to work on a subject that could not help but flatter one of the reigning *littérateurs* of the day.

The novel is built around three principal characters. Edward and May Dupont-Gunther are spoiled offspring of the landowning class in the Landes region, while Claude Favereau is of peasant stock, but with a strong mystical bent. The social juxtaposition, already presented in *L'Enfant chargé de chaînes* in the scenes contrasting Jean-Paul and the worker Georges Elie, is developed in more detail here. Claude is also a former seminarian, the first of many that Mauriac will present in the years ahead. In addition, Mauriac introduces a number of adult representatives of the ascendant bourgeoisie in Bordeaux (Mme Gonzalès, M. and Mme Castagnède) and in Paris (Mme Tziegel, Jacques Berbinet, and the poet Gennaro). He satirizes these characters severely, making fun of their ignorance, bad taste, and social pretensions. This novel is still readable today but remains essentially one-dimensional. In stressing that the flesh and blood of the title function primarily to help those with money and power to close ranks in order to keep outsiders at bay, it is limited by its all too apparent social message. Yet, the atmosphere that would later become emblematic of Mauriac's fictional universe does begin to come into focus here. In *L'Enfant chargé de chaînes,* Jean-Paul was originally from Johanet and later returned there, but the sense of place is not fully developed in that first novel. Johanet remains little more than a background setting. Here, on the contrary, the wealthy young Edward, although not born in the fictional Lur (the transposition of Mauriac's home at Malagar, perched on a hilltop overlooking the river in the distance and surrounded on all sides by the Mauriac grapevines), does spend two weeks there and becomes enchanted by the place, almost as if he had spent his whole childhood there. Mauriac, although going in the wrong direction for the time being as far as his ultimate style would be concerned, was stumbling here for the first time onto his authentic atmosphere.

Claude Favereau, the former seminarian, is the child of local share-croppers. He has spent the last few summers reading and taking care of the library of "the master," M. Dupont-Gunther, who owns the land tilled by Claude's parents. Just having left the seminary, he has a premonition that something will happen during this first summer now that he is home for good. When Claude falls in love with May Dupont-Gunther, he is following the dictates of his nature, without concern for social barriers. After they have exchanged a furtive kiss, May rejects him and marries instead the young man that her father has selected, even embracing Catholicism as part of the arrangement. Claude is convinced that May loves him and does not understand that the lure of money and security can be so strong that it can make people turn their backs on carnal desire and the pagan claims of the body. As for her brother Edward, his love affair with Edith Gonzalès, daughter of his father's ex-mistress, leads nowhere but to despair.

To fully understand Mauriac's fiction, a reader should be acquainted with the traditional Catholic teaching on the relationship between grace and nature. Essential to our understanding of this relationship is the idea that grace is quite distinct from nature, and is added on to nature by God. It is thus through the divine gift of grace that man participates in the life of God. In this novel, Mauriac uses these concepts and also introduces for the first time in his work the theme of vicarious suffering. According to this mystical doctrine, called in French *la réversibilité des mérites,* the graces gained by one person through prayer or suffering can be credited to another. Belief in this mystical exchange has been essential to Christianity from the earliest times. The suffering and death of Jesus, which were incurred, according to church teaching, to achieve the salvation of all men, are the model that all Christians should strive to imitate. This doctrine underlies the belief in the efficacy of prayers said on behalf of others, as well as sufferings and sacrifices incurred to the same end (which thus become a form of nonverbal prayer). The very idea of *imitatio Christi* is inconceivable without pain and suffering. Thus, the devout Christian has a dual obligation, which involves not only loving others, but also sacrificing himself for them as Christ did.[2] In the early years of this century, this doctrine enjoyed wide popular acceptance and was common currency in seminaries.

Thus, in a pact made between Edward and Claude, the latter offers to accept responsibility for all of Edward's sins. Edward, without taking this proposal too seriously, goes along with the idea. When he finally dies at his own hand, Claude, at his bedside, hears the unbeliever say in his final agony that "faith saves us" (*ORTC,* 1:323). Is Edward able to say these words because of grace made available to him through the sufferings of Claude? And is he ultimately "saved" because of this grace? If we read the novel this way and concede that Edward the unbeliever has died a Christian death despite his apparent suicide attempt, *La Chair et le sang* can be considered Mauriac's first attempt to write a "Catholic novel," that is, a novel of conversion in which a character is saved through the operation of divine grace. It has generally not been recognized as such, mostly because critics have been distracted by its social attacks on the bourgeoisie. Nonetheless, this is a real and important dimension to the book. The novel not only shows Mauriac breaking new ground in terms of atmosphere, but also reveals him to be using the theme of vicarious suffering to evoke the workings of grace in the soul of one of his characters. In this respect the novel foreshadows later works like *Ce qui était perdu* (1930), *Les Anges noirs* (1933), and *L'Agneau* (1956).

Préséances (1921)

Préséances (*Questions of Precedence,* 1958) continues Mauriac's attempt to write a Balzacian novel of social analysis. The manuscripts of the novel show clearly that from the beginning his goal was to satirize maliciously the bourgeoisie of Bordeaux and its surrounding area. The first-person narrator of the novel remains unnamed, but we do know that he and his sister Florence are children of a wealthy Landes lumber magnate. They seek to penetrate even higher social spheres by marrying into the great Bordeaux wine families. This quest offers Mauriac an ideal pretext to satirize such families, who owe their wealth to the cultivation of the Bordeaux grape. The young men in this social group, usually with English first names, rarely venture outside tightly circumscribed circles. Since the principal concern of their families seems to be to maintain their place in society at all costs, Florence and her brother face a daunting challenge.

Florence's principal advantages are her personal wealth and beauty. Mauriac, clearly under the influence of Proust in writing this novel, emphasizes in his depiction of the *grande bourgeoisie* of Bordeaux the same characteristics encountered among the snobs of Proust's *A la recherche du temps perdu:* vanity, social climbing, and blind submission to the prevailing social code. Before Florence finally achieves her goal and captures Harry Maucoudinet, a scion of one of the illustrious wine-growing families, she passes through a rather strange relationship with Augustin, a character reminiscent of Claude Favereau of *La Chair et le sang.* As the son of a defrocked priest who had once been a brilliant theologian but later turned his back on Catholicism and became an enemy of the church, Augustin has been raised in a social no-man's-land. Socially, he is an *enfant sauvage* (wild child), as completely outside any known social grouping as Florence and her brother are a part of theirs. He reminds us of the great French poet Arthur Rimbaud, whose work meant so much to Mauriac. Having written all his great poems before the age of 25, Rimbaud disappeared and was heard from again by other writers only indirectly and sporadically.[3]

Augustin gradually becomes the central character of the first half of the novel, as Florence grows interested in him despite his being physically unattractive and devoid of social pedigree. He attracts her because he combines poetic instinct with an analytically brilliant mind: there is no one like him among the young men that Florence usually encounters. Combining a malicious coquetry with unbridled curiosity (one of the ways in which the rich in Mauriac's fiction overcome their ennui), she flirts with Augustin and encourages him to fall in love with her. But just as she achieves her goal, she also brings off the most ambitious project of her life: betrothal and marriage to Harry, the uninteresting but wealthy son of the so-called aristocracy of the cork. When confronted with this betrayal, Augustin disappears. The narrator and his sister feel guilty about their treatment of Augustin, but when Florence realizes that she has made a mistake in turning her back on his love, it is already too late.

The plot of the second part of the novel takes place 12 years later, in 1919 or 1920. We learn that during this interval Florence has sought consolation in the arms of several different lovers. She is unhappy. Her brother, the narrator, has taken advantage of his sister's successful marriage to engineer his own admission into the highest spheres of the Bordeaux bourgeoisie. But in true Proustian fashion, he is no longer interested in such great honors once he has achieved them. The betrayal of Augustin, who has ruined their attachment to their little world by showing them another, freer, more mystical and poetic existence, has engendered feelings of remorse. By the time Augustin returns, the narrator, overcoming his materialism, seems to be coming very close to a conversion to Catholicism. He attributes his change of heart to Augustin, who is portrayed as a spiritual intermediary whose vicarious suffering can redeem others. Augustin himself, before he vanishes once again, is seen to be physically decrepit. He has lost his teeth and endured enormous suffering—alluded to but not clearly described—both in the colonies and in the war. The narrator, on the edge of despair, says to him: "If the salt of the earth loses its taste, who will restore its power? In what country rectory, in what cell is there a monk whose suffering will save me? Only you, Augustin, you have been my incorruptible salt. Until now it's in you that I have tasted it and I can only go on living because of the memory of its bitter taste on my lips" (*ORTC*, 1:431). The diarist ends his narration on a note of hope. His sister, now under the care of a spiritualist, is interested only in speaking to spirits of the dead, while he himself recognizes that he is a better person for having known Augustin. He feels that his soul will be saved because of this experience.

The resemblance in structure and subject matter between *Préséances* and *La Chair et le sang* can be explained in part by the fact that the manuscript of *Préséances* was put aside while Mauriac wrote *La Chair et le sang*. He then came back to *Préséances* and finished it. The obvious resemblances between the two pairs of well-born brothers and sisters as well as between Claude Favereau and Augustin, both of whom are portrayed as unusually intelligent and sensitive country boys, show Mauriac trying to use the same basic ingredients in different combinations. These early novels fail in part because their inner mechanisms are too evident and their desire to edify perhaps too apparent. In retrospect, however, they represent an essential period of apprenticeship in Mauriac's career as a novelist.

The Short Fiction

Mauriac's short fiction appeared during his lifetime in two principal collections: *Trois récits* (1929), (Three stories) and *Plongées* (1938), (Fathomings), which contained another five stories. In addition to these collections, there are two more stories, "Le Visiteur nocturne" and "Le Drôle," which were published separately and not gathered into a collection until publication of the *Oeuvres complètes*. These 10 stories represent the only short fiction that Mauriac chose to pass on to posterity.

With the exception of "Un Homme de lettres" and "Le Démon de la Connaissance," all the stories are more or less directly related to

Mauriac's novels. In some cases the connection is obvious, as for instance the two stories dealing with the character of Thérèse Desqueyroux. But even here, the apparent relationship is more complex than it seems at first. In the case of "Thérèse chez le docteur," for example, themes are developed that range far beyond what we usually associate with the character of Thérèse. In fact, it can be argued that she is a mere pretext for treatment of such themes.

Mauriac's short fiction, including the still unpublished stories in the Bibliothèque Jacques Doucet, are a minor, but interesting and at times important part of Mauriac's total oeuvre. They have not as yet been studied in any systematic way either on their own merits or in terms of the ways in which they help to illuminate the novels. The following discussion is a first critical and analytical attempt at such a study.

"Le Visiteur nocturne" (1920)

When Mauriac gathered together the texts to be placed in his *Oeuvres complètes,* he selected only one story from among several published immediately after World War I. "Le Visiteur nocturne" (The nocturnal visitor) first appeared in May 1920 in the *Revue des Jeunes.* The story seems to be a further development of the character Augustin of *Préséances,* the novel that Mauriac was working on at the same time.

In this brief story, a young would-be writer named Octave, living in a bourgeois setting in Paris, is visited late at night by a former classmate from secondary school whom he has not seen in eight years. Gabriel, who had wanted to become a seminarian but could not because of financial difficulties, is now passing through Paris on his way to Bordeaux from Charleville, a city in the north of France where Rimbaud was born. He has been exploited these last few years while working for meager wages in a private school in order to support his sickly parents. Now he is returning to Bordeaux in order to embark on a ship destined for Dakar, where he has been offered a job. He will be leaving shortly aboard *L'Afrique.* Unfortunately, Octave does not extend a very warm welcome to his old friend, who wants to reminisce about the adolescent experiences that still mean so much to him. Octave begrudgingly allows his friend to sleep on the sofa and does not even get up to wish him farewell in the morning.

It is only after Gabriel's departure that Octave begins to feel remorse. He forces his memory to overcome the obstacle of all the recent events of his life in Paris and return to the school in Bordeaux where he knew

Gabriel. He realizes that in not welcoming Gabriel properly, he has turned his back on an important part of his own life. He thus boards a train for Bordeaux to catch up to his friend before he leaves, but to no avail. He not only arrives after the departure of *L'Afrique,* but learns the next day that the ship has sunk in a storm. As the story ends, Octave is hastening to visit a church. Gabriel's abrupt return into his life has clearly been an occasion of grace, for in the closing scene we find the somewhat decadent and self-absorbed Octave kneeling next to a poor man at the back of the church.

In this story, Mauriac pits the purity and innocence of Gabriel against the calculating selfishness of Octave. The references to Rimbaud are unmistakable—both Charleville and the flight to Africa—for Mauriac was still quite conscious of his debt to Rimbaud at this time and wanted to acknowledge it. The story shares the same concerns raised in *Préséances* and may be read as a companion text to that novel.

"Un Homme de lettres" (1926)

"Un Homme de lettres" (A man of letters) is one of Mauriac's most important short stories. It was first published in the *NRF* in July 1926 and later appeared in *Trois récits.* Written in 1926, at the beginning of the spiritual crisis that culminated in the publication of *Ce qui était perdu* in 1930, it tells us a great deal about the *souffrance amoureuse (ORTC,* 1:995) that had caused so much turmoil in Mauriac's life.

This story, which is more a portrait than a true narrative, is told by an unidentified male writer about his friend Gabrielle and her lover of 15 years, the writer Jérôme, who has left her for Berthe, an older woman with two children. The narrator, through his conversations with Gabrielle, elicits testimony about her years of total sacrifice to Jérôme, a well-known playwright. She has tolerated his past escapades, knowing that he would always come back, but she is upset now because his departure seems irrevocable.

Through the narrator's separate discussions with Gabrielle and Jérôme, the monstrous selfishness of the "man of letters" is laid bare. Critics generally agree that Mauriac to a certain extent is writing about his own selfish tendencies as he tried to expropriate the experiences that came into his life for eventual transformation into art. It is a bleak portrait of what he could have become if the "conversion" of 1928 had not taken place. The adoring female is the tortured and oppressed party, for her suffering seems to be necessary for the success of the weak and insecure writer. At the end of the story, Jérôme has also left Berthe and her two children; he is last seen going off in a taxi—with no guarantee at all that he is returning to Gabrielle. The story is not so much about the couple as about how the creative partner must use the other to nourish his art.

It is unclear whether Mauriac ever intended to develop this idea into a novel. Although it bears no direct relationship to any of the novels, the story shares a sense of atmosphere with *Ce qui était perdu,* with Jérôme, the insecure writer at the center of the story, foreshadowing Marcel, the failed poet of the novel.

"Coups de couteau" (1926)

"Coups de couteau" ("Stab Wounds") was written shortly after "Un Homme de lettres" and first appeared in the *Revue des Deux Mondes* in October 1926. It was later included in *Trois récits.* As he had done in "Un Homme de lettres," Mauriac develops once again the theme of the self-ishness and monstrosity of the creative artist. This theme, combined with the stifling Parisian atmosphere centered on the world of art and artists, links the story to *Ce qui était perdu.* Jérôme, the playwright of the earlier story, here becomes Louis, a painter. Once again, there is a couple at the center of the action. To Mauriac, the study of the couple, an enduring theme in western literature, had entered a new phase in the 1920s, with the widespread acceptance of divorce among the social elites. Thus, although divorce is an alternative for Louis, who is infatuated with Andrée (herself a wife and mother) and who no longer loves his wife, Elizabeth, he cannot bring himself to break the invisible chain that binds him.

Mauriac analyzes willpower as an important factor in love, since it can affect a conscious decision to remain committed to the lover. The same idea will be taken up later in "Insomnie." As the will becomes weakened, the *souffrance amoureuse* caused by longing to be with the lover and not with the spouse increases. This suffering in turn tends to isolate the couple from the rest of the world. They are so preoccupied with their own (largely self-generated) problems that they shut out the outside world.

Within the realm of love and affection, Mauriac tended to divide people into two separate groups: those who suffer in the name of love and those who impose this same suffering on others. The theme is illustrated quite well at the end of this story, when Louis receives a phone call from Andrée. It is Saturday and she must see him that very afternoon; other-wise she will be unable to survive through the weekend. Previously determined to break up with her, he now drinks in this news like a poison, as if he and his wonderful suffering had no effect on his wife (who has answered the phone). This closing scene shows how the two tendencies are inseparable, for as the masochistic Louis suffers in the name of love, he is also imposing renewed torments on his wife, who loves him.

"Insomnie" (1929)

"Insomnie" (Insomnia) was written in 1927, just after "Coups de Couteau," and was published in 1929 under the title "La Nuit du bourreau de soi-même" (The night of the hangman of oneself). Significantly, Mauriac deliberately held it back and did not publish it in *Trois récits*. One possible explanation for this is that he feared that if he published it together with "Coups de couteau" and "Un Homme de lettres" he would run the risk of revealing too much about his personal life.

The thematic relationship of "Insomnie" to "Coups de couteau" is evident in the opening pages of the story, for the principal protoganists represent the two groups that interested Mauriac most at this time: those who suffer in the name of love, and those who cause this suffering. He not only gives the protagonists the same names used in "Coups de couteau," but also points out the nature of the relationship between the two works. To him, "'Coups de couteau' and 'Insomnie' are like two pieces of wreckage from an unknown vessel, from a novel that was not written, [and] that I couldn't write at that time, since I was, so to speak, too involved in the affair, too directly affected by it" (*OC,* 6:ii; *ORTC,* 1:995). On another occasion, he wrote that "Insomnie" is "the chapter of a novel that I didn't write, and for which 'Coups de couteau' would have been perhaps the prologue. Many dramatic destinies still don't furnish the substance of a novel, because there isn't enough action. The story of the hero of "'Insomnie' can have only one chapter" (*OC,* 6:229–30; *ORTC,* 2:1048). Of course, it is precisely this "chapter" of his life that Mauriac was always reluctant to speak about openly. Read together, however, these two stories begin to provide an understanding of the sentimental aspects of Mauriac's religious crisis of the late 1920s.

"Insomnie," along with "Coups de couteau," stands out in Mauriac's fiction as a road explored but not quite taken. In both works there is no fully developed plot or action. Louis, once again, is a painter, as is the younger Andrée. He is married and his wife and family are away on vacation. In a nightclub Andrée shows interest in another, younger man. Louis, jealous, leaves in a huff and goes home. He knows that Andrée will be unhappy at his jealous departure, but he wants to be home alone and enjoy the feeling of being miserable. He cannot sleep, tossing and turning the whole night. The thoughts that pass through his mind constitute the essence of the story. By being home he is sure to be able to enjoy his suffering, because Andrée, for fear of giving scandal to the domestics and neighbors, cannot come to comfort him in the middle of the night. The story ends on an inconclusive note. The protoganist's suffering is in no way attenuated.

In "Coups de couteau," the emphasis is on the suffering that Louis imposes on his wife when he tells her of his love for Andrée. Here we see what this relationship is doing to him and, in the process, we begin to understand why this essentially sick love attachment can lead nowhere, for Louis is really in love with himself. But he is lucid in his egotism, as he recalls how, as a boy, he had narcissistically kissed his own image in the bathroom mirror.

Just as "Le Rang" and "Le Visiteur nocturne" are related to *Préséances* by their treatment of the themes of money and social rank, "Insomnie," "Coups de couteau," (and indirectly "Un Homme de lettres") are all related in some way to *Ce qui était perdu*—what I call Mauriac's important, but underrated, Parisian novel—by the theme of the artist/adulterer. Mauriac was right when he stated that these stories were aborted remainders of another attempt to write a novel about Parisian artistic circles. To my mind, this apparent failure only enhances the value and interest of *Ce qui était perdu,* which does, to a certain extent, deal with this subject.[4]

"Le Démon de la connaissance" (1928)

This story was also written during Mauriac's crisis of faith in the late 1920s. Published in the *NRF* in July and August 1928, it also appeared in *Trois récits*. In "Coups de couteau" and "Insommie" there exists a genuine tension between the temptations of the flesh and the religious training that Louis, the protagonist, had presumably received as a young man. The incompatability between the two is stressed. In "Le Démon de la connaissance" (The demon of understanding), Mauriac develops this same theme from a slightly different point of view by exploring how a young man can decide to become a priest in part because he considers himself so physically unattractive as to be unlovable. This story once again shows Mauriac's obsession, during these crisis years, with the relationship between love and suffering.

Lange and Maryan share an intellectual and artistic quest. Lange is more sensitive to literature, while Maryan prefers to study philosophy.

Thus it is Lange who will become a novelist and who will recount the details of this relationship from his particular point of view. The story is a thinly veiled transposition of Mauriac's boyhood friendship with André Lacaze, who later became a priest and remained true to his calling until death. At some time during their friendship, which fluctuated over the years, Mauriac and Lacaze seem to have had an argument, during which the priest accused the novelist of convincing him as a boy that he was too unattractive to please a girl. This, claimed Lacaze, was the origin of his religious vocation. In the story Maryan (Lacaze) tells his friend: "If I made the mistake of going into the seminary, if I began life with this mistake, you alone are responsible" (*ORTC*, 2:234). Mauriac later admitted in his *Bloc-Notes* that, "He reproached me later in life for having made him so conscious of his ugliness that he decided to go into the seminary" (*BN*, 4:451).

There is little if any action in this story, which, like the others just considered, concentrates on the evocation of a state of mind. For Maryan, the great challenge in life is to understand the mystery of existence, but his philosophical and theological investigations will be inevitably flawed by the heartsickness and isolation that characterize his conviction that he is unlovable. At the end of the story Maryan is sick of life and ready to die, if only to finally know what comes after death. Like the artist Louis of "Coups de couteau" and "Insomnie," he is at an impasse, unable to move forward, immobilized by self-absorption.

"Le Démon de la connaissance" is yet another evocation of the difficulties that Mauriac encountered during these years. Although it is not directly related to any of the novels, he would explore this theme again in *Les Chemins de la Mer* (1939) (*The Unknown Sea*, 1948), and base the entire novel *Galigaï* (1952) (*The Loved and the Unloved*, 1953) on it. In these later works, however, it is female characters who are unable to become objects of desire for the men they love.

"Le Drôle" (1933)

"Le Drôle" (The oddball), published in 1933, was specially commissioned for a series of books written by great writers for little children. It tells of a crucial episode in the life of Ernest Romazilhe, a spoiled boy in a provincial family. About 10 years old, he is so spoiled that he has never attended school and has already caused the resignation of 17 nannies. A new nanny, Mlle Thibaud, arrives in her small provincial town as the story opens. Even before she gets off the train, she learns of the challenge that awaits her when a traveler tells her what a terror the boy is. After sizing up the nature of the power that the boy exercises over the entire household, she comes to the conclusion that she will never be able to educate this boy, let alone cure him of his tyrannical ways, as long as his father, his grandmother, and the family maid are there to wait on him. Once she has persuaded the three of them to leave the house and take up residence temporarily at their country home, she is able to deal directly with Ernest. By the end of the story she has succeeded in domesticating him, first by sharing with him her love of animals and later by discovering that his love of music is his Achilles heel.

This story can be connected to Mauriac's novels in a number of ways. One possibility is that Ernest could be considered a childhood portrait of Fernand Casenave of *Génitrix*. On firmer ground, the maid, named Seconde, reminds us of Marie de Lados of *Genitrix* and Cadette of *Le Baiser au lépreux*. Finally, Mlle Thibaud's taming of this little Nero through music reminds us of both *Le Sagouin*, in which Guillou's father plays the piano, and *Le Mal*, in which Fanny seduces Fabien through music.

The resemblance to *Le Sagouin* (1951), (*The Little Misery*, 1952) is the most striking, for both Ernest and Guillou are marginal figures. The one is spoiled by adults, who are largely responsible for making him what he has become, while the other is mistreated in a different way by his family. Their similarity lies in their sense of isolation within these dysfunctional families. In each case it is a teacher from outside the family who is able to help the child. "Le Drôle," unlike *Le Sagouin*, has a happy ending—a somewhat unusual occurence in Mauriac's fiction, but the story had to end like this if it was to fit into the series for which it had been commissioned. Perhaps it is in part for this reason that "Le Drôle" is so captivating and delightful to read. Since Mauriac did not include it in either of his two collections, and seems to have published it as an afterthought at the end of volume 10 of his *Oeuvres complètes,* it tends to be overlooked. Nonetheless the portrait that it provides of the relationship between the little Nero of the title and the dysfunctional family of which he is a part makes this a very modern work.

"Thérèse chez le docteur" (1933)

"Thérèse chez le docteur" ("Thérèse and the Doctor," 1947) first appeared in *Candide* in 1933 and was one of the five stories published in *Plongées*. As we recall, *Thérèse Desqueyroux* had originally been drafted in the form of a confession made by Thérèse to the parish priest.[5] Mauriac rewrote this first draft, adopting instead a third-person point of view. In

the novel, when Thérèse returns home from the courthouse, she is ready
to discuss her crime and to ask her husband, Bernard, for forgiveness,
but he does not want to talk. This desire for confession should be kept in
mind when reading "Thérèse chez le docteur." In this story, ten years
have passed since Thérèse left Bernard on the rue Royale. She has had a
number of lovers, including Jean Azévédo and later Phili, the narrator's
son-in-law from *Noeud de vipères*. Because of her feelings of guilt and
anguish, she is still seeking a confessor. This is why she comes to Dr.
Schwartz's apartment late at night.

Mauriac uses a framing device in this story, a rare occurrence in his
work: the discussion between Thérèse and the psychiatrist is framed by
another, quite different story, which probes the relationship between Dr.
Schwartz and his wife. Thus, the title of the story notwithstanding,
Thérèse is not the exclusive focus of this work, for the authorial voice
accords as much importance to the failed love relationship of the
Schwartzes.

Thérèse's late arrival at Dr. Schwartz's apartment can be explained
perhaps in part because he seems to have given her assurances at an earlier meeting (in a nightclub) that she could visit him at any time if she
felt the need to do so. When Thérèse comes to see Dr. Schwartz at his
home, where he has his office, she is entering a form of confessional, but
in a perverted form. The great doctor is professionally successful, but he
has been alienated from his wife for the last 20 years. It is a rainy night
and Dr. Schwartz's wife, Catherine, is upset by this sudden arrival of a
patient. She tries to relax and regain her composure, but sounds from
other apartments, above, below, and elsewhere on the sixth floor, not to
mention traffic in the street below, disturb her. There is no silence in this
particular confessional. Catherine reminds her husband that he had previously told her about this somewhat strange woman, whom he had met
two years earlier, and she voices her fear at having him receive such people in their apartment so late in the evening. The friction between them
reminds us of the marital strife between the spouses in "Un Homme de
lettres" and "Coups de couteau". The unhappy and disunited couples in
Le Désert de l'Amour and *Noeud de viperès* also come to mind, but here
there are no children.

Dr. Schwartz refers to the couch on which he places his patients as his
"confessional." His name clearly indicates that he symbolizes
Freudianism as well as Freud's Germanic and Jewish backgrounds. Since
the name means "black" in German, it also evokes the priest, whose traditional garb is black. As Catherine overhears Thérèse's confession, she

becomes aware of the difference in the treatment that the doctor accords to her and to this particular patient. Thus, everything that Thérèse says takes on a possible double and contrastive meaning. Gradually, as she listens to Thérèse speak about her love affairs with Jean Azévédo and Phili, Catherine realizes that she is really not listening to this conversation to protect her husband in case Thérèse is carrying a gun, but to eavesdrop on his work. She realizes that she hates both her husband and his work, because he explains everything in terms of an unconscious sexual drive, even going so far as to advise that one can calm the mind by giving the body all the pleasure it wants. Thus, she thinks to herself: "thousands of unhappy people had stammered and repeated their lies, while trying to discover the secret of their existence which they claimed to know nothing of" (*ORTC*, 3:5).

This is a harsh condemnation of the man who pretends to be a rival to the priest. Mauriac's grotesque caricature and simplistic reduction of psychoanalysis is no doubt unfair, but he intends to show no mercy to his adversary. The strong polemic tone that is found so often in his journalism creeps in here and becomes a major element in the story. Thus, Catherine's thoughts continue: "As with his other victims, he would encourage her to indulge all her appetites. Freeing the mind by satisfying the flesh; that's what his method was all about. The same filthy key was used to interpret heroism, crime, sanctity, self-renunciation" (*ORTC*, 3:13). Through Catherine, Mauriac expresses his own fundamental reason for attacking psychoanalysis: it attacks the notion of sin by weakening the feelings of guilt that Catholic theology traditionally attaches to the sex drive, which of course he had been taught to suppress since childhood; in taking this stance, psychoanalysis threatens the sacred preeminence of the priest, who alone is able to absolve guilt through the sacrament of confession.

Mauriac skillfully intertwines the Thérèse/Dr. Schwartz narrative with the framing narrative of Dr. Schwartz/Catherine in order to contrast the parallel thoughts and feelings of the two women while allowing the narrative voice to attack the scientific claims of psychoanalysis. Since the mysterious visitor is clutching her handbag when she arrives, the doctor's wife thinks that she might be carrying a pistol. This is her excuse for listening to the confession that is about to take place. Through this device the narrative voice is able to draw out the contradictions between Dr. Schwartz as a professional and as a husband.

The first part of Thérèse's confession, in which she tells of her amorous adventures, evokes the atmosphere of both *Ce qui était perdu* and *Le Mal.* The theme of drug use (alcohol, cocaine, etc.) on the fringes of a decadent bourgeois society brings to mind what I call Mauriac's Parisian novels, but it shows the self-absorbed characters in a slightly different light. Instead of seeing them in the habitual nightclubs or bars, racing their cars or stealing away to hotel rooms, we see Thérèse in the equivalent of what would become their church, the psychiatrist's office. It is this strong Parisian flavor that also serves to distance this story from the novel *Thérèse Desqueyroux,* which is thoroughly immersed in the lore and culture of les Landes, and to which the story is only superficially related.

The story ends when Catherine hears her husband cry out. She enters the room to find him hiding behind his desk while Thérèse stands against the wall with her hand in her purse. Dr. Schwartz had called for help, thinking that Thérèse was going to shoot him when in fact she was simply reaching for something in her handbag. Catherine now shows the visitor to the door, but not before Thérèse accuses Dr. Schwartz of being a thief because he charges money to treat the soul without really believing in its existence. After Thérèse leaves, Catherine can finally tell her husband that she no longer loves him, no doubt because of his cowardice, as Jacques Petit suggests (*ORTC,* 3:988), but also because of his haughty manner with the sincere and vulnerable patient.

At the time of writing the story, Mauriac took a dim view of psychoanalysis. During his career he would oscillate between acceptance and rejection of Freud's views about the human personality, but at this particular time he was clearly having quite negative thoughts. This is perhaps why he portrays Thérèse's confessor, Dr. Elisée Schwartz, in a very unsympathetic manner. Since Mauriac displayed a good deal of interest in the same subjects that Freud studied, scholars have begun in recent years to probe this possible relationship.[6] In fact, it can be said that Mauriac's principal convictions as a novelist correspond rather well to Freud's basic doctrines on the human personality. Thus, Mauriac's belief throughout his life in the power of heredity corresponds roughly to Freud's theory of the id; his preoccupation with the power of the church and family in the life of the young Catholic hero corresponds in a way to what Freud called the superego; and his self-conscious development of himself as a person and as an artist makes one think of the fragile Freudian ego navigating in the perilous waters between the id and superego. Mauriac and Freud, after all, were interested in the same things: the hidden forces that make people behave the way they do. But since Mauriac was a steadfast Catholic and Freud an atheist, they used completely different sets of words and images to express themselves.

One useful way to think of Mauriac's possible relationship to Freud is to picture him working between the "old" and the "new," that is, to situate him somewhere between traditional Catholic theologians on the one hand and Freud and his disciples on the other. At the same time, we must bear in mind that even if Mauriac did read Freud—and the evidence here is fragmentary, even contradictory as to what he read and when he read it—he almost certainly did not make an effort to understand Freud any more than he tried to understand the technical and specialized writings of theologians. He was simply not inclined to digest such materials, which were never able to hold his attention for very long. Mauriac's strength lay in language and style, not in philosophy and science. Thus, in his fictional work he never tried to prove or validate the theoretical work of any thinker, including Freud.

"Thérèse chez le docteur" is one of Mauriac's most successful pieces. From a purely artistic point of view, Mauriac's objection to psychoanalysis is perhaps best expressed when Thérèse says to the doctor: "Do you believe in the devil, doctor? Do you believe that evil is a person?" (*ORTC,* 3:15). Mauriac obviously believed that the answer to this question had to be in the affirmative, since to the Catholic novelist, evil, like goodness, must be incarnate. This is why, in an edifying novel like *Ce qui était perdu,* he had created a Satan figure like Hervé de Blénauge. Likewise, both Gradère in *Les Anges noirs* (1936) and Landin in *Les Chemins de la mer* (1939), would be assigned similar roles. For Mauriac, the stakes are high in this story, for virtually his entire fictional universe depends on the reader's acceptance of evil as a personalized entity. Psychoanalysis, which sees the same human problems that Mauriac analyzed in his fiction as disorders to be treated scientifically and not as problems with metaphysical roots, seemed to him to challenge the very foundations of his art. Thus, he goes for the Freudian jugular in this story. Thanks to its concision, sophisticated framing structure, and passionate defense, however indirect, of the Catholic novelist's reason for being, "Thérèse chez le docteur" stands out as one of Mauriac's minor masterpieces. It deserves to be rediscovered and more widely read.

"Thérèse à l'hôtel" (1933)

"Thérèse à l'hôtel" ("Thérèse at the Hotel," 1947) was written sometime after "Thérèse chez le docteur" and first published in *Candide* in August 1933. It was later included in *Plongées.* It takes the form of a monologue in which Thérèse recounts a meeting with a young man in a

hotel. The encounter leads nowhere when Thérèse, seeking to initiate a
relationship with the young man when she meets him, realizes that he
feels sorry for her and wants to save her. (Fanny and Fabien in *Le Mal*
come to mind in this regard). Whereas the earlier story was finely structured, this one is open-ended, with no clear denouement. In addition,
Thérèse's interior monologue reads like the examination of conscience
that would precede a confession. The young man seems to be a future
priest, the person who could eventually hear her confession, but their
meeting leads nowhere. This structure suggests that "Thérèse à l'hôtel"
might very well have been a first draft of what would eventually become
La Fin de la nuit. As in that novel, Thérèse is paradoxically both free to
pursue further adventures with still more lovers, and a prisoner held
hostage by the memory of her earlier act: the attempted murder of her
husband.

"Le Rang" (1936)

It is unclear when "Le Rang" (Rank) was written, but it was first published in *Candide* in March 1936 and appeared later in *Plongées*. There is
no surviving manuscript of the story, which Jacques Petit thinks was
written in 1936.[7]

Based on a maternal grandaunt, a *genitrix* figure who had dominated
her children to such an extent that they never married, this story is one
of Mauriac's most pessimistic works. It is linked by this theme to
Genitrix as well as to several other novels in which the dominating mother stifles the development of her children.

Mauriac builds this story around an image. Hector and Hortense
Bellade discuss the fact that their cousin, Auguste Duprouy, has spent an
unusual amount of money on his dead sister's funeral. Auguste, the last
of a dying lineage, had grown up under the controlling influence of his
mother, a widow. Since the Duprouy family did not have much money
but still had a certain "rank" in society that they had to maintain,
Hector Bellade and his wife had given them a small monthly subsidy for
years. This enabled the girls to devote their time to work in the local
parish. Since the Duprouys had essentially lived on handouts from their
cousin and his wife, Hortense sends her husband to enquire of Auguste
why he has spent so much on the funeral. The essence of the story is the
conversation between the two men.

Auguste tells of his mother's domination of him and his two sisters,
and describes in detail how a local priest had attempted to arrange a
marriage between him and a wealthy young girl of their social rank in

need of a husband. Of course, even though both Auguste and the girl wanted to marry, the plans fell through because of the mother's opposition. Before Auguste finishes telling his story he faints—from hunger, for he has no money to buy food. Hector takes him to a restaurant, brings him back home, and gives him extra money in addition to the regular monthly allowance. Several months later Hector receives word from the police that his cousin has died of natural causes, simply a lack of nourishment. When Hortense insists that they will pay to have him buried with his mother and two sisters, because then he will be happy for eternity, Hector responds ironically, "Do you think so?" On this somber note the story ends. The domineering mother of this story is one of the most monstrous in all of Mauriac's fiction. In keeping her children for herself, she forced them all to live tragically lonely and unfulfilled lives.

"Conte de Noël" (1938)

"Conte de Noël" (A Christmas story) was the only work to appear in *Plongeés* that had not already been published elsewhere. The title is misleading, for the story has very little to do with Christmas and very much to do with what is perhaps the major theme in Mauriac's fiction: a son's struggle for emancipation from a dominating mother.

The first-person narrative is related by Yves Frontenac, the young poet of *Le Mystère Frontenac*. He is calling to mind events that took place many years before in the school playground when he was seven years old. His friend Jean de Blaye, teased by the other boys because of his long blond curls, comes in for special abuse from the class bully, Campagne, because he still believes that Jesus comes down the chimney on Christmas Eve to bring presents to children. He holds this belief because his mother told him the story was true. Two weeks later, when classes resume after Christmas, Jean's hair is cut very short. When Yves asks him about Christmas, his only response is that his mother will no longer put things over on him. The shorn curls seem to symbolize the break with the mother. A year later he and his family move away from Bordeaux.

In the last section of the story, Yves is now a student in Paris, where he meets Jean de Blaye's brother, Philippe, in a bar. He learns that Jean as an adolescent broke open the strongbox in which his mother had kept his boyhood curls. This action symbolizes a desire to free himself from his mother's control. Later, after having lived a less than exemplary life, he died in ignominy in a hospital in Saigon.

Yves Frontenac now looks back on his chance meeting with Jean de Blaye's brother as the event that made him decide to become a fiction writer. Since the story helped him to understand his own childhood, which was also dominated by the influence of a powerful mother, the desire to tell Jean de Blaye's story (and to make the connection between the mother's stifling love in his childhood and his unsuccessful life as an adult) confirms that he should really be a novelist and not a poet.

Chapter Three
The Novels of Maturity

Le Baiser au lépreux (1922)

Le Baiser au lépreux (*The Kiss to the Leper,* 1923) is Mauriac's first masterpiece. The book was a bestseller in its day and helped to consolidate Mauriac's reputation among the small group of Parisian intellectuals who already knew him as a novelist and critic. When the novel was published in London the following year and in Amsterdam in 1924, Mauriac suddenly had an international reputation and was a force to be reckoned with.[1] He would later gleefully note that with this book he found not only his style and atmosphere but also his audience. He also recalled that it had caused him no small amount of joy to see one of his major detractors, Paul Souday, bristle at his success: "*Kiss to the Leper* is that point in my career when I found both my style and my readers: I recall the slight feeling of intoxication as the book went through several editions and the pleasure that I got out of Paul Souday's discomfort" (*OC,* 1:ii; *ORTC,* 1:990). We see here a good example of Mauriac's natural instinct, whether in literature or in politics, to go for an enemy's jugular. Souday, who for years had been a lively skeptic of Catholic novels, especially Mauriac's, was particularly upset to see him succeed.[2]

Drawing once again on the distilled memories of people he knew from his childhood and adolescence, Mauriac created the leper of the title, Jean Péloueyre, and the girl destined to become his wife, Noémi d'Artiailh (magnificent regional names that complement the novel's seductive title). This time, however, Mauriac devised a plot that was more credible and engaging than any he had used before. "None of the characters of *Kiss to the Leper* is invented," he wrote: "it's their story I invent. I could put a name alongside each Péloueyre, I knew each one of them in the old house in Villandraut, on the street called . . . However, none of them lived through the experiences that I imagined for them" (*OC,* 1:ii; *ORTC,* 1:990). Despite his familiarity with his characters' real-life models, here for the first time Mauriac creates

characters that are truly removed from his own personal experiences. It
is this quality that distances *Le Baiser au lépreux* from its predecessors.

Jean Péloueyre is the only child of a wealthy landowner, M. Jérôme.
He lives in a large three-story stone house in Villandraut (modeled after
the Mauriac home in Saint-Symphorien) with his father and their maid,
Cadette. The novel opens in the month of August, *la canicule,* the hottest
period of the year. Between one and three in the afternoon all is quiet,
since everyone, but especially M. Jérôme, is taking a nap. This is a good
time for Jean to slip out of the house to see his friend Robert Pieuchon.
The molten air, like water in a swimming pool, encompasses him as he
walks furtively through town, hoping none of the local people will see
him. He is known in town as an oddball. When he walks down the
street he talks and laughs to himself, engaging in a kind of pantomime
that people find amusing. When he gets to Robert's house, his friend is
not there, for the family has gone out to lunch. But Jean is invited to
wait in Robert's room for his friend to return.

There he looks at the titles of books that Robert has bought for his
summer reading. They hint of a world forever closed to Jean: *Aphrodite,*
The Latin Orgy, Diary of a Chambermaid. But another book attracts his
attention, the *Selected Writings* of Nietzsche, in which he reads of the difference between the good and the bad, the strong and the weak. One
passage in particular catches his eye: "What is good? Everything that
exalts in man the feeling of power, the will to power, power itself. What
is bad? Everything that has its roots in weakness. Let the weak and the
unsuccessful perish: and let's help them to disappear! What is more
harmful than any vice? The pity that underlies action on behalf of the
weak and socially inferior: Christianity" (*ORTC,* 1:449).[3] Nietzsche's
denunciation of Christianity as a psychological panacea for the weak sets
Jean to thinking about how ugly he is and the degree to which he has
taken refuge in religious belief. Like his father, who is also a believer and
a regular churchgoer, Jean has lived a life of faith since birth. But now
he wonders, whether he has become a slave to religion, using it as a
refuge to keep from looking more critically at himself. He thinks, for
example, of his friend Daniel Trasis, who has gone off to Paris to seek his
fortune. If, like Daniel, he were physically pleasing to women, would he
be going to Sunday mass with all the old ladies and servants? The theme
of the Nietzschean will to power thus becomes an essential motif in the
novel: how will a "weak" person like Jean Péloueyre become "strong"?

Jean's mother is already deceased, and all contact with her family has
been lost. Thus, his father's older sister, Félicité Casenave, is his principal

living female relative. A widow, she lives only for her own son, Fernand. She looks at her sickly brother and his odd son, a replica of the father, and is reassured that both will die soon, leaving all their money to her and her son. But Jean's father has a surprise in store for her and gradually he reveals it to his son: he will arrange a marriage for Jean to the beautiful Noémi d'Artiailh, who belongs to a respectable, but penurious, local family. In so doing he will achieve three goals: his son will have a wife and companion, Jean and Noémi will perhaps have children to thwart his sister's ambitions, and he will acquire a nurse to watch over him in his last days. M. Jérôme's selfishness is apparent from the beginning of the novel, when we learn of his rage if anyone disturbs him during his sacrosanct afternoon nap. It is clear that this arranged marriage is intended more to satisfy his own needs and desires than Jean's.

The marriage between Jean and Noémi is arranged and carried off despite the girl's reservations. M. Jérôme has used the parish priest as the go-between and tells Jean that the curé is responsible for the whole scheme. He assures his son that the priest is worried about the 23-year-old Jean and wants to see him settled in a solid marriage. But Jean does not doubt that his father is behind everything, pulling the strings. When Jean tells his father that this pretty girl will find him repulsive, M. Jérôme at first insists that the parish priest must get what he wants, once again laying blame for the whole plan at the curé's feet. But then he admits his own interest in arranging this marriage for his son: he will force his son through this humiliating experience in order to block the ambitions of his sister and her handsome young son, who is also a highly visible local politician. So what is really involved here is not Jean's happiness, but money and inheritance, spite and jealousy. Jean and Noémi will be the victims of this plot.

Money, family, love, and desire are all basic ingredients of Mauriac's best fiction, and each element is in place here. Noémi has been trained to obey her parents and to follow the advice of her confessor. The point is made that she does not read novels (how different she is in this respect from Thérèse Desqueyroux, whom Mauriac would create only a few years later), and thus lacks a fully developed imagination. Although she is able to experience elementary sexual desire, she is incapable of focusing on Jean as an object of that desire. When she voices her concern to her parents, they respond with a sentence that would become one of the most often quoted lines from all of Mauriac's fiction: "You don't turn down Péloueyre's son." Encapsulated in this laconic formula is all that is understood as coming with that son: "You don't refuse the income generated by your sharecroppers, the farms, the flocks of sheep, the silverware, the linens dating back ten generations and all folded neatly in wide, high and fragrant wardrobes, and the close relationships with the best people in the region. You don't turn down Péloueyre's son" (*ORTC,* 1:464).

The marriage takes place, and with it the tragedy of this pathetic soul is set in motion. Mauriac makes much of the sexual incompatibility between the two young people, while still treating the subject in a restrained and delicate manner. In the 1920s, however, such subject matter was explosive, especially when mixed with incense and holy water according to the Mauriac formula. The omniscient third-person narrative voice tells us that before her marriage Noémi "gazed with pity on her chaste body, which was still intact, burning with life but with a vegetal freshness. What would the oddball do to this body? She knew that he would have the right to any caress that he desired, including that mysterious and frightful one after which a child would be born" (*ORTC,* 1:464). Such passages shocked conservative Catholic sensibilities at the time. The consummation of Jean and Noémi's marriage offers another example of Mauriac's frank approach to sex, generously tinged with Jansenist guilt and shame: "Behind the cretonne curtains, two guardian angels shielded their shamed faces. Jean Péloueyre had to struggle a long time, first against his own frigidity, then against an inert body. At dawn a weak groan marked the end of a struggle that had lasted six hours. Covered with sweat, Jean Péloueyre—more hideous than a worm alongside the cadaver from which it has just emerged—didn't dare budge" (*ORTC,* 1:466). Mauriac's recognizable Catholic worldview, which here explicitly acknowledges the existence of guardian angels, dared to incorporate sex in a direct manner. In doing so, he gave voice to his own personal obsessions and made many enemies for himself among conservative Catholics and other traditionalists.

Jean's humiliation in the face of his wife's revulsion overwhelms him. He invents a pretext to go off to Paris so as not to be near her. With the complicity of the parish priest, he convinces his father and wife to let him go. He tells them that he needs several weeks or perhaps months to complete a study of a topic of local historical interest, and that it is only in Paris that he will be able to find the documents he needs. M. Jérôme, who does not want to see his son escape his grasp, is consoled by the thought that Noémi will remain behind to wait on him.

Jean goes off to Paris and begins his research, but this does not keep him from thinking of the master/slave relationship depicted by Nietzsche. Each afternoon he sits at the Café de la Paix—the same place

where Thérèse will be left when Bernard Desqueyroux abandons her—
and watches the sad faces of the passersby. He has rethought the
Nietzschean challenge in terms of his own Catholic convictions and is
planning to write a book entitled *Volonté de puissance et sainteté* (The will
to power and sainthood), which would point out that to be a Christian is
not necessarily to be a "slave" in the Nietzschean sense of the word. He
would argue in this book that among Christians there are also "masters,"
since the saints, the great religious orders, and the Catholic Church as a
whole in its universal claims and perennial nature reflect a will to exercise power over others. The reader gets to know and understand Jean
better during this period of exile. Although he is physically unattractive,
he is a thinker and intellectually alive. The young man who might seem
at first glance to be a Nietzschean weakling is gradually becoming something quite different.

Spring finally comes. Jean has been in Paris since December. One day
a letter arrives from the parish priest calling him back home but without
giving any reason. This latest intervention in Jean's life has been
prompted by the content of Noémi's weekly confession; she has related
nothing specific, but the priest still senses that something is wrong.
What he senses is supplied for us by the narrative voice: since her marriage, Noémi's body has been awakened to sexual pleasure while her
heart has remained untouched. Chance would also have it that a man
intent on seducing her, a young doctor in a neighboring village, enters
her life at this time. Not long after Jean returns home, his own weakened state is such that Noémi and M. Jérôme become worried about his
health. Although Jean's father cannot bear to think that anyone but he
can be sick in their household, and does not want to share Noémi's
attention with his son, he recognizes the gravity of the situation and
summons the doctor. But since the village physician, Dr. Pieuchon, is
unable to come (he is at home tending to his own son, who is dying of
tuberculosis), his young colleague, the same one who is determined to
seduce Noémi, is called in to visit Jean. In a magnificent scene, in which
Jean and his father are both unaware of Noémi's attraction to the young
doctor, it is decided that Jean does not yet have tuberculosis but that he
is an excellent candidate for it because of his generally weak physical
state and because, after all, his mother had died from the same illness.
Noémi comports herself with dignity despite the presence in her house
of the handsome young doctor.

Despite the doctor's orders to remain in bed in order to build up his
strength, Jean insists on going out walking every afternoon. Noémi and

her father-in-law let him go, even though they know that he needs bed rest. It is only a month later, when Dr. Pieuchon's son finally dies, that she realizes that Jean has been at the boy's bedside each afternoon, ostensibly comforting him, but also perhaps trying to contract from him the illness that will serve to hasten his own death. Jean's illness soon becomes apparent. He is dying and he knows it. Félicité Casenave and her son tell all who will listen that M. Jérôme is too stingy to send his son away to a mountain sanatorium, where he would have more of a chance of being cured, while Noémi drives from her mind all thoughts of the young doctor who had briefly attracted her attention. The village priest now comes into sharper focus, for he had been instrumental in both sending Jean away and calling him back. His personal agony in watching Jean suffer is highlighted by the fact that his interference in the young man's private life had been motivated by good intentions: he was sincerely trying to do God's work. Scrupulous in the extreme, he sees now that he has become too closely involved in the lives of others, and he reproaches himself for trying to be more than he really wants to be: a simple country priest serving as God's instrument for the salvation of souls. But there is an ironic twist to this feeling of guilt, for the priest, after all, has realized his goal: he has indeed helped to save Jean's soul. And Jean himself, now courageously facing death and thereby imposing his own will upon an impossible situation, has proven that he is anything but a weakling.

Jean Péloueyre dies and Noémi, provided that she not remarry, is made the sole heir of the family fortune. In an epilogue, we see Noémi three years later. Her life is empty since she has nothing to do and no children to care for. Since she has begun to put on weight, Dr. Pieuchon wants her to walk an hour each day. In the last scene of the novel she is walking in the country, through the vast pine forests. By coincidence, she recognizes the horse and carriage belonging to the young doctor. Her instincts attract her to him as he is leaving one of the shacks in which her sharecroppers are lodged. But in a sudden revelation, she realizes that her destiny is one of renunciation. Given her social situation, she really has no other choice than to remain faithful to the memory of her deceased husband. The townspeople consider her an admirable widow for having nursed her dying husband and remained faithful to him after death, while her parents and her father-in-law would be aghast if she were to even consider remarriage. Thus trapped, and realizing it, she flees into the woods so as not to meet the young doctor face to face. She has given to Jean Péloueyre "those kisses that in earlier times the lips of saints gave to lepers" *ORTC*, 1: 487), and in so doing has become a kind of saint herself: "Small, she was condemned to greatness; a slave, she was destined to reign" (*ORTC*, 1:499).

In this, his first masterpiece, Mauriac's mordant irony makes it clear that Noémi's "greatness" is possible in part only because, in his view, the church is overly involved with the things of this world. Noémi is caught in a web of social relationships in which the church plays an important but somewhat questionable role. To Mauriac, the form of Catholicism, which buttresses the social system in this provincial town, and the substance of Catholicism (reflected in Jean's reading about the lives of the saints and his own exemplary life of self-sacrifice for the benefit of others) are two completely different matters. Noémi, of course, is not equipped to understand this distinction, but her experience enables the alert reader to do so.[4]

Le Fleuve de feu (1923)

While writing *Le Baiser au lépreux,* Mauriac also worked on *Le Fleuve de feu (The River of Fire,* 1954). Daniel Trasis, a friend of Jean Péloueyre, and the principal character of *Le Fleuve de feu,* was originally intended as a fully developed presence in the previous novel. But as Mauriac developed each novel, he opted for concision rather than development, for focus on one individual crisis rather than dispersion of interest. Thus, in *Le Baiser au lépreux,* Daniel Trasis is really no more than a name mentioned in the text; he is the friend whom Jean Péloueyre admires from afar, and who has gone off to Paris to establish himself as a writer. Likewise, in *Le Fleuve de feu,* in which Daniel is the central character, Jean Péloueyre is little more than a name. Interestingly, two other characters from *Le Baiser au lépreux* will also provide the focus of a separate novel: the interplay between Jean's aunt Félicité Casenave and her son Fernand becomes the central concern of *Genitrix.*

The original title for this novel was *La Pureté perdue* (Lost purity), suggesting that Mauriac intended to focus the reader's attention on the state of humanity after passing through the innocent phase of childhood. Daniel Trasis is a young hedonist who, like his friend Raymond Courrèges (of whom we shall learn much more in *Le Désert de l'amour),* establishes seduction of women as a major priority in his life. But at the same time he is also nostalgic for his lost innocence. He cultivates this feeling through his recollections of Marie Ransinangue, a girl his own age from his native town who serves for him as a kind of remote guardian angel. Raymond Courrèges, on the other hand, is characterized as an evil and satanic influence. Marie is in a Carmelite convent during most of the action of the novel, praying for the salvation of Daniel's soul, while Raymond is living by his wits on the fringes of Parisian society. Daniel, in the middle, is attracted to both of these polar opposites.

At the beginning of the action, recounted by Mauriac's customary third-person omniscient narrator, we find Daniel Trasis alone in a remote hotel in the French Pyrenees. In adopting this locale, Mauriac was evoking the two months that he had spent in a similar hotel during the early summer of 1919. He was still weak since his return from Salonika and needed complete rest to overcome his pulmonary ailment, diagnosed as pleurisy at the time. Here, in the small town of Argelès, Mauriac would situate the only one of his novels in which the principal action takes place away from the two settings he knew best—the Landes and Paris.

It seems that the sight of two women at the hotel provided the initial inspiration for the novel. To this mental image Mauriac added his clear memories of boredom and fatigue, and transplanted the character of Daniel Trasis from *Le Baiser au lépreux* to this new setting and plot.

Daniel has come to the remote hotel to escape his mistress and to carry out promises that he has made to himself. Like Jean Péloueyre, he seems to have read Nietzsche. Having resolved to stay away from Paris for another two weeks, he is determined to keep faith with himself. Both of his parents are already deceased and now, in his early twenties, he is a survivor of the trench warfare of World War I. He is an utterly modern hero—skeptical, hedonistic, and rootless. His only link with the past, a picture of his granduncle, whom he calls "le Vieux de la Sesque" and who is not much different from "le Vieux de Maltaverne," whom we will encounter in *Un Adolescent d'autrefois* almost a half-century later, is virtually the only element in the novel that links it with the familiar motifs of "Mauriac country."

Daniel is attracted to a young woman, Gisèle de Plailly, who checks into the hotel alone. His attempts to initiate conversations with her lead nowhere. When he overhears that she is waiting for the arrival of a friend, Mme de Villeron, Daniel becomes jealous, wondering about the nature of their relationship and what role this person might play in Gisèle's life. Could there be some kind of mystical link between them? We already know that Marie Ransinangue, who had been his friend in early adolescence and who, despite their friendship, had never been corrupted by him, made a vow to become a nun and to enter a cloister for the rest of her life if Daniel were permitted by God to return safely from the war. Thus, when he came back in 1918, wounded but fully recovered, she had entered a Carmelite convent in Toulouse and had not been heard from again. Marie's vicarious suffering on behalf of Daniel provides a mystical link between them. But what kind of mystical link exists between the mysterious Gisèle de Plailly and "la Villeron," as Daniel calls her? The mystery of identity and relationship is heightened when Mme de Villeron arrives in the company of a little girl, Marie, who calls her "mémé" (grandmother). By this time Daniel has already gotten to know Gisèle and has been struck by her apparent vulgarity: she smokes, her manner of speaking is more frank and straightforward than he would like, and she does not seem, like so many girls from a bourgeois background, to have marriage in the back of her mind. Reality is not living up to the initial vision that he had created in his mind of a pure and vulnerable virgin.

When Mme de Villeron arrives, Daniel (who judges all women primarily in sexual terms) decides that she is incapable of erotic pleasure. Modeled in part on Mauriac's own mother, Mme de Villeron prefigures Brigette Pian of *La Pharisienne*. She is the kind of person who exercises moral authority over others, who directs their consciences and thus does not fit into the narrow categories in which Daniel classifies women. Derisively, he refers to her as *"la dernière des dernières"* (last of the last), a term that had been used throughout the war years to justify "the war to end all wars." On first impression he places her "last" as a hopelessly unattractive female, but he will soon be forced to change his assessment of her. Since he sees only with the eyes of desire, he will have to learn a new way of seeing in order to measure her true worth.

Gradually Daniel learns that the trio of Gisèle/Mme de Villeron/Marie is much more complicated than he had imagined. The child is not the granddaughter of "la Villeron," but is in fact Gisèle's daughter, thus proving to Daniel that Gisèle is not the virgin he had supposed her to be. Despite this disappointment he goes ahead with his plans for conquest and succeeds. When Gisèle reveals to him the circumstances in which she became pregnant and bore a child out of wedlock, the recounting of her experience is reminiscent of the short story "La Paroisse morte," (The dead parish)[5] and of several chapters of an aborted novel (see chapter 1, note 17) that are to be found among Mauriac's papers in the Bibliothèque Jacques Doucet.

As a poor girl raised on a farm that, by the end of the war, was just behind the front lines, Gisèle would go into Paris each day on the train to escape her lonely life with her father. On one of her trips she encounters a soldier on leave. They sit next to each other in a darkened movie house; touching each other in the dark leads them to a hotel room, where they meet regularly for the next five days. After this unnamed young man returns to the front and is killed, Gisèle bears his child. This episode is unique in Mauriac's fiction. Written soon after the war, when memories of that great conflict were fresh in his mind, it encapsulates the whole panorama of bizarre events that could take place in the unprecedented atmosphere created by the war. This part of the novel, in particular the sordid meeting in the darkened movie house, is naturalistic in style and effect and shows how Mauriac was tempted to incorporate into his own work some of the elements of the *roman social,* a novel depicting lower-class life and conveying a social message, before hitting upon his own particular style.

Mme de Villeron, a friend of Gisèle's family since her childhood, assumes responsibility for the child as if it were her own. As a childless widow, she has resolved to seek spiritual perfection. In addition to traditional acts of piety, she is particularly interested in helping young women like Gisèle who have fallen. In her own way, she wants to make the weak strong: "Her religious passion revolved around the lost coin and the prodigal son who, fresh from the embrace of his lover, was more beloved than the oldest son" (*ORTC,* 1:560). Mauriac, interested at this time in studying the "strong" side of Catholicism and thereby implicitly refuting those who see in it only a refuge for the "weak," develops the powerful and dominating aspect of Mme de Villeron's personality. Thus, she "spoke with a persuasive voice that resounded with authority. Directrice of consciences, obviously; more adroit than a priest in the guidance of souls; she was one of those women for whom clinics and labor unions are nothing more than fish ponds, reservoirs of people to be saved" (*ORTC,* 1:542). By the end of the novel, Lucile de Villeron will have succeeded in pulling her spiritual charge from the all-consuming "river of fire" of carnal temptation. Also, having achieved the Jansenist ideal of mastery over the urgings of the flesh, she sees herself as morally better equipped to raise Marie and thus convinces Gisèle to give the child over to her. She then withdraws to the country in Normandy, where her home and fortune are, while Gisèle returns to her native village in the dreary suburbs northeast of Paris. Lucile is "strong," and she has conquered herself. But in doing so she has cut herself off from any genuine experiences of human emotion, and her need to dominate others is perhaps a compensation for this void in her life.

In the final scene, Daniel Trasis, seated at a sidewalk café opposite the Gare du Nord, decides that he wants to see Gisèle one more time. He takes the train to the suburbs and walks the remaining five kilometers to her village. It is Sunday morning and the bells in the village church are ringing, calling the faithful to mass. He is determined to see and to possess Gisèle once more, but when he finally does see her, she is playing the harmonium in church. This is a new Gisèle that he discovers, one who has been fortified by Mme de Villeron. She is so enraptured as she plays, seemingly enveloped in an ecstasy of divine grace, that she looks like a portrait of the Virgin Mary being assumed into heaven. Daniel watches as Gisèle receives communion and returns to her seat. He continues to watch her for a long moment and, when nothing happens and she remains motionless, he decides that he must impose his will on the situation. Thus, he tells himself that if she does not look up in three minutes, he will renounce his plans for seduction and leave her forever. This young disciple of Nietzsche, whom we first met in an isolated hotel in the Pyrenees where he had gone to escape his lover and conquer his personal appetites, is now counting off the minutes after which he will turn his back on Gisèle. As the novel ends, he is going out the door of the church, having first placed his hand in the font of holy water placed nearby. Daniel has been defeated in his plan to lure Gisèle back into the "river of fire," while Gisèle has emerged from the final confrontation without even being aware of her victory. While this denouement may seem somewhat contrived, it is consistent with the moral uplift that takes place in the last section of the novel. Gisèle, who has been conscious of how abject her condition is, of how low she has fallen, now reigns. The initial vision that we had of her—through Daniel's eyes—of an innocent virgin, was first attenuated by the more vulgar aspects of her speech and deportment. From there she was revealed to be a completely fallen woman. But here, as the novel ends, she has been regenerated to the extent that the narrator actually compares her to the Virgin Mary.

Le Fleuve de feu is as close as Mauriac ever came to writing a *roman social*. It is perhaps in part for this reason that it remains undervalued— both by him and, in general, by his critics. In the preface to his *Oeuvres complètes,* Mauriac passed rapidly over the novel as if it were an embarassment, claiming that only the first 50 pages or so of the text (which deal primarily with the atmosphere of the old hotel in the Pyrenees), are truly representative of his work. And yet he still had to admit that "Gisèle de Plailly exists in spite of everything because so many readers have remained faithful to this lost girl" (*OC,* 1:iii; *ORTC,* 1:990-91). Although the temptation to write in a naturalistic style was probably barely remembered 30 years later, it was a real option for him as a neophyte in 1920. Reading this part of the novel today, in which the action takes place elsewhere than on the usual "planète Mauriac," we find the author painting one of his starkest, yet most convincing portraits of the solitude and isolation that characterize life in the "modern" era. This path is the one that Mauriac, however briefly, was tempted to follow, but decided instead to reject. The last part of *Fleuve de feu* offers a good example of this road not taken.

Modern readers have been slow to fully appreciate this novel, which did not even appear in an English translation until 1954. If Mauriac himself expressed reservations about it in the 1950s, we can hardly be surprised when one of his most attentive readers, André Séailles, devotes no more than a paragraph to the book in his study of Mauriac's works, dismissing the novel because "the story of this child-mother has lost much of its meaning, principally because of the change that has taken place in morals."[6] It can be argued, however, that this change in morals is irrelevent. While probing the inner workings of the human mind, this novel focuses on the problems of control and domination, hints at the action of divine grace within Gisèle's soul, and portrays graphically the difference between carnal desire (eros) on the one hand and selfless love and commitment (agape) on the other. *Fleuve de feu* is the last novel that Mauriac wrote before discovering his mature style, and in certain respects it is the most appealing of his early works.

Genitrix (1923)

Genitrix (*Genitrix,* 1930 and 1950) was conceived by Mauriac (without his quite realizing it) while he was writing *Le Baiser au lépreux.* He had intended the earlier novel to be somewhat longer, dealing with several branches of the Péloueyre and Casenave families, but decided instead to limit its scope and create a completely separate work from the material he had left out.

Genitrix has only two principal characters, Félicité Casenave, the *genitrix,* or powerful dominating mother, and her son Fernand. The latter's wife, Mathilde, dies shortly after the beginning of the novel, allowing the narrative voice to focus on the problematic mother/son relationship in the context of past generations and the ongoing obsession with money and property.

The novel opens at a moment of crisis. Mathilde is lying in bed, gravely ill after a delivery that was poorly handled by the local midwife. She has lost a lot of blood and is running a very high fever. She has been left alone at the far end of the family's large home, for her husband sleeps at the other end of the house in the room adjoining his mother's. Her physical separation from them is symbolic of the psychological isolation in which they have kept her. Although married to Fernand, she is still an outsider in the Casenave family and plays a secondary role in her husband's life. In *Le Baiser au lépreux* the fierce anticlericalism of Fernand and his mother is a strong counterpoint to the faith and piety of Jean Péloueyre. Here Mauriac attenuates somewhat this aspect of their personalities, but he still insists on their lack of faith. In contrast to them, Marie de Lados, the faithful old family servant, exemplifies through her piety and humility another approach to life.

After Mathilde dies, Fernand's attitude toward his mother changes precipitately. "There are some men who are capable only of loving against someone," the narrator tells us, and Fernand is surely such a person (*ORTC*, 1:634). His whole life has been devoted to irritating his mother. Until his marriage, when he was already bordering on the age of 50, the only other sexual relationship he had ever pursued was with a mistress in Bordeaux whom he visited periodically and whom his mother accepted grudgingly as his "habit." But for Fernand, who clearly did not love this woman, part of the pleasure of the relationship—and perhaps the most important part—was the distress it caused his mother. In addition, each of these psychological victories over Félicité was accompanied by the ritual of mending fences afterward. In marrying Mathilde, Fernand repeated the type of maneuver he had employed with his mistress, the only difference being that with Matilde the stakes were greater. Mathilde actually entered their home and ate at their table, whereas the mistress remained in Bordeaux. Confronted by this menace, Félicité succeeded in isolating her daughter-in-law after only a few weeks, driving her off to the far end of the house. The death of Mathilde is an apparent victory for Félicité, but it creates a situation in which the mother and the son are alone again. At this juncture, true to his nature, Fernand turns against his mother and, in opposition to her, loves the dead Mathilde.

Abandoned by her son, Félicité languishes and loses her desire to live. But before her death she realizes that her son, in continuing to make her suffer as he always has, but now refusing to be reconciled with her, is treating her the same way that they both had treated Mathilde. His unceasing psychological war against his mother culminates in the accusation that she is responsible for Mathilde's death. When Félicité argues that the girl died of natural causes, Fernand insists that his mother had killed her gradually each day.

A few months later Félicité dies. At her burial, the neighbors think they are witnessing an extraordinary display of filial attachment when Fernand seems to be trying to jump into his mother's grave. What he is in fact doing is leaning over as far as he can to look at the casket holding Mathilde's remains.

Now Fernand is alone—or almost alone. The old servant Marie de Lados, whose simple faith he has never been able to share or understand, is the only person left in his life. He banishes her from the house momentarily (and in doing so acts very much like his mother) when he thinks that Marie's daughter is trying to extort money from him. But in the closing scene of the novel, old Marie returns to him and places her aged hand on his forehead. He has nothing to live for, and Marie's return probably indicates that she will prepare him for death.

Genitrix is one of Mauriac's greatest masterpieces, not only for its powerful depiction of an unhealthy love relationship, but also for its many stylistic features. Often noted by critics is the special atmosphere in the Casenave house created by the fact that it is located adjacent to a railroad station. Many events in the novel are situated with respect to the coming and going of trains and the effect that this has on the house, that is, the shaking and rattling of windows and furniture. The train is a structuring device used to link the torment, pain, and suffering of the characters. Thus, when Fernand is obsessed and guilt-ridden by the thought that his wife has actually died from neglect, he hears the same train that Mathilde had heard the previous day on her deathbed.

The conflict between the simple faith of Marie de Lados and the anticlericalism of the Casenaves highlights again a dichotomy found in Mauriac's own family, which he instinctively incorporated into his novels. Finally, the theme of death pervades the novel—from the opening scene, which depicts Mathilde on her deathbed to the last one, when Fernand himself is ready to die in the company of the third female to whom he feels a close attachment, Marie de Lados.[7]

Le Mal (1935)

Le Mal (The Enemy, 1952) occupies a unique place in Mauriac's fiction of this period. He worked on it intermittently between 1917 and 1924 and allowed parts of it to be published in the literary review *Demain* in April 1924. But when he finally completed the text, he "was so unhappy with this botched novel that I decided at the last minute not to publish it," he tells us in the preface to the *Oeuvres complètes,* where he relegates it to volume 6, far from the other novelistic successes of the 1920s (*ORTC,* 1:994). He finally decided to publish the book in 1935, at a completely different stage of his career, but since it was written in the 1920s it will be discussed here.

Le Mal is a novel of apprenticeship, a bildungsroman that tells of the coming of age of Fabien Dézaymeries, a young man from the Landes region who learns in Paris about the world of adulthood. His initiation is presided over by an older woman, Fanny, whose physical desire for him reminds us of Phèdre's passion for Hippolyte in the classical seventeenth-century play by Racine. At the end of this process, the boy of 22 will have become a man. This work, like *Ce qui était perdu,* which would follow a few years later, is one that I call a "Parisian" novel because its focus is more clearly on Paris than on the Landes. In addition, it deals with the aesthetics of modern painting and music, and provides a portrait of the decadent Parisian artistic milieu of the 1920s. Most of the action of the novel takes place in Paris and a good deal of it is based on Mauriac's personal experiences as a young man away from home for the first time in the early years of the century. Fabien, like Mauriac, comes from an austere religious background; his father is dead and his mother quite devout. He is now a student at the prestigious Ecole des Chartes, hoping to become an archivist, and is living in relatively humble circumstances in student lodgings while making his way in artistic and avant-garde literary circles.

Fabien has been raised by his Jansenist mother, Marie, in the belief that anything having to do with the flesh is evil. His older brother, Joseph, who shares his mother's piety, dies of tuberculosis, leaving Fabien an only child. The principal outside influence in their family is his mother's girlhood friend Fanny Barrett, an orphan of French and Irish background who had been raised by an uncle in Bordeaux. In contrast to the bourgeoisie of the Landes region, whose kinship relations are strictly regulated by marriage, Fanny is both unattached and an outsider. Like so many people in Mauriac's fiction who do not come from solid bourgeois homes, she lives in a dangerous world without roots or parental guidance. Thus, Fanny grows to womanhood without the religious beliefs that would, in Mauriac's view, attenuate her natural sensuality. She reappears from time to time and stays in the guest room that Marie, by now a widow, keeps ready for her. But when on one particular visit Fanny seems to be unduly interested in Fabien, she is banished from the house by her hostess and asked never to return.

Marie, in the hope of buttressing her son's religious faith, suggests that he make a pilgrimage to Rome, but he never makes it that far. Feeling no religious inspiration in retracing the footsteps of St. Francis of Assisi in Italy and perhaps untouched by divine grace, he decides to travel to Venice and not to Rome. His mother's perfectly laid plans, made with the best of intentions (that is, to expose him to the graces that can come from visiting important religious sites while at the same time mortifying herself by living without her beloved son's presence), will lead to results that are quite the opposite of what she had hoped. Not long after Fabien's arrival in Venice, where he experiences deep solitude for the first time and perhaps also a complete absence of grace, he meets Fanny quite by accident in a hotel lobby. The narrative voice makes it clear that Fabien is in a state of emotional disarray when he meets her. Although his belief in God is intact, he is in a weakened moral state since he is far from home and alone. In this situation, the diabolic Cyrus Bargues, a British ballet dancer and friend of Fanny, strikes up a conversation with Fabien in the lobby and serves as the intermediary who will bring Fabien and Fanny together. The hero now enters a period of apprenticeship in the ways of the world. He returns to Paris with Fanny, he living in his student quarters in the Latin quarter and she in her fashionable apartment on the Right Bank.

Fabien is initiated fully into the experience of love and is exposed at the same time to the world of modern painting and music, but his background and upbringing have not prepared him to understand these expressions of the avant-garde. Each time he comes to the realization that he does not belong in this world of unlimited self-indulgence and experimentation, he intimates to Fanny that he wants to leave her, but when he does so she threatens to commit suicide. Finally, after several months of tension, Fabien decides to drop out of school. The process of initiation has of necessity consumed so much of his time that the bourgeois security offered by the Ecole des Chartes must be sacrificed. The prospect of spending his whole life in dusty archives is no longer of interest when compared to the self-indulgent pleasures Fanny and her circle can offer him.

When Fabien meets Colombe, the illegitimate daughter of Fanny's current husband, he idealizes her and hopes for salvation in this life by combining sexual fulfillment with love in a permanent bourgeois relationship: marriage. He now bestows upon Colombe (which means pigeon or dove in French) the nickname Palombe, after the species of pigeon that migrates through the Landes region each year. In a dream vision, he also imagines the two of them burning together as one flame in his native Landes, which of course represents nature and purity, qualities that are sorely lacking in their Parisian milieu. When Fanny discovers the affection that the two young people have for each other, she tries to commit suicide but, as is usually the case in Mauriac's novels, her attempt is unsuccessful. While recovering, however, she realizes that her relationship with Fabien is now ended and that she no longer has power over him. As for Fabien, he too struggles to achieve a new level of equilibrium, for now his passionate appetites are under control. The period of initiation has been completed and this young bourgeois hero is now ready to get serious about life and to take his place in the world.

Le Mal, like *Le Fleuve de feu,* takes place for the most part outside of Mauriac country and explores in depth a different social milieu. The original manuscript of the novel dates back to the period at the end of World War I when Mauriac was experimenting with different types of fiction in search of his own particular style and atmosphere. In fact, the earliest version of Fabien was a young officer returning home from active duty, indicating that the novel was conceived originally when Mauriac had not yet opted to devote himself definitively to writing psychological novels with a strong religious dimension rather than Balzacian novels with a predominantly sociological and political content. Another clue that this novel is in certain respects linked to Mauriac's earliest work is its strong autobiographical dimension. Quite a number of details seem to be lifted and transposed from his own personal experience.

Mauriac ends the novel by telling us that this new period in his hero's life "is where it would be appropriate to begin the real story of Fabien Dézaymeries, to which the preceding story would be a prologue" (*ORTC,* 1:734). He was conscious of the fact that many Catholic critics condemned him for exploiting his own Catholic social milieu to write what they considered scabrous novels. Thus, he seems to be conceding to them here that he does indeed believe it to be important to tell the story of the struggle for perfection that follows upon the usually sinful initiation experience. But then why doesn't he write such a novel of moral uplift? His answer is that since grace is a "mysterious protagonist" whose actions are difficult to decipher, he cannot do so: "What artist would dare to imitate the deceptive workings of grace, the mysterious protagonist? It is our slavery and our misery that human passion is the only subject we can depict without lying" (*ORTC,* 1:734). Like Racine, he still preferred in the early 1920s, when he wrote the novel, to depict human passions without compromise, leaving out the "edifying" episodes that follow conversion.

An interesting character in the novel is Fabien's friend and classmate at the Ecole des Chartes, Jacques Maïnz. He is one of the rare Jews to appear in Mauriac's fiction despite the fact that Mauriac had many Jewish friends, including his confessor the Abbé Altermann, a convert to Catholicism. Maïnz plays the role of guardian angel for Fabien and in this sense counterbalances Cyrus Bargues, who is clearly a Satan figure. Together, they enrich the novel's dichotomies—Paris/Landes, Fanny/ Marie, nature/grace. It is Maïnz who admires Fabien and helps him when in need, in particular calling a doctor and visiting him faithfully during the illness that follows the final breakup with Fanny. Maïnz's kindness and generosity are such that he is even called a Simon of Cyrene, the man who in Roman Catholic tradition helped Jesus carry his cross, a gesture that is commemorated today in the rite of the stations of the cross. Maïnz stands in rather stark contrast to Dr. Schwartz, the Jewish psychiatrist in "Thérèse chez le docteur," whose portrait is somewhat less than sympathetic.

The struggle between nature and grace is at the heart of this novel. Fabien and his mother, as practicing Catholics, are aware of the world of grace because their upbringing and education have made it real for them. They believe that grace works with nature and builds upon it, but is nonetheless fundamentally powerless to change it. Fanny, on the other hand, knows nothing of this realm and is presented to us as a creature of nature who follows her instincts to satisfy her various appetites. She represents for Mauriac that vast majority of the population of our planet who have no knowledge of Christianity and its claims: "One would think that she had no part in Adam's sin—a small, solitary destiny evolving outside of all redemption. God was responsive to neither her heart nor her reason" (ORTC, 1:651). Christianity, as a historical religion, is something that the human being learns about from others, since its beliefs and doctrines are not inscribed in nature. Mauriac presents this constant battle between the two through vivid imagery: just as local villagers must struggle to keep the sacred ground of the village cemetery from being taken over by nature (ORTC, 1:660), or fight constantly to keep the forest from reclaiming fields tilled by human hands (ORTC, 1:666), so also Fabien struggles to maintain purity in at least a part of his soul. Of course, Christianity is not only a set of religious doctrines, but also a way of life, and the class-conscious Catholics among whom Fabien is born and raised must sometimes put on moral blinders (represented symbolically by the giant pine trees that surround their homes, depriving them of direct sunlight) to protect their vision of life.

Mauriac is well aware of the weakness and contradictions of his own social milieu, but this is not to say that Fanny and her friends, as children of nature, do not wear blinders of their own, have any more true human freedom, or are any happier. They often appear to have no solid guidelines by which to live their lives and seem hopelessly sunk in the mire of selfishness and materialism. Perhaps the true gauge of the success of this novel is the degree to which Mauriac makes the opposition between these forces of compelling interest to the reader. *Le Mal* is not generally considered one of Mauriac's greatest achievements, but it still makes for interesting reading and contains many magnificent passages.

Le Désert de l'amour (1925)

Le Désert de l'amour (The Desert of Love, 1929 and 1949), which received the Grand Prize from the French Academy in 1925, is the novel that definitively established Mauriac as a mainstream writer. In its early drafts the novel changes direction several times, but it never forsakes the initial vision of a seducer who is haunted by the memory of a woman who had rebuffed him years before. The woman in question, Maria Cross, is nine years his senior. Through her Mauriac tries to develop the polar opposites of the female image in Christian tradition: woman as the cause of carnal temptation (Eve), and woman as the consoling mother figure (Mary, the mother of Jesus).

The action of the novel begins and ends in Paris, but in between these scenes there is a long flashback to events that occurred 17 years earlier in the Bordeaux suburb of Talence. In the opening lines, the narrative voice tells us: "For years Raymond Courrèges had kept alive the hope of meeting up with Maria Cross, against whom he ardently desired to take vengeance" (*ORTC,* 1:737). Raymond, like Daniel Trasis, is a Don Juan figure who has little difficulty seducing and then abandoning women. Now 35 years old, he goes to a nightclub in the rue Duphot in search of pleasure, but also in the hope of seeing Maria Cross again. On this particular occasion she appears in the company of her husband, Victor Larousselle, a wealthy businessman from Bordeaux. As Raymond sits at a table staring at Maria and her husband at the bar, his thoughts wander back to his first meeting with her when he was barely 18 years old. They met while riding the streetcar every afternoon, he on his way home from school and she returning from the cemetery, where her only child was buried. A troubled teenager with what would now be termed low self-esteem, he feels his life changing when Maria invites him to her house.

When he later learns that she is a kept woman, he resolves to make her
his lover. Unfortunately, in his subsequent attempts to put this idea into
practice, he relies more on force than on persuasion, thus triggering the
rejection that might not have occurred had he been more subtle.

Back in the present, Raymond sees his chance to take vengeance. By
coincidence, his father is in Paris attending a medical convention. He is
about 70 years old now, and Raymond has not seen him for many years,
having broken with his parents and his sister over a quarrel involving an
inheritance. During the flashback that comprises the long middle section
of the novel, we learn that Dr. Courrèges, unfulfilled in his marriage,
had fallen in love with Maria Cross while caring for her son, but had
never acted on his passion. His family and professional life, as well as his
solid social rank in Bordeaux society, would not have permitted such a
liaison.

Mauriac adroitly pulls all the pieces together in the third part of the
novel, as the action shifts back to the nightclub in Paris. Victor Larousselle
recognizes Raymond as the son of Dr. Courrèges and introduces himself.
Since he wants to flirt with two girls at the bar, he leaves Maria with
Raymond. Raymond steers the conversation back to Talence, but Maria
makes it clear that whatever happened then is of no significance to her
now. Still a kept woman at that time, she has now become a true *bourgeoise,*
since Larousselle married her upon the death of his wife. Victor's son, who
has grown up to be a successful young man, has in fact insisted that his
father marry Maria. He is just the opposite of Raymond, who, as the son
and grandson of doctors, has achieved virtually nothing in life. Thus, it is
principally to her stepson that Maria owes her respectability; it is he who
has replaced her dead son, just as Raymond might have, however briefly, if
things had gone differently 17 years earlier.

As the evening progresses, Maria observes that her husband is drink-
ing too much. When he falls off his stool, he cuts himself with his glass.
His hand begins to bleed profusely. Raymond accompanies them back to
their apartment, hoping that this will give him the opportunity to be
alone with Maria and humiliate her. When Maria attempts to call the
family doctor there is no answer, and of course the ethos of bourgeois
respectability does not allow her to awaken their servants, who are asleep
upstairs on the seventh floor, and let them see their master in such a
drunken state. Raymond then offers to call his father. Thus, Mauriac
brings together the father and son who have not communicated in years,
and increases the irony by joining them with Maria Cross, the object of
both their long-standing obsessions. Raymond now realizes that his

father's presence will keep him from taking vengeance on Maria by seducing her (if indeed that is even possible). After Larousselle is examined by the aging doctor, Raymond asks Maria if they can see each other again, but she does not encourage him. Finally, the father and son leave, and the doctor tells Raymond that he had committed adultery with Maria in his heart many times over the years.

Who is Maria Cross and how does she come to exert such power over men? It is helpful to see her as Mauriac did: an unstable and unpredictable character oscillating between the poles represented by Eve and Mary. She is an object of desire for both Raymond Courrèges and his father, while for her personally sex causes feelings of disgust. If anything, it is primarily a duty to be discharged, a price that must be paid to achieve motherhood. Like so many of Mauriac's heroines, from Gisèle de Plailly and Mme de Villeron of *Le Fleuve de feu* to Brigitte Pian of *La Pharisienne,* the strongest feelings of these characters are maternal. In the case of Maria, who surely belongs in their company, there is an ironic twist because others—especially other women—perceive her to be a kept woman, living in sin because she seeks pleasure more than anything else. When she attends a public event like the theater or opera in Bordeaux with Victor Larousselle, respectable bourgeois women whisper behind her back and point at her. Indeed, Mme Courrèges, before her death, is one such person.

But Maria's own explanation for her situation is quite different. As she tells Raymond, she became Larousselle's mistress only because she found herself a widow with a child to support and no source of income. Likewise, if she cultivated her relationship with Dr. Courrèges, who would leave pressing professional and family obligations to be with her, it was for the benefit of her sickly son, François. But while she pleads that her sense of motherhood has governed her behavior, she is also lucid and intelligent enough (and in this respect she prefigures Thérèse Desqueyroux) to understand how others can come to form negative opinions about her. "All my acts," she tells Raymond, "have an innocent side turned toward me and an abominable side turned toward the world. But perhaps it's the world that sees the truth" (*ORTC,* 1:810). Although Dr. Courrèges is probably wrong when he sees in her a "saint" (*ORTC,* 1:802), we can understand why he has so much esteem for her. She is intelligent, reads books, and can understand him much better than his wife, who is interested only in her household.

In the last scene of the flashback portion of the novel, Dr. Courrèges is called out in the middle of the night to treat Maria, who has sustained a head injury from an apparent suicide attempt. He goes to her, even though his own health is in a precarious state at the time. When he arrives at Maria's house, he finds her in a state of delirium. He sits by her bedside and listens to her speak with a kind of "confused elegance" (*ORTC,* 1:838), and of course the subject is sex. Her deepest and most disturbing thoughts come out strangely in this monologue, which seems intended to help the reader understand the inner workings of her mind. "I'm not made for erotic pleasure" (*ORTC,* 1:838), she declares to whoever will listen. And if we are not quite sure at first what she means, she goes on to explain that for her, just as thunder always accompanies lightning, disgust always accompanies sex.

It is in part because of this revelation that we are not surprised by Maria's reaction to Raymond when the action of the novel returns to the present. Now a perfectly respectable *bourgeoise,* she seems to be happy to arouse desire in Raymond, but is clearly not interested in a sexual liaison. He is still deceiving himself when he thinks he will finally be able to seduce her after almost two decades.

It is not difficult to see why *Le Désert de l'amour* was so successful in its day. Dealing with desire, adultery, and frigidity within a Catholic context, it delighted one family of French readers—the non-Catholic intelligentsia and certain liberal Catholics—while shocking traditional Catholics, among whose number Mauriac officially included himself. If there is any novel of the 1920s that justifies the criticisms leveled at Mauriac by Catholic critics, it is this one. One of the best studies of the Catholic novel in English, Conor Cruise O'Brien's *Maria Cross: Imaginative Patterns in a Group of Catholic Writers,* assigns to this novel a central place in Mauriac's fictional oeuvre.[8] Nonetheless, I would argue that in relation to Mauriac's masterpieces, this novel today seems contrived. The father's and son's obsession with the same woman is farfetched, and it is difficult to understand why Maria, so predictably bourgeois and so frigid, can also be such a femme fatale. Of all Mauriac's successful novels of the 1920s, this one seems to have aged the most.

Thérèse Desqueyroux (1927)

Thérèse Desqueyroux (Thérèse, 1928 and 1947), by virtually any criterion, is Mauriac's most famous and successful novel. When a group of writers chaired by Colette was called upon in May 1950 to select the 12 best novels of the first half of the twentieth century, *Thérèse* was included in their number.[9] In addition, its continued popularity accounts for

Mauriac's position as one of the most successful authors ever to be published in the Livre de Poche paperback series. When Mauriac looked back on this novel while working on *Le Romancier et ses personnages* (1933) (The novelist and his characters), he put his finger on why this character has appealed to so many successive generations of readers. It is "the element of mystery, of uncertainty, of the possible," that endears her to us and that has helped "to keep alive among us her depressing shadow" (*ORTC*, 1:849).

At the heart of the mystery of Thérèse Desqueyroux is the question of why she has tried to kill her husband. Mauriac had originally conceived of Thérèse as a young Catholic girl whose story we learn of only after the fact, as she confesses her sin to the parish priest. The fragment that contains her confession, and which is in fact the first draft of the novel, is entitled *Conscience, instinct divin* and is only about 10 pages in length. In transforming the original inspiration for Thérèse into the novel as we know it, Mauriac drew on a key mental image: the family as a cage that imprisons its victims. Since 1906, he had been carrying around in his mind memories of Mme Canaby, a woman who had been brought to trial in a Bordeaux courtroom for attempting to poison her husband. It was a celebrated case at the time and Mauriac apparently attended several sessions of the trial. Twenty years later, while transforming this experience into a novel, he still retained some basic elements of the case, for Thérèse uses the same poison as Mme Canaby, obtains it through the use of a forged prescription as Mme Canaby did, and has the same kind of strained relationship with her husband. There is thus a real historical character at the heart of this novel.[10] Mme Canaby, however, was sentenced to spend 15 months in prison—not for attempting to poison her husband (who, like Bernard, testified on her behalf), but because she had falsified the prescription. In the preface to the novel, Mauriac imagines his heroine already imprisoned, but the prison in question is her bourgeois family. "How many times, through the living prison bars of a family have I seen you turning about, like a wolf, your cruel and sad eyes staring at me" (*ORTC*, 2:17). This basic overlapping of the ideas of family and prison is at the heart of the novel.

As the novel opens, Thérèse, in the company of her father and her attorney, is emerging from the courthouse where she has been exonerated of the charge of attempting to kill her husband. This verdict has been reached in large part through her husband's complicity and her father's political connections. The first six chapters of the novel, almost half of the total work, relay to us the thoughts that go through her mind as she returns home alone in the train to face her husband once again. These chapters serve to relate to us all that has come before and to set the stage for her reunion with Bernard and the other members of the family. She goes over in her mind her relationship with Bernard, his half-sister Anne, who is at once a friend and a rival, and Jean Azévédo, a young Jewish student who represents freedom, the life of the mind, and escape from the bonds of the family. At the same time that she recalls these relationships, she wonders what it will be like to see Bernard again. The physical surroundings in which she sits during these first chapters set the tone for the rest of the novel. She is alone in a darkened train compartment whose door is closed. She may not be going to jail, but symbolically she is already in prison. The cramped, confined space in the train prefigures that of her family—a cage consisting of the institution of marriage itself, her extended family, and provincial society as a whole, which assumes a place for her and a role for her to play.

The narrative line of *Thérèse* is relatively simple and direct. Thérèse, née Laroque, has married Bernard Desqueyroux, believing their union to be based on love—a concept she barely understands when she goes to the altar—when it is in reality merely an alliance between families, supporting only their interests. Thérèse had lost her mother when still a child (a circumstance that of course links her to Mauriac himself, who never knew his father), and when she marries it is in part because her father is now ready to be rid of her. Despite her Republican freethinking background, Thérèse is allied with Bernard, whose family attachments and loyalties are solidly Catholic. She does share with him, however, her love of her vast landholdings (and the wealth that they bring). From the beginning Thérèse is also attracted to Bernard because of his stepsister Anne de la Trave, whose widowed mother has married Bernard's father. There is a strange attraction of opposites between the two girls. Anne, raised in the traditional manner, attends Catholic school while Thérèse goes to the lycée. Anne is outwardly pious, innocent, even naive, with little sense of intellectual inquisitiveness, while Thérèse is forever reading, analyzing, trying to think for herself. Anne and Thérèse have almost nothing in common except the desire to be together. Nevertheless, Thérèse seems to feel threatened and competes with her friend. They are a young female couple and, as such, remind us of the pairs of young male friends that populate Mauriac's fiction and usually compete with each other.[11] As we shall see, while Anne is rebelling against her family's wishes by falling in love with Jean Azévédo, Thérèse is settling into marriage. When she also puts a pin through Azévédo's picture, she seems to be expressing a desire to kill Anne's happiness as well. When Anne later gives in to her family and agrees to marry a young man they have selected for her, Thérèse rebels against her own married state by trying to kill her husband. Her attachment to Anne is much stronger and more powerful than she realizes.

If Thérèse had been born Catholic, she would have been a good candidate to become a pharisee. Like Mauriac's mother and fictional characters such as Mme de Villeron of *Le Fleuve de feu,* Mme de Blénauge of *Ce qui était perdu,* and Brigette Pian of *La Pharisienne,* Thérèse is animated from the beginning by a desire for purity, expressed as a revulsion against human sexuality. From her wedding day through her honeymoon, she suffers through the agony of physically belonging to her husband. The page that Mauriac devotes to their honeymoon is one of his most famous, as he deftly contrasts Bernard's lust against Thérèse's frigidity: "He was enclosed in his pleasure like those young piglets that it's fun to watch through the fence when they sniff their happiness in the trough—('and I was the trough' thought Thérèse)" (*ORTC,* 2:38). Marriage has been stripped of its romance.

When Thérèse returns from her honeymoon, she learns of Anne's ecstatic love for Jean Azévédo, whose summer home is located nearby. Jealous of Anne's happiness while she herself is so disillusioned, she goes along with Bernard's request to help break up this affair, for he and his family have already selected a suitable mate from their own social group. While Anne is away on a trip with her mother (and mistakenly believes that Thérèse is looking after her interests), Thérèse meets with Jean Azévédo. She quickly learns that he does not take this flirtation with Anne seriously. He intends to continue his studies in Paris in the fall, and his description of the freedom of his life in Paris contrasts with Thérèse's lonely sense of imprisonment among the pine forests of the Landes. By having his wife talk to Jean, Bernard is unwittingly achieving just the opposite of what he intended. Since Jean Azévédo is not interested in Anne, their relationship would have dissolved without any outside intervention. But when Thérèse talks to Azévédo and hears him speak of Paris and freedom, her feelings of restlessness are only reinforced. When Anne returns to Argelouse without having received a letter from Jean, she is upset to learn that he has already left for Paris without leaving either a message or an address. She does not realize that Thérèse has betrayed her.

The birth of Thérèse's daughter, Marie, brings no respite from her sense of incarceration. On a scorching summer day a forest fire begins several miles off on the family's property. The fire presents a grave family crisis, since the loss of pine trees has an immediate effect on actual income (reduction in the total amount of resin produced) and also affects the long-term value of the land. In the confusion caused by this catastrophe, Thérèse notices that her husband takes a double dose of the arsenic that has been prescribed for his heart problem. When he becomes sick afterward, Thérèse decides to experiment to see if she can provoke the same reaction by doubling the dose again. This first gesture seems motivated by curiosity as much as anything else. When she realizes what she has discovered—and at the same time Bernard does not know what is making him sick—Thérèse continues to give him overdoses until he has to be taken to a hospital in Bordeaux. At this point the family doctor discovers that the arsenic prescriptions have been falsified: Bernard has been poisoned by his wife. It is for this reason that criminal charges are brought against her. But at this point the families also close ranks to avoid scandal. So as not to jeopardize Thérèse's father's political career or disrail Anne's planned marriage to the hand-picked young Deguilhem, Bernard will testify on her behalf.

Now begins the second half of the novel. Still unsure of her motives in committing her crime, Thérèse hopes that when she gets back home she will be able to discuss everything with Bernard and to "confess" if need be, but he does not want to talk. In fact, he has already devised a family plan that will forestall any real attempt at communication and reconciliation. She will be imprisoned in her room, although she will retain the right to walk in the woods. The solitary compartment of the railroad car will now be replaced by her bedroom. She will also be expected to accompany her husband to mass on Sundays in order to convey the impression that the family considers her innocent. She is then offered a deal. If she will put on her best behavior for the Deguilhems (who, being suspicious, will not let their son marry Anne until every member of her family has been personally inspected), Bernard will eventually reward her with freedom. She will be allowed to move to Paris, where she will live off the income generated by her land, while Marie will remain behind and be raised by her father and his family. Thérèse agrees to this arrangement, which is designed to secure Anne's "happiness." In reality, however, she is agreeing to incarcerate Anne in a loveless bourgeois marriage in order to engineer her own escape from such a union. Anne's imprisonment becomes the necessary condition for the acquisition of her own freedom. Once again she does not hesitate to betray her friend.

In the final scene of the novel, Bernard and Thérèse are saying their final good-byes at the Café de la Paix. When it seems that some type of genuine communication might finally take place between them, perhaps leading to a reconciliation and Thérèse's reinsertion into the family system, a few sharp words from her put an end to this possibility. At the end of the scene she is left alone on a Paris sidewalk. She has achieved her emancipation.

Mauriac goes out of his way to convince us that Thérèse's struggle is for personal liberation from the family and its constraints. Thus, Thérèse is not physically attractive: she is not a seductress or femme fatale who wants to use her physical attributes for personal pleasure or amorous adventures. On four different occasions, the narrative voice tells us that she is not beautiful but instead exerts a certain charm on people. The neighbors, for instance, say of her that "you don't wonder if she is pretty or ugly, you just give in to her charm" (*ORTC,* 2:27).[12] Mauriac does this to focus our attention on her interior struggle as well as to underline his own personal bond with her. She cannot free herself until she redefines her relationship to the family. "The family! Thérèse let her cigarette go out; staring straight ahead, she looked at the cage with its innumerable living bars, this cage furnished with ears and eyes" (*ORTC,* 2:58–59).

No other Mauriac novel plays up the importance of sex and sexual desire more successfully than *Thérèse.* By juxtaposing the anarchic powers of unconscious desire with the straitjacket of a proper bourgeois family, Mauriac was concocting an explosive mixture, which he underscores through his use of language. Thus, before her marriage, Thérèse is pure, and is compared to an angel. This is her "real life," a kind of "paradise" before sex becomes a part of it. Afterward, she feels "disgust" and "shame"; she has been "soiled." Her paradise has been turned into a "prison," her real life has become "death," and the angel that she had been is now a "monster." Since Bernard's desire transforms him into a beast who is unable to take into account the psychological needs of his wife, Thérèse comes to look upon the sex act as a kind of crime. She is the victim of the crime, and her protective response is frigidity. If anything can explain her later act, it is this immense disappointment. Since sex for her is not accompanied by any feeling, she becomes jealous of Anne and her romantic love for Jean Azévédo. Disappointment also explains why she spends so much time reading. Books become for her both an escape from an unpleasant reality and an opportunity to learn about possible solutions to her problem.

Thérèse's desire for freedom and recognition cannot be fulfilled in a social system in which the family unit establishes money and the maintenance of outward appearances as its principal values. What actually goes on between her and Bernard in their private moments together is of litle or no importance to the family. It is for this reason that Thérèse must learn to suppress desire and stifle any personal interests that she might have. There is simply little or no room for individual expression in such a system. In a powerful image, Thérèse comes to understand that "here all the vehicles are just the right size, that is, just wide enough that their wheels fit smoothly into the tracks made by the donkey carts" (*ORTC*, 2:59). So also, each new family member must accept the assumed code of conduct. Mauriac's particular stroke of genius in creating this novel was to present in a credible female character the clash between the search for individual freedom and bourgeois society's policy of channeling and controlling such desires. It is for this reason that Thérèse remains a compelling character for a contemporary reader: her strongly felt but poorly articulated (even to herself) desires run counter to the values of the social system in which she finds herself. Also, by having Thérèse come from a Republican, freethinking and not a Catholic background, Mauriac ensures that her frustrations in achieving freedom and lucidity cannot be blamed on religion. She is thus a truly "modern" heroine who is rebelling against the social system, without being sure what her eventual identity within that system will be.

We should not interpret Thérèse's longing for freedom as a rejection of the bourgeois or capitalist system, which posits money as the basic necessity in life. One of the pleasing things about Thérèse as a character is that she incarnates many of the contradictions that we readers feel. Thus, she finds it quite normal that she and Bernard should marry because their landholdings are contiguous. In addition, she had originally been attracted to Bernard because of his family and the order that it represents: "never had she seemed more reasonable than at the time of their engagement: she was becoming part of a family unit, finding her own niche in it, and becoming part of the order of things" (*ORTC*, 2:35). Nor does Thérèse question the idea, even as she is being left by herself at the end of the novel, that she will enjoy a steady income for the rest of her life without having to work. The sharecroppers who work on her land will, through their labor, assure her physical comfort and financial security. She accepts this situation without question as she continues to search inside herself for personal happiness. Finally, Thérèse also accepts the family's need to put up a dignified facade, since they have been wealthy for only two generations (the more recent the wealth, the greater the need for such a facade, the narrative voice tells us). She is thus resigned if necessary to share the fate of her maternal grandmother, Julie Bellade, who, because of an indiscretion that is never made clear, has been erased from the family's collective memory. Pictures of her have been destroyed and no one talks about her. Thérèse realizes that the same thing will probably happen to her.

The multilayered complexity of Thérèse has endeared her to several generations of readers. One reason she continues to attract us so much is that Mauriac encapsulates in a female character so many of his own personal obsessions and contradictions. A somewhat homely half-orphan like him, she wants to assert her own rights against the family. Like Mauriac, she has a great love for the land and respect for money and power, but realizes that she does not fit comfortably into the system. She simply cannot be content to play the role of the wife of a wealthy provincial landowner, despite the superficial attractions of such a life. Like Mauriac, she breaks with all the traditional institutions that surround and inhibit her existence in order to flee to the safe haven that Paris symbolizes. There she will eventually find her freedom. Thérèse is Mauriac's greatest character (and the novel, with *Le Noeud de vipères,* his greatest masterpiece), for she embodies so much of the inner turmoil of the newly liberated twentieth-century bourgeois female. As he wrote this novel, Mauriac too was being torn apart inside by despair caused by desires which, if he had acted upon them openly, might very well have destroyed his own family and possibly even his career. Mauriac's genius consisted here once again in transforming his own inner turmoil and raising it to the level of art. This supreme achievement marks the end of this period of his development.[13]

Chapter Four
Toward the Catholic Novel

As Mauriac was undergoing his spiritual crisis of the late 1920s, he slowly began to realize that there was a contradiction between what he believed as a man of faith and what he projected into his novels. After all, there was a good deal of justification for Gide's observation that Mauriac the writer seemed to prefer Mammon to God. Furthermore, with the exception of *La Chair et le sang,* one would be hard-pressed to call the works written up to this time truly "Catholic novels." Defining what is meant by this term can be a daunting enterprise, but a few words are in order before considering the next phase of Mauriac's career.

J. C. Whitehouse makes a useful distinction between two kinds of Catholic writing. The first is "practical and calculating" and "is aimed ultimately at influence and control."[1] Treatises of a liturgical or devotional nature clearly fit into this category, as do apologies and polemics. On various occasions Mauriac worked in each of these areas. The Catholic writer in Whitehouse's second category works specifically in the realm of the imaginary and has "a sensibility formed and influenced by a specific faith, which contains concepts of man's nature and destiny." The work produced by this second type of Catholic writer is an "expression of a personal reaction to human life and a personal vision of it" (241). The subjective vision of the Catholic novelist, therefore, may sometimes seem to have more in common with that of an atheist or agnostic than with the objective and demonstrative works of the first category of Catholic writers.

John Cruickshank adds another important element to the definition when he writes that the Catholic novelist, as a believer, "regards no portrayal of human experience as complete unless it takes into account an element of divine transcendence operative in human affairs. He is thus faced with the formally paradoxical task of translating the ineffable into words, of setting forth convincing human evidence of divine providence."[2]

80

One must also avoid confusing the terms *Catholic novelist* and *Catholic novel*, for not every novel written by a Catholic novelist will be a truly Catholic novel. As Maurice Bruézière has written:

> One can be a professional writer and a practicing Catholic without necessarily being a Catholic writer. This term has been used exclusively for creative writers whose inspiration has been deeply influenced by their faith. For a Mauriac or a Bernanos, this presence of faith in their work goes without saying. More discreet in the novels of [Marcel] Jouhandeau and, in the case of [Julian] Green, closely associated with the theme of the invisible, it is nonetheless latent and widely diffused in the work of each of these authors and allows us to also include them in the multi-faceted tradition of Catholic literature."[3]

One advantage of Bruézière's yardstick is its flexibility: there are varying degrees of "Catholicity" in the work of different Catholic novelists. But to be more precise, Bruézière might have added that within a given writer's oeuvre, some novels are clearly more Catholic than others. Thus, for instance, as we shall see below, Mauriac's *La Pharisienne* is, by any criterion, a truly Catholic novel, and to Jacques Petit it is perhaps the most Catholic of all his novels: *"La Pharisienne* is Mauriac's most explicitly religious novel; one of the rare ones in which the character of the priest is not merely a sketch, if not an outright caricature; the only one in which the religious life of the characters becomes the very subject matter of the novel" (*ORTC,* 3:1310). Perhaps it is for this reason that Albert Sonnenfeld prefers to talk about the Catholic novel rather than the Catholic novelist, and his useful definition is the one that will be kept in mind in the course of the following analysis: "There is something called the Catholic Novel: it is a novel written by a Catholic, using Catholicism as its informing mythopoeic structure or generative symbolic system, and where the principal and decisive issue is the salvation or damnation of the hero or heroine."[4] According to this criterion, *La Chair et le sang* may be called a Catholic novel while *Thérèse Desqueyroux* should not be.

Destins (1928)

Destins (Lines of Life, 1957) was written hastily, in the space of only a few months. A novel about jealousy, it develops at length the archetypal confrontation between the *séducteur,* who attracts women without even trying to do so, and the *mal-aimé,* who is unsuccessful in making himself attractive to women. But several other "destinies" are also treated in detail, for Mauriac deliberately tried to widen his scope in this novel so that one character would not monopolize the center of interest, as had Jean Péloueyre and Thérèse Desqueyroux. Thus Elizabeth Gornac joins the two young men who confront each other at the center of the work. One is her son Pierre, the pious, self-conscious enemy of the flesh, and the other is Robert Lagave, or Bob, the *séducteur.* A fourth person, Paule de la Sesque, who is in love with Bob, also becomes a fully developed character.

Mauriac situates the Gornac and Lagave families in the wine-growing region of his childhood. The fictional Viridis of *Destins,* like Lur in *La Chair et le sang* and Calèse in *Noeud de vipères,* is a transposition of the family estate at Malagar, which is located on the north side, or right bank, of the Garonne River. This is the property that Mauriac inherited from his paternal ancestors. We recall that it is on the other side of the Garonne, at Saint-Symphorien, the country home adjacent to the Landes pine forest, that Mauriac situated the action of many of his other novels. Thus, for example, Johannet in *L'Enfant chargé de chaînes,* Saint-Clair in *Thérèse Desqueyroux* and *La Fin de la nuit,* Hostens in *Noeud de vipères,* Liogeats in *Les Anges noirs,* Larzujon in *La Pharisienne* and *L'Agneau,* Maltaverne in *Un Adolescent d'autrefois,* and Bourideys in *Le Mystère Frontenac,* are all fictional representations of Saint-Symphorien.

After establishing an image of the hereditary roots of the two families, Mauriac shifts the focus of the action to Bob Lagave and his bourgeois parents in Paris. His father, Augustin, is a government official who serves the state with Republican zeal. Having started off in life as a Catholic, he attended a minor seminary as a boy. But as he grew to manhood he fell under the sway of his family's neighbor, old man Gornac, and went over to the anticlerical "other" side. From then on he excelled in school, passed the major competitive exams, and rose to the high post of auditor of government accounts.

Augustin's great disappointment in life is his son Robert, or Bob, who has never done well in school or shown adequate respect and admiration for his father's accomplishments. He comes and goes from the family apartment at will, and his parents have little control over him. Now in his early twenties, he works as an interior decorator for wealthy people and socializes with a group of people who do not accept traditional bourgeois values. The drugs, alcohol, free love, even bisexuality that are integral to his social set separate him from his parents. But Bob's life suddenly changes when an attack of pleurisy forces him to take to his bed. His friends, who hitherto did not show their faces in front of his parents, now come to his home to visit him. Bob's father is so shocked by their appearance and demeanor that he decides to send his son to recuperate at his mother's home at Viridis.

Now the action shifts to Mauriac country, where Bob takes up residence with his old grandmother Maria and is in close contact with the Gornac neighbors, old Jean (who had been his father's benefactor) and his widowed daughter-in-law Elizabeth. Having already lost his sons, old man Gornac, like Jean Péloueyre's father in *Le Baiser au lépreux* and Alain Forcas's father in *Ce qui était perdu,* barely clings to life. Of Elizabeth's own sons, one is deceased and the surviving one, Pierre, lives in Paris, where he seems to belong to a group of socially conscious Catholics, like the *Sillon* group to which Mauriac himself belonged as a youth and which he had satirized in *L'Enfant chargé de chaînes.*

The action quickly builds to a climax. Bob awaits a visit from a young woman, Paule de la Sesque, who belongs to one of the best families in the region. Elizabeth, in the absence of her own son, observes that what she thought were her maternal feelings toward Bob are becoming mixed with jealousy at the thought that Paule is coming. Nonetheless, she is willing to act as his accomplice, agreeing to put the girl up in her own house, for old Maria would be shocked to know that á young woman was visiting her grandson unchaperoned. Paule's arrival is accompanied by intensely hot and sunny weather, with the threat of forest fires. She and Bob spend the day walking in the woods so that neither Maria nor old man Gornac are even aware of her presence. The summer heat and the towering pines about to burst into flame symbolize their desire for each other. Just before they come back to Elizabeth's house in the evening, Pierre returns from Paris. When Paule comes into the house (Bob has left her at the doorstep and gone to his grandmother's house), Pierre tells her about Bob's degenerate life in Paris and says that she is foolish to consider herself engaged to such a person. Paule is shaken and departs early the next morning, leaving a note for Bob in which she asks for time to think things over.

Now begins a period of rain, or the threat of rain. Mauriac skillfully changes the atmosphere of the novel to signal that Bob will not be saved through Paule's love. When he finds out what has happened behind his back, he punches Pierre in a fit of rage (one of the few violent scenes in all of Mauriac's fiction). He then takes to his room and begins drowning his sorrows in alcohol. One afternoon, when Elizabeth comes to comfort him, he tries to seduce her, causing her even more chagrin but also indicating to her that her own confused feelings toward him are more than merely maternal. After this, his friends from Paris come to fetch him and he drives off with them, only to die in a car accident in the rain a few days later.

At first Pierre holds himself responsible for Bob's death. But when he learns that Bob had lived for two hours after the accident and thus had time to make his last confession, he is grateful, believing that he has saved Bob's soul. Mauriac clearly intends for us to see him as a male pharisee figure, able to rationalize his shortcomings by convincing himself that he is an instrument of God's will. What had at first seemed like a selfish and destructive act of denunciation that caused Paule to leave Bob can now be mystically reinterpreted as a courageous act leading to the salvation of Bob's soul. Finally, Bob's body is returned to the local village for burial, giving Elizabeth one last opportunity to realize that her heart was attached to him even though she is 48 years old and shows signs of aging. When she confesses to the local priest what she considers her sin of desire, he assures her that no sin has been committed and that God does not expect people to stifle natural movements of the heart.

As Mauriac was writing this novel in late 1926 and early 1927, he was entering the most serious phase of the spiritual crisis that culminated in his "conversion" of late 1928. Later he would write about this phase of his life: "If ever I was supposed to give up my Christian faith, the time had come" (*OC,* 8:105; *ORTC,* 2:993).[5] Despite his intention to enlarge the scope of the novel to include four principal characters, in reality only one—Elizabeth—emerges as the central focus of the work. Tortured by her impossible love for and attraction to a man who is young enough to be her son, she reminds us of Racine's Phèdre; it is no accident that Mauriac was also working on his *Vie de Jean Racine* (1928) while he was writing this novel. Because of her awareness of her weakness in lusting after her stepson, young Hyppolite, Phèdre arouses compassion in Mauriac, whose crisis seems to have been caused in large part by his sentimental attraction to a younger person. He had already transposed this obsession through the characters of Fanny in *Le Mal* and Maria Cross in *Le Désert de l'amour,* taking up again the theme of *souffrance amoureuse* that he had dealt with most explicitly in the short story "Insomnie." The portrait of Elizabeth Gornac develops this type of relationship again in yet another setting. Mauriac writes of his own frustration as well as that of Phèdre and Elizabeth Gornac when he depicts the power and attraction of carnal union with the beloved: "No safety valve is needed other than the body of the beloved," the narrative voice tells us: "it hides us, defends us, it protects us against mankind, against the night, against the unknown. Courage must come easily for two people united in the flesh" (*ORTC,* 2:150). This is one of Mauriac's most ardent expressions of the power of Cybele and the pagan rites of the flesh.

Elizabeth is considerably more innocent than Fanny and Maria Cross. Whereas Fanny had been frankly lubricious and Maria somewhat more problematic, though clearly not innocent in the way she led on the young Raymond Courrèges, Elizabeth is moved at first by maternal feelings that slowly get the better of her. Before meeting Bob she has been content to live in the country caring for her sickly father-in-law and running the family vineyards. When Bob appears she is moved by a maternal instinct to care for him and even to help him receive a visit from Paule de la Sesque—a liberated woman for the time—without arousing the suspicion of either Bob's grandmother or her father-in-law. When Bob tries to take her by force, she is shocked and repels him, only to have him tell her that she should have taken advantage of this opportunity and that in the future she will surely regret not having done so (*ORTC,* 2:179). Likewise, Paule insults her later by telling her that at her age and in her physical condition, disinterest is the only possible form that love can take (*ORTC,* 2:189). Elizabeth's trauma is thus caused in part by the disequilibrum between what her heart tells her and what is socially acceptable for a middle-aged woman in her situation. When she confesses to the parish priest what she thinks was her sin of lust, he reassures her that merely being attracted to Bob was not a sin. In using the confessional, Mauriac is obviously exploiting the Catholic world of sign and symbol, but it would be inexact to call this work a fully developed Catholic novel. It is, however, an important step in that direction.

Despite Elizabeth's eventual emergence as the principal center of interest in the novel, the theme of the battle between the *séducteur* and the *mal-aimé* is also present here in the rivalry between Bob and Pierre. They of course reproduce other problematic male couples like Jacques and his cousin in *La Robe prétexte,* Claude and Edward in *La Chair et le sang,* and Augustin and the narrator in *Préséances.* Finally, alcohol also plays an important role here, for it causes the death of both Elizabeth's husband and Bob. Although Mauriac saw *Destins* as a pessimistic work, it is in fact a much more hopeful novel than he realized, and it clearly points the way toward the more consciously Catholic novels that were to follow.

Ce qui était perdu (1930)

After his "conversion" of 1928, Mauriac determined to put the past behind him and to become a "Catholic novelist" in the true sense of the word. His aim now was to attempt to save the souls of his principal characters and to edify his readers. Signaling this intention, the title of the first novel to be written in the wake of the crisis, *Ce qui était perdu*, *(That Which was Lost*, 1950), is taken from a verse in the Gospel of Matthew: "The Son of Man has come to save that which was lost" (18:11).

The death of Mauriac's mother in June 1929 extended for just a few more months the spiritual crisis that for the most part was over by this time. If he decided to write more edifying novels starting with *Ce qui était perdu* it was in part to make up to his mother those things that he had denied her before her death. It is important to recall that Mauriac saw very little of his mother during the last few years of her life and was deeply unhappy and guilt-ridden that he had not stopped to see her as he was passing through Bordeaux a few days before her death. He incorporated this incident a few years later into the novel *Le Mystère Frontenac* (1933), and we still find him conscious of this lapse 30 years later in the *Nouveaux Mémoires intérieurs (OA*, 763–764). Thus, Mme de Blénauge of *Ce qui était perdu* is a thinly veiled transposition of his mother in which he tries to paint a lasting portrait of her personality.

About two years passed between the composition of *Destins*, completed around February 1927, and *Ce qui était perdu*, begun around September 1929 (just two months or so after his mother's death). Two novellas appeared during this interval, but most of his time was devoted to writings of a religious and personal nature, such as *Souffrance et bonheur du chrétien (Sufferings and Happiness of the Christian*, 1931) and his biography of Pascal entitled *Blaise Pascal et sa soeur Jacqueline (Blaise Pascal and His Sister Jacqueline*, 1931). For this reason it would seem that from *Destins*, which deals with a feared loss of faith yet sees it recovered in the redemption of middle-aged Elizabeth Gornac, to *Ce qui était perdu*, there is but a small step taken on the psychological and spiritual levels. Mauriac's crisis of faith is clearly working itself out, and as it does the desire to edify the reader becomes more readily apparent. He is now prepared, from a spiritual point of view, to openly hint at the workings of grace in his characters' souls. The reading of Pascal that took place during the conversion process, and that was continuing as he wrote *Ce qui était perdu*, has a tangible effect on this novel. At the same time, on a purely artistic level, a more serious progression is noticeable in terms of the "desire to enlarge" the scope of the novel (*ORTC*, 3:925). This tendency would continue from *Destins* through *Ce qui était perdu* and *Les Anges noirs* (1936) to *Les Chemins de la Mer* (1939).

The writings of Blaise Pascal affected Mauriac from the days of his youth, but he achieved a deeper understanding of the great Jansenist philosopher's thought during the years of his personal crisis. His biography of Pascal reflects this interest. Mauriac draws from Pascal not only his rather somber worldview, but also a very precise notion of the "three orders" of existence. Two basic dichotomies are essential to Pascal's thought: one between the corruption of human nature and the redemption of mankind through Jesus Christ, and the other between the man with faith and the man without faith. It is on top of this latter polarity that Pascal posits the existence of the three orders of existence: body, mind, and charity. To him, there is an infinite distance between these orders, so that just as mind exists on a plane infinitely higher than that of body, the plane of charity is infinitely higher than that of mind. Thus, as Hugh M. Davidson has written, "The senses of many fundamental terms have then to be reinterpreted on three instead of two levels. . . . But it is not hard to translate from the double to the triple ordering, from the diptych to the triptych. The situation of the man-apart-from-God corresponds to the first and second levels of the hierarchical scale,— that is, to men and things as bodies first, then to men as thinking beings; man-with-God corresponds to the top level of charity and supernature."[6]

On the artistic level, Mauriac tried to write a longer, more complex novel when undertaking *Ce qui était perdu* because his successful short novels, which usually focused on only one character, as in *Le Baiser au lépreux* or *Thérèse Desqueyroux*, went against the contemporary trend toward the *roman fleuve*, or cycle novel. These long works of the pre-television era, which dealt with a large number of characters and usually chronicled their lives through a series of separately published novels, were very much in vogue in the years between the wars.[7] Without going so far as to write a *roman fleuve* of his own, Mauriac in *Ce qui était perdu* is writing a more complex novel, in which he manifests a definite concern for form and structure.

As in *Destins*, he wants to deal equally with several characters. Dividing the novel into 23 chapters, he attempts to develop complete portraits of six principal characters. Each chapter contains in its first sentence the name of the character who will be the principal subject of

concern. In addition, these six characters are grouped into two intersect-
ing triangles. In the first triangle are the married couple Hervé and Irène
de Blénauge, and Hervé's mother Mme de Blénauge; in the second we
find Marcel Revaux and his wife, Tota, along with Tota's brother, Alain
Forcas. No other of Mauriac's novels seems as concerned with geometric
form. The two groups evolve independently of each other, as in a cycle
novel, but are linked through the relationship between Hervé and
Marcel. Finally, there is barely any sense of nature in this novel,
Mauriac's most urban work. By situating the action almost exclusively in
Paris, he is able to achieve a stifling, almost hellish, atmosphere.

Seven of the novel's 23 chapters are situated in Irène's bedroom (the
smallest circle in this hell), the rest elsewhere in the modern Babylon.
Mauriac presents Hervé as a truly diabolical figure, someone who is forever turning what is innocent into something evil. Likewise, Marcel is a
failed writer. It is as if Mauriac had taken two aspects of his own life
experience and given them to each of these characters. The two sides of
Mauriac's life—bourgeois comfort with its requirement to maintain outward appearances of control and sobriety, and the world of art, which
allows for the expression of one's deepest, most powerful and secret
drives—are symbolized by the relationship between Hervé and Marcel.
Hervé's locus is Mauriac's bourgeois apartment with the fancy address in
the sixteenth arrondissement. Marcel, on the other hand, is associated
with Parisian nightlife of the 1920s, especially the nightclub *Boeuf sur le
toit,* where Mauriac was so fond of meeting his friends from the art
world. The intimate bond that is established between them serves both
a technical and a symbolic function: it unites the characters from the two
triangles and also conveys a sense of the tension that Mauriac felt within
himself in the months following his conversion.

In the first triangle Mauriac situates Hervé, wealthy and idle, and his
sickly wife, Irène, who is bedridden and dependent upon drugs. The
third character, Hervé's mother, is a pharisee figure who, as mentioned
above, owes much to Mauriac's own mother and maternal grandmother.
Her faith and pious practice are contrasted to her daughter-in-law's
agnosticism.

Irène is unique among Mauriac's freethinking characters, for the anticlerical overtones that usually accompany such a philosophical point of
view are absent here. In fact, there is something almost saintly about
Irène, for as a child of divorced parents, she has always tried to create personal relationships with others, principally by doing volunteer work
among the sick and the poor. Although she fancies herself a rationalist

and spends much of her free time reading Nietzsche, Irène senses a need for religious fulfillment. But since her husband (who has married her only for her money) continually lies and cheats on her, her health deteriorates to the point where she depends more and more on medication to make the pain of her life go away. Thus, when Irène dies of a drug overdose, the question arises as to whether her death is intentional or accidental. Suicide is a difficult thing for a Christian to account for, and a Catholic writer like Mauriac cannot allow a character to commit suicide, especially in what is intended to be his first Catholic novel. Thus, Irène calls out in her sleep as she is dying: "But, sliding into the abyss, she recognized, she perceived, she called out finally to this love by its name, which is above all other names" (*ORTC*, 2:341). Mauriac later makes it clear that Irène has not committed suicide, when the parish priest assures Mme de Blénauge in the confessional that she has been saved: "the master inspires me to tell you 'she was absent but I was there'" (*ORTC*, 2:350). Thus, there can be no doubt that grace has triumphed, even if the authorial hand might be somewhat less than well hidden in this drama of salvation.

Irène says of Mme de Blénauge, "Catholicism, that's my mother-in-law" (*ORTC*, 2:347). She says this not in a reproachful fashion, but in a matter-of-fact way that recognizes in Mme de Blénauge the traditional piety that characterized pre–Vatican II spirituality. She is forever sticking her hand into the large purse that she lugs around with her in order to secretly recite her rosary. As a true "pharisee," Mme de Blénauge is not a hypocrite. She loves her daughter-in-law and castigates her son for mistreating her. But although everything she does is sincere, she still falls short of Mauriac's standard of charity because she is more interested in incurring merits with God than in following the law of love. We get a glimpse of the inner workings of her formalistic mind when, after the death of her daughter-in-law, she confesses to the parish priest what she thinks are her sins. Because she had arranged for Hervé to marry Irène and later acted toward her as a pharisee and not as a true Christian, she holds herself guilty of causing the death of her daughter-in-law. This is one of the most powerful scenes in the novel and ends with her confessor's mystical assurance that Irène's soul has been saved. Through this character, Mauriac brings his mother to life one more time: even Mme de Blénauge's bedroom is a faithful re-creation of his mother's. But at the same time, Mauriac's expression of filial devotion does not shy away from depicting the blemishes in her character—in particular the pharisee element in her personality, which would be studied in more detail a decade later through the character of Brigitte Pian in *La Pharisienne*.

The members of the second triangle are younger, and their immediate concerns are quite different. Marcel, at 37, is a writer who has run out of inspiration. Married now to the 18-year-old Tota, whom he met while they were both taking the cure for drug addiction, he realizes not only that he no longer has anything to say to his readers, but also that he is unloved. Whereas the couple in the first triangle is solidly bourgeois, this couple operates on the fringes of the world of art.

Tota's brother, Alain Forcas, is only a year older than his sister, and very much in love with her. The theme of incest, so persistent in Mauriac's novels over the years, represents an irrational carnal instinct in the order of nature, which in Pascalian terms is the lowest of the three orders. But it can be turned into a source of moral uplift in the order of charity if the flawed character, aware of the temptation, cooperates with divine grace to overcome it.

In the first triangle, it is Irène's death that provokes the crisis leading to Mme de Blénauge's discovery of the primacy of love over devotional practice. Her spiritual uplift is contingent upon her making this discovery. In the second triangle, it is Marcel and Tota's frank discussion of her incestuous love for her brother that leads to the final crisis. When Tota, both to hurt her husband and to convince herself that his accusations are not true, is ready to give herself to William, a young man in their social circle, Alain appears at the last minute to save her. He announces that their father has taken ill. As they leave for the south of France to see him before he dies, Alain realizes that he has a religious vocation and is being called to the priesthood. Like Irène de Blénauge, he is also being saved through a direct infusion of divine grace.

Within this second triangle, incest operates as the unifying device: Alain and Tota's father is also the father of his own sister's child. Alain's redemption is thus contingent upon recognition of and victory over his own incestuous temptations.

While in *Destins* the use of drugs was mentioned only in passing, it is a constant motif in *Ce qui était perdu*. In fact, it is this very theme that makes the novel so interesting to us today, when modern man seeks escape in drugs on a scale never before imagined. Virtually each major character is dependent on drugs in some way. In Mauriac's other novels, dependence on drugs, especially alcohol, is usually emblematic of a character flaw. But here drug use is so pervasive that the author seems to be getting at something else: it is as if the body's dependence on drugs, which disrupt the natural order of things, is a paradigm for the soul's rejection of grace in the order of charity. Mauriac's insistence suggests to us that if major characters do not receive divine grace, it is perhaps because they are incapable of working with it. Drugs and drug addiction seem to come naturally in this urban setting, where people are cut off from all contact with nature. Mme de Blénauge, whose husband has already committed suicide through a drug overdose, tries to hide Irène's drugs from her in order to cut her dependency, but there is no hope when two doctors are treating her, each with his own diagnosis.

Mauriac later called this book his first truly Catholic novel. "*Les Anges noirs* and *Ce qui était perdu,* along with *Le Noeud de vipères,* are my only novels that deserve to be called, without reservation Catholic—the only ones that are completely based on Revelation" (*OC,* 3:ii; *ORTC,* 2:883). As the title of the novel indicates, he is concerned about souls, and Mauriac clearly wants to save as many as possible of the characters presented here. Thus, in addition to Irène de Blénauge and Alain, others also seem to be saved. The merits earned by Irène through her suffering and death drive Hervé back toward his mother, whose love seems to save him. Likewise, Tota is at the very least spared further temptations to incest through her brother's vow of celibacy.

Ce qui était perdu has been largely overlooked by Mauriac scholars. Perhaps the author himself led the way in this negative evaluation of the work, for he considered it to be a failure. Writing the preface to the volume of the *Oeuvres complètes* that appeared in the 1950s, he commented, "Of all my novels, perhaps this is the one about which I have the deepest regrets, because it's the first draft of what could have been a great book. Incomplete, hastily written, it bears witness to a kind of fear of a dangerous subject." He then added: "written at the time of my life when I was most preoccupied with religion, *Ce qui était perdu* suffered visibly from the desire to edify and the fear of giving scandal" (*OC,* 3:i; *ORTC,* 2:883). In my view, this rejection is unwarranted. Mauriac, writing in the 1950s, had technical reservations about having "saved" Irène, an apparent suicide, and having redeemed the pharisee figure of Mme de Blénauge. From a purely personal point of view, he could also see that he had put a great deal of himself into this novel and preferred 20 years later that this period of his life be consigned to oblivion. Nonetheless, because of its structure, characterization and themes, *Ce qui était perdu* deserves to be rediscovered. A true Catholic novel, it shows the workings of grace in the souls of several characters without their being aware of it (and in so doing sets the tone for the works to come) and tells us more than Mauriac realized about the inner turmoil that plagued him at a critical period of his life.

Le Noeud de vipères (1932)

For years Mauriac had been carrying about the idea for a novel that would also be a confession—the great and universal cathartic experience of pre–Vatican II Catholic spirituality. Confession, one of the Church's seven traditional sacraments, is much less widely practiced now, but in the 1930s it was still one of the defining aspects of the Catholic experience. Thus, it should not surprise us that the first draft of what would later become *Thérèse*, entitled *Conscience, instinct divin,* is a confession made by Thérèse to the parish priest. Mauriac also reports on Mme de Blénauge's confession to the parish priest in *Ce qui était perdu*, his first truly "Catholic novel." Here, in *Noeud de vipères (Vipers' Tangle,* 1933), arguably the most Catholic of all his works, the act of confession is the very essence of the novel. But in this case Louis, the central figure, will confess not to a priest but to his wife, Isa. He is dying, and before he leaves this world he wants to settle accounts with her, perhaps even make up with her. Their whole married existence of some 40 years has been one long misunderstanding, and over the course of time the children have sided with Isa against him. He is now alone and isolated, but he still has one weapon over which the others have no control: his fortune.

There is most likely a family anecdote (or ancedotes) at the heart of this novel. Mauriac alluded on several occasions to his mother's family's fortune, which was administered by an uncle, an anticlerical intent on disinheriting Mauriac's mother and her five children. The uncle presumably intended to will his money to an illegitimate son whom he had rarely if ever seen. But his sudden death in the arms of his mistress before he could carry out this threat (whether it was real or imagined on the part of Claire Mauriac and her children) disposed of the problem. Another family anecdote revolves around the death of Mauriac's maternal grandmother. As she lay dying, the family members supposedly asked among themselves whether it would be appropriate to open her strongbox before she died. In this scenario, the fear and anguish associated with finding out who gets what (i.e., the power of money) overcomes the law of love. Mauriac takes this image and places it at the center of the novel. The box and all it contains—deeds, stocks, bonds, cash and other valuables—becomes the ultimate weapon. Louis's children wonder if they should open it before he dies, for they are anxious to find out if they are going to be punished for having sided with their mother all these years.

Like *Thérèse Desqueyroux,* whose first half consists of a long flashback as Thérèse returns home from the courthouse after her acquittal, *Noeud de vipères* also recounts earlier events in order to bring the action up to the present, this time with the device of Louis pondering the past in order to write a letter to his wife. The letter becomes the substance and text of the first half of the novel.

As in the earlier masterpiece, money, land, and property are at the heart of the action. Louis ends the first paragraph of his letter to Isa by assuring her that there will be no surprises in store for her: the strongbox containing the deeds, titles, and certificates that represent the family wealth are all in their usual place.

Isa, from the very beginning, is an integral part of the story, for the letter that Louis is writing loses its meaning without an addressee. This is an especially critical element if the letter is interpreted as a form of confession. Louis's intention as he begins his narrative is not to confess in any religious sense but simply to force Isa to hear his side of the story. He looks at this process with the eyes of a freethinker and a lawyer: he simply wants to justify himself and set the record straight before he dies. But he does not realize as he begins to write that divine grace will soon invade his soul. What begins as a cold and calculating settlement of accounts becomes gradually a confession in which, unbeknownst to its author, a religious conversion is taking place.

Mauriac would often begin a novel in the first person and then later rewrite it from a third-person point of view. He seems to have often felt more comfortable projecting himself into the mind of his major character at the outset in order to get his novel started. In subsequent drafts, he would then become more objective and give the story over to a third-person voice to describe the character. Thus, *Thérèse Desqueyroux* began as a first-person confession to the parish priest; similarly, the original 17 pages of *Le Baiser au lépreux* were also written in the first person. But in *Le Noeud de vipères* the letter/confession written in the first person serves Mauriac's goals admirably, and he apparently realized that no change of point of view would be desirable. Since Louis is an outsider in Ida's family and has been isolated by them during his whole adulthood, a subjective appreciation of the effect of their behavior on him is quite appropriate. One does not expect complete objectivity in a letter/confession of this kind.

As in *Thérèse,* the theme of land and money, according to the traditional Mauriac formula, is mixed from the outset with sex. Louis, sprung from peasant stock, has become eligible to marry into Isa's social circle because of his family's acquired wealth and his own university degrees. He feels uneasy, however, because Isa's parents make fun of his mother (although born a peasant, she has amassed a considerable fortune thanks to her thrift and shrewd real estate dealings). But when Isa, after their marriage, lets slip that she had been previously engaged to someone from her own social milieu, Louis is overcome with jealousy. He imagines the rival, whom Isa loved, as a handsome and athletic *séducteur,* possessed of qualities that he himself lacks, and he is not consoled by the fact that her marriage to Rodolphe could not take place only because of his family's concern that two of Isa's brothers had already died of tuberculosis. Already conscious that he is a *mal-aimé,* homely and seemingly unworthy of love (compounding the disadvantage of his peasant background), Louis concludes that Isa and her family had selected him only because they feared that their daughter might be unmarriageable and that he, despite his origins, was at least acceptable. Since he is convinced that she made so much of this earlier engagement (but did she really, or is Louis inflating this event to justify his own subsequent behavior?) only to make him miserable, this initial breakdown in communication will lead to frustration bordering on hatred for the rest of their adult lives and will poison the lives of their children as well.

Instead of inquiring about his wife's earlier emotional relationship, Louis retreats into his shell, devoting most of his energies for the rest of his life to increasing his own fortune and planning vengeance on his wife and family. There will be hardly any consolations for him along the way. His daughter Marie, the only one of his children to show him any warmth and tenderness, dies in childhood. His friendship with his wife's widowed sister, Marinette, also brings light into his life, but only until she marries again. Marinette's son, Luc, is a third cause of joy, but his life is tragically cut short during World War I. Finally, and significantly, the country priest at their vacation home at Calèse (a fictional transformation of Mauriac's own family home at Malagar) has also helped to give some meaning to his life. The kindness, gentleness and sincerity of the Abbé Ardouin, the most fully developed priest in Mauriac's fiction up to this point, are in marked contrast to the pharisaism of Isa's family. He also foreshadows the Abbé Calou of *La Pharisienne,* and is a source of grace for Louis.

The letter/confession format constitutes the first 11 chapters of the novel. Like Thérèse's interior monologue as she returns home from the courthouse, this structuring mechanism brings us up to date on the action and prepares us for the dramatic second half of the novel, which is about the same length as the first and is written in the form of a diary. Louis is in Paris, lodging in a third-rate boardinghouse in order to save money. Having overheard his wife and children plotting to disinherit him by having him declared incompetent, he has come to Paris by himself despite his failing health. He now confides in his diary the countermeasures that he has decided to take to thwart their initiative. He seeks out his illegitimate son, Robert. When he meets the young man, whom he had never seen before, he is astonished to see that Robert bears an astonishing physical resemblance to him, but otherwise he is unimpressed. He tells Robert of his intention to leave him his whole fortune; but the young man, afraid of legal problems after the death of his father, reveals Louis's plans to the family. When Louis learns of his betrayal, he upbraids Robert, but still provides him with a comfortable inheritance.

Louis's health falters again, forcing him to remain in Paris for a few more days. When he receives a telegram informing him of the sudden death of his wife, he hastens back to Bordeaux to attend her funeral. His family does not know what to make of his behavior when he seems to show true remorse over her death. After all, this is the man who had always insisted on eating meat on Friday (the famous "côtelette du vendredi") in order to express his rejection of his wife's Catholicism. But now, after scolding them for attempting to have him declared incompetent and for plotting with Robert, he announces that they can have all his possessions. He keeps for himself only the summer residence at Calèse and a small annuity to cover his expenses.

A short time later, Louis's granddaughter Janine (the child of Louis' daughter Geneviève and her husband, Alfred) escapes from a convalescent home where her parents have placed her because of a nervous disorder. They also want to keep her from running after her profligate husband, Phili, who is a *séducteur* like Bob Lagave of *Destins*. She joins her grandfather at Calèse and brightens the last days of his life. Janine is different from the other members of the family in that she blindly follows the law of love in her life, even when it leads to personal disaster. Thus, despite her husband's philandering, she still loves him. Her presence at her grandfather's side can be taken to represent divine grace as it works within his soul to effect complete and total devotion to the divine will—that is, to bring him once and for all from the side of justice to that of love. When Louis dies a few weeks later, he is in the act of writing in his diary a sentence that suggests that he has been converted and that the love he has discovered in the world is nothing other than a reflection of the presence of God in his life.

In an epilogue to the novel we learn of the reactions of Louis's children to the discovery of the letter and diary. His son Hubert, in a letter to Geneviève, uses these writings as proof that his father was insane, thus justifying his own previous actions. In contrast, Janine testifies in a letter to Hubert that her grandfather underwent conversion in his last days. She asks him to let her read the diary as a chronicle of that experience. She also adds crucial information not included in the diary: that her grandfather had met three times with the country priest, had confessed his sins, and intended to take communion for the first time at Christmas. These last pieces of information, when added to the content of the letter/confession/diary, indicate clearly that Louis has undergone the process of conversion.

His obsession with money places Louis in the company of other famous misers of French literature, like Molière's Harpagon and Balzac's Grandet. But here the vice is overcome through the process of religious conversion. The power of grace transforms Louis's character and presumably wipes out in God's eyes the negative effect of the years that preceded his conversion. The true meaning of his ability to give all of his money to his children, even though he knows that they despise him, can be fully measured only when we appreciate the extent to which money had previously governed the major decisions in his life. An opportunity earlier in his career to try his hand at writing or politics was aborted because it would have kept him from maximizing his income as an attorney. Later, if he frequented houses of prostitution instead of becoming involved with lovers, it was because he preferred to know in advance the price of everything. His summer vacations had always been spent at Calèse, even though this meant that he would be trapped there with his wife's family, because it enabled him to save money. While in Paris on the trip to visit Robert, he stays in a run-down boardinghouse, and in the restaurant he orders cheese for dessert because it is the cheapest item on the menu. His stinginess is probably the principal reason that he considers his sister-in-law Marinette such a noble soul. He is unable to understand how she could remarry after the death of her aged husband when to do so means renouncing the seven million francs that he left her provided she not remarry. He still cannot understand her action, but the model of her example is perhaps not without effect upon him in the Pascalian order of charity. Significantly, her son Luc, before his death, reflects this same kind of selfless innocence with a similarly positive effect on Louis.

The exercise of free will is often impeded by hereditary factors in Mauriac's fiction. These hereditary factors can be physical (predisposition to tuberculosis is the most common) or, more important for him as a novelist, psychological (antisocial behavior or an obsession). Thus, Louis attributes his quarrelsome nature to his father and his miserly instincts to his mother. This is an easy way for him to avoid complete responsibility for his actions. The narrative voice in Mauriac's fiction often seems to mock people who believe in the power of heredity, but at the same time the author subverts this high-minded moralizing by providing in his novels so many examples of its power. Thus, in *Thérèse Desqueyroux,* Anne's family is rebuked by the narrator for believing that Jean Azévédo's family might have hereditary defects. Yet Thérèse, in attempting to kill her husband, replicates the antisocial conduct of her maternal grandmother in rebelling against the interests of the family, thus seeming to confirm the power of heredity. Likewise, in *Ce qui était perdu* we are told that people are free to live their own lives, yet Alain Forcas and his sister Tota feel drawn to each other incestuously, as their father and his own sister had been. In *Le Noeud de vipères,* Louis's obsession with money is explained as a hereditary trait inherited from his mother in the Pascalian orders of body and mind, but he is finally able to overcome this hereditary limitation when he allows his will to work in concert with divine grace in the Pascalian order of charity.

If one applies Albert Sonnenfeld's working definition of the Catholic novel to *Le Noeud de vipères,* the work clearly belongs to this genre. As a novel of conversion that attempts to portray the working of grace in a soul (without the person's complete awareness), it is a Catholic novel in the fullest sense of the term. It is also a masterpiece of psychological fiction that is written, as usual, in Mauriac's clear and deceptively simple style. For all these reasons the novel has attracted a good deal of critical attention ever since its publication. In recent years. Jacques Monférier has argued that *Le Noeud de vipères* is an intensely personal novel that comes exactly in the middle of a 15-year period of turmoil in Mauriac's life.[8] He makes a convincing case that it is by design Mauriac's most Catholic novel. Monférier points out, among other things, that Mauriac seems to have originally intended to end the novel with Isa's death in chapter 17. Judging by the fact that after a short interval Mauriac continued the story in a new notebook (the first 17 chapters had filled most of two notebooks), Monférier concludes that Louis's spiritual adventure comes to the forefront in the last three chapters because Mauriac decided to give a new meaning to the novel, which was not foreseen or intended when he started out. Thus, in his view, *Le Noeud de vipères* began as a novel about a miser and his family and became a novel of conversion

only as it was being written. For Monférier, this evolution signals definitively the end of Mauriac's crisis of faith and also reveals that Mauriac
was attempting to convert his readers by making them sympathize in
their hearts (but not necessarily with their reason) with what is happening in Louis's own heart.

Le Mystère Frontenac (1933)

Mauriac underwent surgery for throat cancer in 1932. Since he was
only in his midforties at the time, the pathology and its removal were a
traumatic experience for him. During his convalescence his wife and children rallied around him and, thanks in part to their love and support, he
made a complete recovery. Nonetheless, he spoke with a raspy voice,
sometimes barely audible, for the rest of his life. Later he was to joke
that if he was so young when voted into membership among the 40
"immortals" of the French Academy in 1933, it was only because those
who voted for him probably thought that he would die soon anyway.
The experience of a lengthy and serious illness requiring many hours of
solitude in his sickbed explains in part the genesis of Le Mystère Frontenac
(The Frontenac Mystery, 1952). The novel is intended as a paean to the
experience of family life.

"I conceived of Le Mystère Frontenac as a hymn to the family in the
wake of a serious operation and the illness, during which the members of
the family took care of me with such devotion," Mauriac wrote in 1951.
"If I was to die, I would not have wanted Le Noeud de vipères to be my last
book" (OC, 4:ii; ORTC, 2:886). That this novel is intended as a tribute
to his family is quite obvious, but I would also argue that another compelling reason for its creation was to repay the spiritual debts that he still
felt were outstanding to his mother. She had already inspired to a large
extent the character of Mme de Blénauge in Ce qui était perdu, but that
portrait had not been without blemish. In Le Mystère Frontenac certain
aspects of her rigoristic personality are softened considerably, as the delicate and sensitive little boy with the drooping eyelid tries to make up to
his mother for not stopping to see her in Bordeaux shortly before her
death.

Le Mystère Frontenac occupies a special position in Mauriac's oeuvre, for
its autobiographical elements are more evident than usual. The habitual
process of transformation is less elaborate. Two characters in the novel,
Blanche Frontenac and her brother-in-law Xavier, are based directly on
Mauriac's mother, Claire, and his uncle, Louis. The five Frontenac chil-

dren, three boys and two girls, also correspond to the five children in Mauriac's family, although he does cover his tracks a bit more in portraying the children, especially the youngest one, Yves, who reminds us so much of Mauriac himself. It is for this reason that Mauriac later referred to the novel as "mémoires imaginaires" (*OC,* 4:i; *ORTC,* 2:885). To him, the novel was generally "true," but it also contained invention and transposition. This creative process becomes evident if we compare the novel to his autobiographical essay, *Commencements d'une vie* (The beginnings of a life) (1932), which treats the same period in his life. The novel's hybrid nature is further underscored when we remember that Mauriac published it in the fourth volume of his *Oeuvres complètes,* in the company of other autobiographical texts, and in fact noted in the introduction that several of his relatives had been upset by it at the time, thinking that they had been unfairly portrayed (*OC,* 4:i–ii; *ORTC,* 2:885).[9] Despite all this confusion, scholars today generally read the book as a novel.

The novel is divided into two sections of about equal length. Part 1 vividly establishes the atmosphere in Bordeaux and the surrounding countryside at the turn of the century. Michel Frontenac has died young, leaving his wife Blanche with five children to care for. As is so often the case in Mauriac's fiction, one parent is from a strict Catholic background (in this case it is Blanche) while the spouse is from an anticlerical Republican family. Xavier Frontenac, who shares the political convictions of his deceased brother, has assumed responsibility for helping his sister-in-law raise the children. He has a law office in Angoulême, several hours away by train, but comes every two weeks for a brief visit in order to check up on everybody's welfare and to look over the books of the family-owned lumber company. We soon learn that Xavier has a secret, and this explains in part why he does not move to Bordeaux to be in daily contact with his nieces and nephews. He has a mistress, Joséfa, and because she is of a much lower social stratum, he does not dare introduce her to his family. Mauriac also introduces the five children—the boys, Jean-Louis, José, and Yves; and their sisters, Danièle and Marie. The principal occurrences during Part 1 are Yves's discovery of his literary vocation (which is encouraged by Jean-Louis) and Jean-Louis's decision to renounce his plans to do graduate work in philosophy in Paris in order to take over the family business. The other children are not depicted with as much detail as these two. Finally, the daily life of the family is portrayed in part against the background of their apartment in Bordeaux, but especially in their home in Bourideys (Saint-Symphorien) on the edge of the pine forests that are the source of their wealth. The boys go hunting along the same trails that their uncle and father had followed 30 years before and they too respond to the pagan call of the river, La Hure, that runs through their property. Some of Mauriac's most lyrical pages are found in the first part of *Le Mystère Frontenac*.

In the second half of the novel, Yves begins the pursuit of his literary career in Paris, hobnobbing with monied and decadent Englishmen and Americans. On a trip to a resort in the southwest of France, he makes a surprise visit to his mother while passing through Bordeaux. Going back through the city on the return trip to Paris, he would like to surprise her again but does not dare ask his friends to go out of their way. Since they are determined to get back to Paris that very day, he lacks the courage to ask them to stop for a few minutes at his mother's apartment. When he learns a few days later of her death, he is overcome with guilt. These touching pages are brutally honest and strongly felt by Mauriac, as he shares with the reader his own feelings of filial attachment to his mother and the residual guilt resulting from not having stopped to visit her one last time.

The action of Part 2 is propelled forward when Uncle Xavier falls ill. Joséfa dares to come to the Frontenac house to inform his relatives of his condition and to invite them to his bedside. Mauriac contrasts their mockery of her lower-class clothing and demeanor with her devotion to them and their interests as if she herself were an officially recognized member of the family. Gradually the family members overcome their class prejudice and come to like her. All the children except José (who is in the army in Morocco) visit Xavier before he dies, thus revealing to him that they have found out his secret—which, at this point, does not bother them. Yves will later come to realize that Joséfa, through her love and devotion and despite her lower-class origins, has become a part of the family "mystery": "Yves realized that humble Joséfa had entered into the Frontenac mystery, that she was a part of it and that nothing could ever detach her from it. Of course, she had a right to [family] photos and to a letter on New Year's Day" (*ORTC,* 2:670).

The mysterious connections that bind all the members of the family are further explored when Yves, back in Paris, takes an overdose of sleeping pills in despair over the infidelity of a girl he loves. The Paris nightclub scene of the 1920s, already evoked in some detail in *Le Désert de l'amour* and *Le Mal,* reappears here. But strangely and mysteriously (and this helps to explain the meaning of the title) Jean-Louis has a premonition that Yves needs him. He hastens to Paris and arrives in time to be at Yves's bedside when he regains consciousness. He then nurses him back to health. As the novel ends, Yves realizes that the mystery of his family's union is a reflection of divine love. As Jean-Louis sleeps beside him in his room, he remembers his mother and her pious devotion. The closing image in his mind is that of "the cluster, forever close, of the mother and five children. . . . The Frontenac mystery was escaping destruction, because it was a reflection of eternal love refracted through a family" (*ORTC*, 2:673).

This "hymn to the family" is replete with references to the pious domestic universe that Mauriac knew as a child. As such, it offers a good example of the degrees that exist in characterizing a given work as a Catholic novel. Although it can be argued that *Le Mystère Frontenac* is a Catholic novel in the strictest sense of the term (because it deals with the issue of salvation through Jean-Louis's mysterious awareness that his brother needs him and his efforts to nurse him back to health), this would be overstating the case unnecessarily. *Le Mystère Frontenac* is a truly Catholic novel but in a manner that is completely different from, say, *Le Noeud de vipères,* a novel of religious conversion. Exploiting the Catholic world of belief as reflected in a very pious family, it is a heartwarming work that uplifts and edifies, but does so without ignoring the problems, both internal and external, that families must confront in order to survive. Thus, it posits that the living faith of each member of the family is an important part of this program of survival. Finally, it also depicts a gifted son's faithful attachment to his mother, with religious belief obviously being one of the most important qualities he has inherited from her. *Le Mystère Frontenac*, despite its hybrid nature, remains for many readers one of Mauriac's most endearing works. It is also one of his most stunning achievements as a novelist.[10]

As Mauriac experimented with various forms of the Catholic novel during the 1930s, he also maintained an interest in writing longer novels with more fully developed characters. *Ce qui était perdu, Le Noeud de vipères,* and *Le Mystère Frontenac* are quite different from one another, yet each in its way can be called a Catholic novel. None of them, however, brings back characters from earlier works, which is one of the fundamental traits of the cycle novel. Mauriac would begin to explore such possibilities in the novels written during the remainder of the decade, while also continuing to focus on basic religious questions.

Chapter Five

The Longer Novels of the Late 1930s

As Mauriac continued to explore the aesthetic possibilities of the Catholic novel, he also attempted to write longer works with more fully developed characters. He therefore began to resurrect important characters from earlier works and to depict them later in life, in new settings. This is the case not only with Thérèse Desqueyroux, but also with Alain and Tota Forcas of *Ce qui était perdu*.

La Fin de la nuit (1935)

Mauriac had written two short stories about the character of Thérèse Desqueyroux before devoting a novel to her. It should also be recalled that she is mentioned in passing in *Ce qui était perdu* (*ORTC*, 2:311–13), when Alain Forcas meets her sitting alone on a park bench at night. Her character is not developed beyond this one scene in *Ce qui était perdu*, but the image of her alone and abandoned in Paris recurs through all the later works in which she appears. In the introduction to *La Fin de la nuit* (*The End of the Night*, 1947), Mauriac voices once again his obsession with this character. He wants to save her, but never having met the priest who could hear her confession, he has not been able to do so. This novel, he tells us, will chronicle her existence to the end of her own personal night. Fifteen years have passed since Bernard left her in Paris. She lives alone, with few social contacts and failing health. Her only steady companion is her servant Anna, who comes to wait on her each day. Her daughter Marie, whom Thérèse has not seen in three years, is now 17 years old. At the beginning of the novel she suddenly appears, having fled to Paris to be near the young student Georges Filhot, whom she loves and wants to marry. Since people in Saint-Clair still talk of Thérèse's crime and circulate rumors about her, the mother and daughter talk about the subject candidly. Marie comes to understand her mother better. But even if the obstacle of Marie's suspicion can be overcome, another one still needs to be addressed. Georges's parents will not give their consent to a wedding because Marie's dowry is insufficient. They want more money to help them in their own business dealings. Learning this, Thérèse volunteers to give all that remains of her own fortune to secure her daughter's happiness.

Thérèse takes matters into her own hands when she goes to Georges's student quarters and tries to convince him to go ahead with the wedding. Her dealing behind her daughter's back reminds us of the parallel scene with Jean Azévédo in *Thérèse,* in which Anne thought that Thérèse was sympathetic to her love for Jean. After Marie returns to Saint-Clair, Georges goes to Thérèse's apartment, where they spend a long evening together. He returns again the next evening and declares his love for her. Thérèse is flattered, happy to know that, even at this age, she can still inspire such interest in a young man; but she also realizes that a serious relationship between herself and Georges is impossible. Thus, to cure Georges of his romantic delusions, she pulls back the hair on her forehead to show him her receding hairline. She then makes him promise to be faithful to Marie for the rest of his life.

Afraid that Georges may have committed suicide, Thérèse goes to his room the next day. He is not there and has not come home all night. Soon his friend Mondoux appears, representing his friend. He announces that Georges no longer wants anything to do with Marie or her mother—he simply wants them to get out of his life. Since Georges does not speak for himself here, it is impossible to know what he really thinks. Thérèse and Mondoux quarrel bitterly, and then she goes back to her apartment convinced that everyone is plotting against her. Her weakened psychological state reflects what life in exile in Paris all these years has done to her.

Soon afterward, Marie returns to Paris to retrieve her mother and bring her back to Saint-Clair. There she gradually nurses Thérèse back to health. When Georges returns for the Christmas holidays, he comes to see Marie one last time. Just before the end of the novel a general reconciliation seems to be taking place as Thérèse, lying in bed, places the hands of the two young people together. This denouement suggests that Marie will be able to combine love and marriage in a way that was always impossible for her mother. But the vision of happiness is subverted a few pages later when it becomes apparent that Marie understands that Georges really loves her mother. Like Catherine of *Les Anges noirs,* Marie appears to be willing to marry a young man who does not love her, content to have only his body rather than nothing at all.

A reader familiar with *Thérèse* cannot help but notice that the latter novel provides a variation on the Anne–Jean Azévédo–Thérèse triangle.

Once again, Thérèse is the intermediary between two would-be lovers. In *Thérèse Desqueyroux* Anne leaves on a trip with her mother thinking that Thérèse is supportive of her love for Jean Azévédo. But in fact Thérèse is bent on destroying their liaison out of jealousy and in order to buy her own freedom: Bernard will not let her go to Paris unless a suitable marriage (with young Deguilhem) can be arranged for Anne. In this novel, Thérèse once again encounters a young man who wants to flirt with her and who is ready to betray the girl who loves him. The major difference is in Thérèse's reaction. In the first novel she bides her time until she can get free. Then, after her arrival in Paris, she begins a liaison with Jean (we learn of this in "Thérèse chez le docteur"). Here, she encourages Georges to a certain point, but finally realizes that she is ruining her daughter's chance to marry for love. Georges, at her cajoling, finally agrees to remain faithful to Marie, even though he has just declared his love for her mother. At the close of the novel, Georges wonders how he will ever be able to live his whole life with Marie, whose very voice he abhors. But he seems willing to do this because of his feelings for her mother. The key to understanding Thérèse's power over Georges is that she has supposedly helped him to understand himself through discussion and analysis of several of his past actions, but the reader finds it difficult to believe that Thérèse has now begun to practice psychoanalysis, albeit as an amateur.

The very fact that Mauriac returned again to the story of Thérèse indicates his ongoing interest not only in this character, but also in the possibilities offered by the cycle novel, so much in vogue at the time. In continuing to develop a character portrayed in an earlier novel, he too was writing a form of cycle novel—but on his own terms. Thus, although he resurrects the character of Thérèse, he does not take the exercise one step further by making the action of this novel cohere with what had come before. *La Fin de la nuit* takes place 15 years after the earlier novel, when Thérèse was only about 19 years old, but suddenly she is 45, having gained a decade somewhere along the way. Likewise, the new novel apparently takes place during the economic crisis of the 1930s, when the fortunes of the Desqueyroux and Filhot families are in jeopardy, but that would place the earlier novel during World War I, which is not the case. Finally, among several other points that one could make, Anne de la Trave, whose role is essential in the first novel, is completely absent from this "sequel." The reason for these inconsistencies is that Mauriac wants to concentrate on Thérèse here, while at the same time subverting the genre of the cycle novel by deliberately refusing to make the various pieces of the Thérèse cycle fit together.

La Fin de la nuit is perhaps the weakest and least credible of Mauriac's novels. Its plot is contrived, and the psychological evolution of the principal characters borders on the implausible. In fact, the Thérèse who emerges in this novel is quite changed. She does not completely contradict her predecessor, but she does act in a far more cruel manner, for she is clearly aware of her ability to do evil and cause harm, even going so far as to secretly rejoice that Georges prefers her to her daughter. In this regard, she reminds us of Hervé in *Ce qui était perdu,* and prefigures both Gradère of *Les Anges noirs* and Landin of *Les Chemins de la mer,* each of whom is depicted as a Satan figure. In each of these works we find Mauriac trying to present a physical incarnation of evil through the creation of such characters. As a Catholic novelist, he does not see evil as a mere concept, but as an incarnation—Satan. When Thérèse herself had said to Dr. Schwartz in "Thérèse chez le docteur," "Do you believe in the devil, Doctor? Do you believe that evil is a person?" she was expressing one of Mauriac's deepest convictions as a novelist. Thus, when he developed such characters, he was trying to convince his readers of the truth and validity of his belief. Nevertheless, *La Fin de la nuit* remains one of Mauriac's least successful novels.

Les Anges noirs (1936)

For a number of years Mauriac had wanted to write a novel about a saint, an intention which was quite consistent with his desire to write novels that would edify and uplift the souls of his readers. Since, in the Catholic tradition, the priest is much more likely to be declared a saint than is a layperson, Mauriac hit upon the character of Alain Forcas of *Ce qui était perdu,* who is now a priest.[1]

As we recall, at the end of that work, Alain comes to realize that he is being called by God to the priesthood, and thus to a life of celibacy. In following this call, he understands that he will have to sublimate his carnal desire for his sister (which she reciprocates). Mauriac wanted to achieve on his own terms what the Catholic novelist Georges Bernanos had done in creating the character of the Abbé Donissan in *Sous le soleil de Satan (Under the Sun of Satan,* 1926). He had been impressed by how the human side of the priest had been presented in that novel and wanted to work along the same lines himself. With this idea at least partially in mind, he wrote *Les Anges noirs (The Dark Angels,* 1950) in 1935, and it appeared the following year. Alain Forcas thus becomes Mauriac's version of a saintly country priest. Ironically—apparently unknown to Mauriac— Bernanos was also writing another novel in which the life of a country priest would be depicted as the central focus. His masterpiece, *Journal d'un curé de campagne (Diary of a Country Priest),* appeared several months after Mauriac's *Les Anges noirs.*

Mauriac's novel opens with a long first-person confession in the form of a letter. Gabriel Gradère, the Satan figure of the book, has decided to write to the local country priest, whom he respects and admires. A former seminarian who has lost his faith and who, on several occasions, seems aware of the physical presence of Satan, Gradère has reached a crisis in his life. He feels a need to communicate with someone and has selected this young priest, who is derided, even despised, by certain members of his parish. The lengthy prologue, in which he tells his life story, is about 30 pages long, or 20 percent of the total work.

The saint and the sinner are juxtaposed from the very beginning of the novel. Ironically, each of them could have chosen a different path in life: Gradère could have become a priest but did not; Alain could have succumbed to his incestuous temptations but did not. The presence in Mauriac's mind of the model of the Abbé Donissan in Bernanos's *Sous le soleil de Satan* must have had an impact, however unconscious, on the novel. For when Bernanos wrote in that work, "Each of us . . . is in turn in some way a criminal or a saint, at times drawn toward the good . . . at others tormented by a mysterious desire for degradation," he was already expressing the central theme of Mauriac's novel.[2]

At 50 years of age, Gradère is still physically attractive. Like Bob Lagave of *Destins,* he is a *séducteur,* for women are naturally drawn to him. But unlike Bob, he has always been fully aware of his powers and is determined to use them. The son of a local sharecropper, he had distinguished himself enough in school to attract the attention of a wealthy landowner who, thinking that he had a vocation for the priesthood, was willing to pay for his seminary education. As a seminarian he spent his summers with two wealthy cousins, Mathilde and Adila Du Buch, who at first treated him like a little brother. He later dropped out of the seminary and continued his education at the university in Bordeaux. But once established in the city he met Aline, a prostitute, who was first his lover and then his employer. He continued to live in Bordeaux, extorting money from Adila Du Buch, who naively thought that he was still a student. She paid most of his bills while he lived on the fringes of society. He eventually seduced Adila, and had a son by her, who was born while Adila was in Spain for an extended visit. Upon her return, Gradère married her, but then left her to follow Aline to Paris, where they continued to work together. This is the essence of Gradère's narrative.

Gradère has come back to Liogeats, a fictionally transposed Saint-Symphorien, to try to extort money from Andrès, the son he had some 22 years earlier with Adila. In Paris Aline has become an alcoholic and can no longer work, even as a prostitute. She has been blackmailing him for years with the threat of exposing facts about his past that he would rather keep secret. Thus, we find at the center of the action, in addition to Alain (the saint) and Gradère (the Satan figure), Alain's sister Tota (even more lustful than she had been in *Ce qui était perdu),* Andrès (who has inherited his mother's extensive land holdings), his mother's cousin Mathilde, and Mathilde's aging husband, Symphorien Desbats, and their daughter Catherine. In bringing forward Alain and Tota from *Ce qui était perdu,* Mauriac is continuing to experiment with the form of the cycle novel, but once again it is on his own terms. *Les Anges noirs* is tightly constructed with a half dozen well-developed characters who are all closely connected to one another. It is an ambitious work in which Mauriac exhibits complete mastery of his material. The novel reads like a thriller, with the apparent outcome seeming to change several times, much like the plot of a classical drama. In fact Mauriac was working on his first play, *Asmodée,* at the time, and this influence perhaps helps to account for the fast pacing of *Les Anges noirs.*

Mathilde and her husband, who is 20 years her senior and whom she married only to merge their respective landholdings, have planned for Catherine to marry Andrès, thereby uniting an even larger land area in one family. But suddenly Catherine refuses. Her decision interrupts the flow of the action and suggests unwanted outcomes. After she is persuaded to go ahead with the wedding for the sake of the family and the land, it is Andrès who now refuses, for he fancies himself in love with Tota (who had picked him up on a train and who is now being kept by him in a nearby hotel).

In the meantime, Catherine and her father want to eliminate Gradère from their midst. To this end, they are in secret contact with Aline, whom they have invited to visit. It is expected that she will embarrass Gradère by her presence and will then take him away to Paris once and for all. The situation would then be appropriate for Catherine and Andrès to go ahead with their wedding plans. When Gradère learns of Aline's travel plans, he intercepts and murders her. He has finally committed the crime that he felt Satan had been pushing him toward all these years. But when he develops pneumonia during the two nights that he spends out in the rain, the first digging Aline's grave and the second killing and burying her, Alain Forcas takes him in. He dies in the rectory, confident that divine grace, mediated through the country priest, has saved him. The novel ends with a handshake between Andrès and Alain, through which it is understood that Andrès will stay away from Tota and will therefore most likely marry Catherine in a loveless union.

A key structuring device in the novel is the small staircase or stoop in front of Alain's rectory in the town square. As a Christ figure, Alain has already ascended these steps and accepted the suffering that is necessary to imitate Christ. When Gradère first returns to Liogeats it is late at night; he notices that the steps have been covered by a *jonchée,* a freshly cut pile of boxwood branches, which, according to local custom, are placed at the entrance of the home of a newly married couple. Several young people have placed these branches on the steps of the rectory after dark to embarrass the young priest in the morning when he goes out. Since, at the beginning of the novel, Tota is living in the rectory with her brother, it is their way of saying that they do not believe that Tota is his sister; they take her to be his lover. Gradère, the fallen angel, is indignant at what they have done and disposes of the branches. Thus, when Alain, who had heard and seen his enemies placing the branches on his doorstep in the middle of the night, comes out in the morning, he is surprised to see that the steps are perfectly clean. He does not yet know that Gradère, whose letter he has just read, has done this. Gradère will later mount the steps himself and die in the bedroom on the second floor before the novel ends. But here, at the beginning of the work, the *jonchée* placed on the staircase by Alain's detractors symbolically and mystically joins the two men. Later, before he dies, Gradère wakes in the middle of the night and sees Alain sleeping in the armchair at his bedside. The young man's face is a double of his own, and Gradère realizes that the young Christ figure watching over him could have followed another path in life. But by this time the grace that Alain has earned through his own suffering will be sufficient to save Gradère.

One of the important questions that the novel raises is whether Gradère is possessed. When citing in his letter to Alain the phrase that an old country priest had once used, "There are certain souls that are given over to him [Satan]" (*ORTC,* 3:233), Gradère seems to be concerned, and at times completely convinced, that he is one of them. This conviction enables him to absolve himself of responsibility for his past and future actions: if Satan has usurped his freedom, he cannot be held accountable for anything that he has done.[3] But Alain cannot believe this as he reads Gradère's letter. He knows as a priest that there is no sin that cannot be forgiven and that Gradère will be forgiven if he will simply recite with a truly repentant heart his long list of sins to a priest in the confessional. Thus, the reader should not be led to believe that this is a pessimistic novel about possession and thus potentially about predestination. On the contrary, it is an optimistic one about freedom and divine grace. Alain Forcas, as a potential saint whose all-too-human side we see clearly, knows what temptation is, especially when it is heightened by the influence of heredity. Like his father, who had an incestuous relationship with his own sister, Alain is attracted to Tota, yet he refuses to yield to this temptation. Having been aided by divine grace, he overcomes it. It is evident that his conviction about freedom and his trust in the power of grace more closely parallel Mauriac's own views on these matters. At the end of the novel it is he who has the last word, for he understands that to work with grace and use one's freedom, one must "give oneself over to the madness of trust in God, and be trusting to the point of madness" (*ORTC*, 3:366).

The brief epilogue to the novel, in which we find all the characters back in the situations they were in before the fallen angel temporarily changed their lives, brings up again the relationship between genetic inheritance and human freedom. Mauriac's propensity to share, at least in part, the essentially pessimistic Jansenist view of the human condition is quite evident here. In special cases man can achieve wonders in the Pascalian order of charity by cooperating with grace, but this does not diminish the power of the lowest of the three orders, that of the body. Grace might win out in a particular case, but the propensity for evil is not only inherent in the human condition, but magnified or diminished by particular hereditary traits. Thus, if grace has won out here, the venom is still in the family blood lines and it can be expected to exert an influence on the life of Gradère's son, Andrès. This is why the final handshake between Alain and Andrès takes place on the rectory steps, which clearly symbolize Calvary. Since Andrès is Gradère's son, he has perhaps inherited a predilection for evil. By shaking hands with Alain, he signals his determination to cooperate with divine grace, for he realizes that, like his father, he must ascend the steps of Calvary. Alain, a saint who has overcome a hereditary penchant for incest, has saved Gradère. Now he will save his son.[4]

Les Chemins de la mer (1939)

Les Chemins de la mer (The Unknown Sea, 1948) appeared originally in installments in 1938 under the title *Mamôna*, whose connotations of money, and the pleasures of the flesh that it can buy, catches a reader's attention more effectively. This is one of those rare cases in which Mauriac's innate flair for imaginative titles betrayed him. In light of the

title, one is reminded of André Gide's cutting remark about Mauriac's
Vie de Jean Racine (1928): that the Catholic novelist was guilty of "a
reassuring compromise which allows [him] to love God without losing
sight of Mammon" (*ORTC*, 3:1198).[5] Mauriac responded with his
essay *Dieu et Mammon* (1929), in which he attempted to express in
detail his views on the problematic relationship between strong
Christian commitment and worldly values. But the writing of this
essay did not by any means solve the problem for Mauriac: he still
remained haunted by the problem of money because of its power to
influence human freedom. It seems that when he began publishing
Mamôna in installments he had already decided that his primary
theme would be money, but the novel's conclusion had not yet been
written. Then, as he completed the work, other themes and a rather
large number of fully developed characters emerged. Although the
motif of money remained at the heart of the novel, its larger ambitions led to a certain amount of confusion, since it seemed to go in
several directions at once. This lack of concentration is especially
obvious in comparison to virtually any of Mauriac's other novels, but
especially his masterpieces. Between the serialized *Mamôna,* which ran
in *Candide* from 14 April to 7 July 1938, and the publication of the
work in book form, Mauriac kept correcting and changing his text,
even after it had appeared in installments. Referring to the many
changes—a rarity in Mauriac's fiction—the judicious Jacques Petit
certainly understates the problem when he concludes: "It seems that
the writing of *Les Chemins de la mer* was very difficult" (*ORTC*, 3:1203).
For all these reasons, this work is perhaps the weakest fictional effort
of Mauriac's career.

The opening scene establishes the theme of money as the root of all
evil. A wealthy bourgeois family, the Révolous, are preparing to
attend a ball sponsored by one of Bordeaux's most socially prominent
families. The family consists of the mother, Lucienne Révolou, her
husband, Oscar (an attorney), and their three children, Julien, Rose,
and Denis. As Lucienne and the children are preparing to leave, a
friend, Léonie Costadot, appears. A wealthy widow, she has found out
that Oscar Révolou has lost his fortune because of shady dealings.
Oscar is not at home, and his wife thinks that he is working at his
office, but actually he is preparing to spend the evening with his mistress, an actress of notorious repute. Léonie Costadot has come directly to their home unannounced because she is concerned about the
safety of her own family fortune. Having left her family's stocks and

bonds in Oscar's keeping, she wants to protect herself from Oscar's financial collapse by having Lucienne sign a legally prepared document that pledges that Oscar will reimburse her for the full amount of her holdings before paying off any of the family's other clients or creditors.

Lucienne and her children are stunned by this news and do not know what to make of it. Nevertheless, she signs the document and Léonie marches off trimphantly. She returns home to inform her sons Pierre and Robert of what she has done. She has preserved their fortune and is exultant over her pluck and foresight, but her children do not see it that way. Robert a medical student who intends to marry Rose Révolou, realizes that his plans have been dealt a shattering blow. He cannot marry Rose if, because of her father's financial ruin, she loses her social standing. Pierre, a close friend of Denis Révolou (and in this they foreshadow Nicholas and Gilles of *Galigaï),* is concerned about the effect that the loss of the family fortune will have on his friend.

The oldest boy, Gaston, is not present, for he, like Oscar Révolou, is a lover of the same actress, "la Lovati." In fact, before the evening is over, Oscar will commit suicide when he learns that "la Lovati" prefers the younger man to him.

Unfortunately, the control exhibited by Mauriac in *Les Anges noirs* is absent in the present novel. Working with a multiplicity of characters becomes more problematic for him as the plot develops. As we recall, he had been tempted by the cycle novel when he wrote *Ce qui était perdu.* There he experimented with a larger number of characters, but he returned to his more traditional, concentrated form in *Noeud de vipères* and *Le Mystère Frontenac.* But, beginning again with *La Fin de la nuit* and *Les Anges noirs,* novels that consciously take up again characters from earlier works, he seemed on one level to be writing a cycle novel while at the same time subverting the genre, mostly through inconsistencies between the earlier and later novels. *Les Chemins de la mer* starts off relatively well, for the many characters are tied together by the idea of money. But as it loses this initial focus, the novel soon fragments into a somewhat disjointed work.

Over the course of the first four chapters, the narrative voice jumps back and forth between the two families to describe the effect that money, or the lack of it, is having on them. But gradually other themes emerge, deflecting attention from the central issue raised at the outset. One of these distractions is the character of Landin, Oscar Révolou's devoted assistant. He seems to have dedicated his life to the service of his master, but gradually we learn of his dark side—including homosexuality, which the narrative voice associates with the work of the devil. After Oscar's suicide, Landin moves to Paris, where he serves different masters in the newspaper business while continuing to lead his secret life. Near the end of the novel, after Pierre meets him in a nightclub, he is mysteriously murdered on his way home. Landin, like Hervé of *Ce qui était perdu* and Gradère of *Les Anges noirs,* is thus another Satan figure from this period of Mauriac's fictional career, but he is not nearly as fully developed as the other two. His presence leads the action off on a tangent that is not structurally integrated into the rest of the work and is another reflection of the novel's lack of internal cohesion.

After the initial revelation that Oscar Révolou has committed suicide and that the family, for all practical purposes, is bankrupt, most of the action takes place at Léognan, a fictional transposition of Château-Lange, a large domain of a hundred acres or so on the outskirts of Bordeaux that had once belonged to the Mauriac family. Léognan is now all that the Révolou family has left. It consists of the land, a large but somewhat dilapidated house, and the smaller building in which the caretakers, M. and Mme Cavailhès, live with their daughter Irène. In Mauriac's family, this large piece of property had belonged to Mauriac's maternal grandmother. It was sold immediately after her death at the turn of the century, but years later, in his *Nouveaux Mémoires intérieurs,* Mauriac lamented that the property had been allowed to escape the family's grasp: "You don't have to be a soothsayer to foresee the appreciation of this property located right at the edge of the city. As an adolescent, I was astonished that my mother and my aunts had been so shortsighted" (*OA,* 735). Mauriac would have been about 17, the same age as Denis Révolou, when he became aware of what had happened to this family property, and in fact Denis in the original draft of the novel is the first-person narrator. It is as if this aspect of the novel were an elaboration of a childhood fantasy, with Denis doing what the young Mauriac had not. The centering of the novel on Léognan, which Denis and his sister are able to revive and make into the basis of a new family fortune, enables Mauriac to develop this idea. It also provides him with a structuring device for the action of the novel after he abandons the earlier plan of contrasting the two families in relationship to money. Of course, inordinate attachment to land, no less than to money, is also a part of "Mammon," and to the extent that the rest of the novel is structured around this property, the work coheres. The problem is that the novel is forced to bear too much weight, with the different characters (including Landin, who is now in Paris) pulling in too many different directions.

As Mauriac had distributed parts of himself between Marcel and Hervé in *Ce qui était perdu,* he also divides himself here between Pierre Costadot and Denis Révolou. When Pierre, at age 18, finds out that his mother has preserved his inheritance by persuading Lucienne Révolou to sign the document, he expresses both his disgust at what his mother has done and his personal fear of the power of money: "I hate money because it holds me in its power" (*ORTC,* 3:561). Pierre's ambition is to become a poet; he has been working on a poem entitled "Atys et Cybèle," in which Atys is a shepherd and Cybèle the earth, or nature. From time to time he reads sections of it aloud and explains what the verses mean. On each of these occasions the development of Atys's sentimental life parallels his own. Thus, when Atys is in love with the nymph Sangaris, Pierre is secretly in love with Rose Révolou, who, he thinks, still loves his brother Robert. Later, when we find Atys discovering God, Pierre has sublimated his carnal love for Rose and is ready to join the army and go off to North Africa to serve a cause that is larger than himself. Pierre believes that in turning his back on his family's obsession with money, he will be able to separate himself from mammon. But as a young would-be artist, he soon learns that "the world," or the realm of unbridled discovery and exploration of power and pleasure, is also a form of mammon.

If Pierre is based largely on Mauriac's experience of having wanted to be a writer as he crossed the bridge from late adolescence to adulthood, Denis is essentially a creature of Mauriac's imagination. Like his creator, he fails his "bac" examination on the first try. But unlike Mauriac, who passed it on his second attempt and then went on to successful university studies, Denis has no such success. He must work to support the family and ransom its property. His marriage to Irène Cavailhès is motivated by a mixture of reason and fleeting passion, not genuine love: primarily, this union will enable him to obtain a loan from Irène's father, which in turn furnishes the capital necessary to begin tilling the land and selling produce in the city. By the end of the novel Denis has become a wealthy young businessman who drives a large, expensive car and belongs to an exclusive tennis club. He is proficient at making money, but has no serious goals beyond this. For Mauriac, Denis represents the road not taken, a speculation about what might have happened if, after he failed his first exam, the Château-Lange property had remained in the family and had fallen to him to develop.

Mauriac disperses his energies in this novel in order to account for the destinies of all the main characters. Julien, the oldest Révolou child, had been a snob and social climber before his father's suicide. He now takes to his bed, unable to cope with life. He also becomes his mother's reason for living, as Lucienne spends most of her time waiting on him. Rose Révolou, aged 22, overcomes the heartbreak and disappointment of her broken engagement and courageously gets on with her life, finding a job as a clerk in a bookstore. Pierre Costadot, who loves Rose with childlike devotion, is so angry with his mother and brother at the abandonment of the poor girl that he takes his share of the inheritance and squanders it in Paris. While there he meets Landin, Oscar Révolou's former assistant, in a nightclub. After he accompanies Landin home in a cab and leaves him at his doorstep, Pierre falls into a drunken stupor. When he awakens the next day he reads in the newspaper that Landin has been murdered and that the police are looking for someone who fits his description. He stays in hiding until the affair blows over. This experience is critical in helping him decide to join the army, where he will serve an ideal larger than his own personal concerns.

At the end of the novel, Mauriac tries to pull together all that has come before when he writes: "The life of most men is a dead-end road and leads to nothing. But others know, from childhood, that they are going toward an unknown sea, . . . they have only to hurl themselves into it or turn back" (*ORTC,* 3:705). If we take the image of the sea, which Mauriac had used earlier in *Ce qui était perdu,* to mean God, then it is apparent that only the elect can reach this goal and then only through suffering. Of all the characters in the novel, only two are called to this special destiny: Pierre, who follows an ideal of service to God and country; and Rose, who seems to be awakened to true religious faith. Mauriac clearly intended this work to be read as a Catholic novel, but by the time he finally finished writing it, he had lost any sense of focus he might have had at the beginning. His intention to depict the clash between Christian and worldly values seems clear enough, but it is never brought to realization in a sustained way. In the end, the faith journeys of Pierre and Rose remain vague at best.

The extensive rewriting of the novel after it had already begun to appear in installments reflects the state of confusion that Mauriac was in as he wrote it. The poor to lukewarm reception accorded *Les Chemins de la mer* raised doubts in Mauriac's own mind about his continuing ability as a novelist. Was he, now into his mid-fifties, running out of inspiration? His interest in writing for the theater suggests that he harbored such doubts.[6] It would take the defeat of France in 1940 and the enforced seclusion at Malagar that followed that debacle for Mauriac to refocus his energies and redirect his inspiration. The result, *La Pharisienne,* would be one of his greatest works.

La Pharisienne (1941)

La Pharisienne (Woman of the Pharisees, 1946) was begun shortly after the fall of France in 1940 and was written hastily, seemingly without interruption, during the dark autumn days of that year. Despite the problems posed by German occupation of the northern half of France, Mauriac was able to obtain the necessary publication approval from the German authorities without too much delay. The book appeared in June 1941 and enjoyed an immense popular success. Although the collaborationist press in the occupied zone wrote hardly a word about it, the fact that it sold 35,000 copies in the first four months after publication suggests that many people read the book as a commentary on their own condition.[7] To be sure, this was a Catholic novel about certain aspects of contemporary spirituality, but it could also be read as an indictment of the political pharisees who had welcomed defeat the previous summer and were now preaching moral regeneration under German hegemony. In short, it was seen by many at the time not only as a *roman catholique* but also as a *roman de l'Occupation.* As the Gaullist Maurice Schumann later put it, it was "a book about issues of the day."[8]

This interpretation might be difficult for readers 50 years later to understand, for the novel at first glance seems as nonpolitical as the rest of Mauriac's fiction. After all, the very title of the novel is taken from the Christian Gospel narratives, in which the Pharisees, a religious sect of the day that was committed to strict observance of Mosaic law, are depicted as implacable foes of Jesus, who preached that a new law of love should replace the old law of rites and rituals. The primary level of discourse in the novel is thus religious in nature, with Brigitte Pian cast in the role of the observant pharisee. Yet strong political currents are perceptible under the surface narrative. The book appeared in such unusual, indeed unprecedented circumstances, that a political interpretation of its meaning was almost impossible to avoid at the time.

Coming as it did after several attempts to write longer and more ambitious novels, *La Pharisienne* continues Mauriac's artistic preoccupations over the preceding decade. Mauriac seems to have given it an inordinate amount of concentrated effort (especially in terms of structure and point of view), in part because the circumstances under which he wrote kept him from the social whirl and distractions of Parisian literary life. Perhaps this forced seclusion also accounts for the fact that this is his most personal novel. As a professional writer with as clear and formal a commitment to Catholicism as any modern French writer has ever had, Mauriac uses the novel to inquire into the degree to which he himself may be a pharisee.

Another reason for Mauriac's intense concentration on this novel is his desire to use the book as a means of responding to Jean-Paul Sartre's bitter attack on him in the February 1939 issue of the *NRF*. As yet largely unknown outside a small circle of Left Bank literati and cognoscenti, Sartre displayed in this article his uncanny ability to invent catchphrases that the public could easily pick up and adopt without really understanding what they meant. A full decade before pop-philosophy expressions like "existence precedes essence" found their way to a large audience of nonphilosophers, informing them of a new approach to life called "existentialism," Sartre was able to attack Mauriac for taking liberties with the "freedom" of his characters; in the process he created a good deal of publicity for himself. Taking special aim at *La Fin de la nuit,* which was indeed a vulnerable spot for Mauriac, Sartre accused the author of playing God with his characters and of too often predicting what was going to happen to them. He ended his essay with a wry phrase that delighted Mauriac's enemies. Attributing to Mauriac the conviction that he could act like God with his creatures, limiting their freedom when it pleased him to do so, Sartre concluded: "God is not an artist. And François Mauriac isn't either."[9]

This attack had a devastating effect on Mauriac. From a distance of a half century, when it is clear that Sartre was a relative failure as a novelist (which he grew to realize himself, never completing the last of the four novels in a cycle that he had announced under the grand title *Les Chemins de la liberté {The Paths of Freedom}*), one might wonder why this was so. Nevertheless, and even though the main points of Sartre's diatribe can be rebutted, Mauriac was so upset by the attack that he continued to verbally assault Sartre for the rest of his life.[10] But it should be remembered that literary tastes were changing in the 1930s, and a new generation of novelists was coming to the fore. The social protest novel, or *roman social,* as exemplified by Céline's *Voyage au bout de la nuit* (*Journey to the End of the Night,* 1932), which had exerted a tremendous influence on Sartre, had redirected the interests and energies of many writers during the rest of the decade. Mauriac, 20 years older than Sartre, and one of the 40 "immortals" of the French Academy, represented just about everything that Sartre abhorred from a religious, social, and political point of view. The two men would be implacable enemies for the next 30 years.

This is not the place to review in detail the content of Sartre's attacks on Mauriac, nor to judge their merit. It can be said, however, that there is some justification for Sartre's accusation that Mauriac is inconsistent in the use of point of view in many of his novels, often allowing his narrator to comment upon things that he has no way of knowing about. To be fair to Mauriac, however, the novel that Sartre was writing at the time, *La Nausée* (1939), as well as the novels that he would publish during the 1940s, sprang from a quite different aesthetic stance. Thus, the claim by Mauriac's defenders—that his only real fault was that he was being true to his own inner voices and not writing a novel according to someone else's recipe—also has some merit. The important thing about this controversy is not whether Sartre was right or wrong, but that Mauriac as an artist suffered greatly because of the attack. The best proof of this is that he seems to have written *La Pharisienne* with one eye looking back over his shoulder at Sartre, always conscious to document for his reader the narrator's source of information. He deliberately discards the omniscient narrator of the earlier novels and seems at first glance to want to adhere more strictly to a single point of view.

La Pharisienne is narrated by Louis Pian, the stepson of Brigitte Pian, the "pharisee" of the title. The events described have taken place many years earlier, for Louis, a mere teenager at the time of the action, is now a grown man. He seems to be telling his story sometime shortly after World War I, while the events that he narrates took place in the early years of the century. Louis uses as many sources as possible to support his assertions about the actions and motivations of the various characters. Although this meticulousness increases the reader's trust of the narrator, it also has an ironic dimension, for as the novel progresses the sources Louis exploits increase in number. They include not only the usual diaries and letters that have fallen into his hands, but also a telegram, eyewitness reports, hearsay, and overheard conversations. It is almost as if Mauriac, in responding to Sartre's criticism about irregularities and inconsistencies in the use of the omniscient narrator, also wanted to show the absurd dimension of such criticism. While on the one hand accepting the validity of Sartre's criticism, he also subverts his seeming surrender by carrying the advice to almost ridiculous extremes.

Certainly Mauriac's most ambitious novel, *La Pharisienne* is arguably his most important and successful work as well. The author himself later confirmed its importance after he became convinced that he had been awarded the Nobel Prize for literature because the psychological and theological issues raised by *La Pharisienne* had struck a responsive chord among readers in Scandinavia.[11] This positive reaction presumably influenced the decision of the Swedish Royal Academy in his favor. While Mauriac's acknowledgment of the importance of the novel enabled him

to quip about his ironic debt of gratitude to Sartre, we should not lose
sight of the fact that *La Pharisienne* is one of Mauriac's masterpieces
(along with *Genitrix, Thérèse Desqueyroux,* and *Le Noeud de vipères*) precisely because it incorporates a new technical approach to the problem of
narration, encompasses a broader vision of life, and has a wider scope
than any of his other novels. At the same time, its unity is generated by
the narrator himself. What is unique about the novel is that it concentrates on one character, Louis Pian, while also fully developing several
others. It thus combines the intense focus of his novels from the 1920s
with his attempt in the 1930s to write longer, more complex novels,
such as *Ce qui était perdu* and *Les Chemins de la mer.* In addition, by having
Louis Pian be both the narrator/spectator and an actor in the drama
(albeit a minor one), Mauriac allows self-discovery to emerge as a major
theme. Thus, as Louis Pian slowly discovers and lays bare the pharisaism
of his stepmother, the reader becomes aware that the narrator is also a
pharisee.

The novel is ostensibly concerned with the spiritual "merits" earned
and accumulated by a sincerely pious person, Brigitte Pian, as she seeks
spiritual perfection. But the reader, through Louis Pian, discovers that
such merits are of dubious value when not leavened by unselfish love for
others. Although Louis is able to see clearly into the actions and motives
of his stepmother, we are also struck by his own blindness about himself.
If one agrees that self-delusion is the common thread that unites all
humanity, it can be said that the essence of the human condition is distilled and treated within the covers of *La Pharisienne.*

There are three major sites around which the novel is structured:
Larzujon (another fictional incarnation of Saint-Symphorien), where
Brigitte Pian lives with her husband and two stepchildren; Balauze (a
transformation of the town of Bazas), linked to Jean de Mirbel; and
Baluzac (a fictionalized Balizac), which is associated with the Abbé
Calou. Each place in this structural triangle is also associated in some
way with love and desire.

There are also three major love triangles in the novel. In the Larzujon
triangle we find Brigitte Pian with M. Puybaraud and Octavie Tranche;
in the Balauze triangle are Jean de Mirbel, his mother, and her lover, the
playwright Raoul; and in the Baluzac triangle the Abbé Calou is at the
center, between Jean de Mirbel and Hortense Voyod. These three sites
and their corresponding triangles are linked through the narrative
recounted by Louis Pian, who is attempting to tell the story, above all, of
his stepmother, who has exerted a tremendous influence on his life. He

cannot tell the whole story without also describing certain actions of other characters in each of the different triangles. Brigitte interacts with each of them to varying degrees and in each case her intention is to be of help to others. However, since she cultivates sanctity the way people learn a foreign language—methodically, step by step, without regard to love for others—her actions all too often achieve the opposite effect of the one desired. Louis Pian's narrative also proceeds on two levels. Thus, his discovery of Brigitte's true identity is accompanied by his own experience of self-discovery.

Brigitte came to marry Octave Pian (the father of the narrator, Louis, and of his sister Michèle) after the death of his wife, Marthe, who had been her cousin. Brigitte had been jealous of Marthe and suspected that her reputation for virtue was unjustified. After Marthe's premature death (which Brigitte later learns was probably a suicide), she makes herself indispensable to Octave, marries him, and sets about raising Louis and Michèle. But since in this novel nothing is what it appears to be— which is one of the reasons readers in 1941 read the book without difficulty as a "novel of the Occupation"—it turns out that Octave is really not the biological father of these children. In fact, he is impotent. The real father is Marthe's unidentified lover, who, when he grew tired of her, inspired the nervous breakdown that led to her suicide. Louis gradually learns all this and puts the pieces together as the novel unfolds.

Michèle, a mere teenager, is in love with one of Louis's classmates, a troubled boy named Jean de Mirbel who does poorly in school—another one of those offshoots of the French aristocracy that Mauriac usually depicted in a somber light to highlight their decadence. Jean's father is deceased and his mother lives elsewhere. Like the social caste that he represents, the boy seems lost, his place in society not clearly defined. When Mme de Mirbel appears early in the novel, it is springtime and she has come to make arrangements for the summer vacation. Since she wants to be rid of the boy in order to indulge her personal vices, she arranges for him to spend the summer alone in the rectory in Baluzac with the Abbé Calou, who often takes in boys like Jean, for companionship and to earn extra income. While she is finalizing these arrangements, Jean begs her to spend the night with him, but she refuses. He is desperate to be with her and to receive some sign of motherly recognition. Determined to find her, he goes out on his bicycle after dark and locates the hotel in Balauze, the nearby town, where she is staying. In order to be able to greet her with a kiss the next morning, he resolves to spend the night sleeping outside on the ground. However, in the middle of the night, as his patience becomes exhausted, Jean experiences an epiphany that forever changes his life. When he climbs a tree in order to look into his mother's room, he discovers that she is not alone, but is making love to Raoul, a well-known Parisian playwright. The scene makes Jean aware of his mother's betrayal: she is more interested in exploration of her own sexuality than she is in him. The goodnight kiss, a kind of Proustian viaticum that he had longed to receive from her as a sign of their attachment, belongs to someone else. He discovers his own painful solitude and isolation in the realization that his mother has a life of her own that is completely separate from his. This disillusionment will affect the rest of his life.

In 1941, those who saw *La Pharisienne* as a "novel of the Occupation" could have associated Mme de Mirbel and her son with the degeneration of the traditional social elites, who projected an image of themselves for public consumption that was at variance with the reality of their lives.

Michèle Pian, the narrator's younger sister, lives under the strict supervision of her stepmother in Larzujon. When one of the local share-croppers informs Brigitte that Michèle spent several hours one afternoon alone with Jean de Mirbel in a shed near the Abbé Calou's house, a crisis erupts. Brigitte insists that Octave agree to place Michèle in a Catholic boarding school in Bordeaux the following fall. Michèle must be sepa-rated from this boy, who causes trouble for everyone and who could very well compromise her future. Brigitte Pian, in wanting to protect Michèle, faithfully reflects the traditional concerns of the Catholic bour-geoisie. In granting her request, Octave seems outwardly to be agreeing with Brigitte, but in fact he is really protecting Michèle (in whom he continues to see and love his deceased but unfaithful wife) from Brigitte. He asks Michèle not to correspond with Jean de Mirbel anymore, and she agrees, but this does not keep her from sending him, via the Abbé Calou, the golden heart-shaped locket that she wears around her neck and that contains snippets of her deceased mother's hair. In 1941, read-ers could see in this situation a breakdown in the traditional alliance among the bourgeoisie, the church, and the aristocracy. Each was inter-preted to be saying one thing but doing another, pursuing one policy outwardly and another secretly.

In Baluzac the Abbé Calou has a bitter enemy, the local pharmacist's wife, Hortense Voyod. Having separated her from her female lover (who had told him of the relationship in confession), he must now pay the price. Hortense decides to take vengeance on the priest by seducing Jean and running off with him. When she succeeds in this design, Jean's mother is shocked. After she complains to church authorities about the abbé's lax supervision of her son, the abbé is banished from the rectory, obliged to give up his parish, and forced to take refuge with his brother's family, where he is considered merely an extra mouth to feed. In seeking to do what his conscience tells him is right—that is, counseling his spiritual charge in confession to break off her relationship with Hortense, taking in the troubled Jean de Mirbel, and cautiously approving the adolescent affection between Jean and Michèle (since he knows that each one is starved for love)—he has suffered only pain and humiliation. For many contemporary readers, the Abbé Calou was emblematic of those priests who followed the law of love and did what was right despite the consequences. His subsequent suffering at the hands of the institutional church could then be seen as the logical outcome of such behavior.

Brigitte's life as a pharisee is given particular emphasis when she intervenes in the lives of M. Puybaraud and Octavie Tranche. Puybaraud is an ex-seminarian who is unable to hold a permanent job.[12] He gives piano lessons to children of the upper bourgeoisie and makes ends meet thanks to a monthly allowance that Brigitte, in carefully measured charity, pays him. Unfortunately, his financial dependence upon her is complicated by a psychological dependence, for she has also become his spiritual director. When he tells her that he has fallen in love with Octavie, a teacher in a local Catholic school, Brigitte forbids them to marry, but they do so nonetheless. Her objection is ostensibly based on the conviction that M. Puybaraud's true vocation is to serve God by becoming a monk, but her real motive (probably unconscious) is control. After their marriage, continuing financial difficulties oblige them to continue to depend on Brigitte for a monthly subsidy, which Brigitte pays even though she is convinced that Puybaraud's true calling lies elsewhere. In this way, she enjoys the satisfaction of accumulating even further merits in God's eyes. Her pleasure is increased by the knowledge that the couple she is helping is aware of her disappointment in them, which gives her the chance to prove to them what a saint she is.

A dramatic scene takes place when Brigitte visits their apartment and learns that they have bought a piano, which they clearly cannot afford, but which they deem essential for their happiness and well-being, since they cannot live without the consolation that music brings. The scene ends with M. Puybaraud boldly refusing to sell the piano and slamming the door in Brigitte's face. The act appears to make a statement to her about their desire for freedom: they do not want to be accountable to anyone. But the next day they decide to apologize, for they recognize that Brigitte is not always able to control her self-righteousness, and it is she after all who pays the rent and provides them with money to live on.

As Brigitte returns home after this scene we also learn what goes on in her mind and, in the process, what the true nature of the pharisee is. She regrets having lost her temper with the Puybarauds, but at the same time tries to convince herself that her anger was justified. She suddenly realizes that her concept of God as an accountant who keeps track of the good and pious deeds performed by those who claim to serve him is not necessarily the correct one. She begins to question the feeling of self-satisfaction that she derives from knowing that she is doing God's work, and is shaken by the realization that she has perhaps gone too far in tampering with the private lives of other people (even though she is doing so with the best of intentions). But when she stops at the cathedral to pray, her thought process is reversed, for she concludes that her doubts are simply another trial sent by God. Therefore, she asks God in her prayer to add this latest trial—the temporary wavering of her habitual feelings of self-righteousness—to her list of merits. Finally, to rid herself of the possible stain of a sin that she is not sure she has even committed, she seeks out a priest and confesses to the sin of anger; but at the same time she justifies her anger as being caused by "legitimate indignation within the guidelines of conscious charity" (*ORTC*, 3:823). Thus, while she seems to be recognizing an infraction against the Christian law of love, she also tells herself that no infraction ever took place.

If Brigitte prescribes harsh medicine for others, it is only because she knows it is good for their souls. Hers is the exquisite pain of righteousness peculiar to the pharisee. This search for spiritual perfection, no matter how well intentioned, repeatedly encounters similar stumbling blocks. In 1941, a politically minded reader could see in Brigitte Pian the hypocritical governing class that ruled the country after the fall of the Third Republic the previous summer. If Octave Pian, Brigitte's husband (aging, impotent, and blind to what is going on around him) is emblematic of Marshall Pétain, Brigitte, the conscientious caretaker, represents those underlings who consoled themselves with the thought that the harsh measures that they had to impose upon others, no matter how difficult or unjust, were nonetheless in their best interests. Brigitte Pian's method of soothing her conscience could easily be imputed to such political leaders of the day.

The problem for Brigitte Pian is the one that confronts anyone who seeks to strive consciously for Christian perfection. Brigitte is not a hypocrite. This point is essential to an understanding of her character. She does not deliberately say one thing, like Molierè's Tartuffe, and do another. On the contrary, her problem is that in seeking to do good, she is interested primarily in her own personal spiritual development. Most people who seek spiritual perfection, as Louis Pian points out, are fully aware of their weaknesses and do not hesitate to attribute to God and to the workings of divine grace any progress that they make. But "Brigitte Pian went in the opposite direction, reinforcing day after day the reasons that she had to thank the creator who had made her such an admirable person" (*ORTC,* 3:822). Reference to St. Mark's Gospel (7:1–23) can also be of help in understanding her problem more clearly. When Jesus rebukes the pharisees, it is because of their emphasis on strict dietary laws, which in turn are based on the idea that impurity comes from without. Jesus turns this belief and practice upside down by proclaiming that spiritual impurity comes not from without, but from within. For him, unless one's acts are based on a pure intention—that is, unless they are rooted first in love—they are impure. Thus, since Brigitte is unable to root her actions in love, whether they be private devotional practices or acts of charity toward those around her, her deeds are, in the words of Jesus, "impure." Brigitte emphasizes the acquisition of ever-increasing "merits" for herself, without any necessary relationship to the expression of love to those around her. The external effect on others (she makes life easier for M. Puybaraud and Octavie by giving them money in the name of Christ) is a reflection of the presumed internal increase in her own merits. In fact, the importance of external effect on others is so important to her that when one of her acts leads to clearly undesirable results (the piano incident described above), she is still able to add it to her list of merits by interpreting it as yet another trial sent by God. Without love, hers is a drama of what Mauriac would later call *la fausse perfection* (false perfection; *ORTC,* 3:926).

Study of the manuscripts of *La Pharisienne* shows that as Mauriac wrote this novel he revised it in a number of instances to tone down or alleviate Brigitte's "monstrosity." He had already created a number of fictional "monsters" over the years (Thérèse being the most famous), and he clearly did not want us to see Brigitte as one of them. Like Mme de Blénauge of *Ce qui était perdu* and Blanche Frontenac of *Le Mystère Frontenac,* she is modeled in part on his mother (and perhaps also on his equally pious maternal grandmother), as well as on his confessor, the Abbé Altermann, who had been his spiritual director during the years of his religious crisis. Mauriac wants us to see Brigitte as essentially sincere, although misguided in her zeal. By the end of the novel, when Brigitte has lost her husband, developed a deep friendship with the Calvinist Dr. Gellis, himself a widower, and come to understand the importance of love, Louis Pian can finally tell us that "she understood now that it's not earning merits that's important, but loving" (*ORTC,* 3:881).[13]

Ironically, as Louis points out that Brigitte has finally come to understand and put into practice the admonition in St. Mark's Gospel, he himself is blind to the growing pharisaism of his own life. By the end of the novel, it is apparent that he is guilty of some of the same sins for which he reproaches Brigitte. Appearing some two decades before the Second Vatican Council, *La Pharisienne* can be read as a scathing denunciation of pre–Vatican II spirituality. That spirituality, which grew out of the Council of Trent in the sixteenth century and which was itself an attempt to respond to objections raised by various Protestant sects and movements of the time, placed great stress on a legalistic sense of "merit" to the detriment of "love." Christian perfection in this sense consists of assembling a long series of building blocks and piling them one on top of another. In such a system, the repetition of pious acts, done with the intention of obtaining merits in God's eyes, risks becoming a goal in itself. Unselfish love of others need not be a component of this process.

There are a number of important links between this novel and Mauriac's previous fictional efforts. Mauriac not only worked hard to soften the "monstrous" side of Brigitte's character, he also bestowed upon her an ability to see into other people's souls. Like M. Coûture in *Asmodeé,* she knows from the beginning that M. Puybaraud's vocation is to enter a Trappist monastery. When she first says this to Puybaraud, he cannot believe her. But when Octavie and her baby die in childbirth, a crisis of faith ensues and by the end of the novel he is indeed a monk. Development and cultivation of the spiritual life as practiced by Brigitte Pian can result, Mauriac seems to be saying, in increased insight into life's hidden realities. It is not a completely vain undertaking. But the process is a perilous one, and the insights that are gained usually come with regard to the lives of others, not oneself.

At the end of the novel, Louis talks about having been sent "to the front" during World War I, where he received packages from Brigitte. This evocation of an earlier war against Germany must have conjured up for readers daily images of "the front" that had crumbled weakly before the German advance a year before this novel appeared. But in the France of 1941, where 14 July and 11 November had been dropped as national holidays by the authorities in favor of 18 May, Joan of Arc's feast day, the new paternalism of the Vichy regime—with its emphasis on the idea that decadence had led to national defeat and disgrace—could be read as another version of Brigitte Pian's quest for spiritual perfection. Many readers saw the same kinds of rationalizations taking place in Brigitte that they witnessed in government policy in 1941. Her desire to regulate her conscience and accumulate additional merit echoed the Vichy political line in a spiritual realm. Pursuing this point of view a bit further, we can interpret Michèle, who needs to be brought under control and whose principal sin in Brigitte's eyes is to love, as an emblem of the non-Communist French Left. She has embraced Jean de Mirbel, who, as a decadent aristocrat, can be seen in one possible reading as an emblem of England. She has loved blindly and placed her affections carelessly. She believes in the legitimacy of the Anglo-French alliance and thus needs to be watched closely. Jean de Mirbel (England) complicates matters even futher, for he has been seduced by Hortense Voyod, who is emblematic of the Communists (the Stalinist Left). Michèle's sin is thus compounded, for she loves someone who is unfaithful to her. Thus, when Louis denounces them to Brigitte (and then excuses himself for having done so), readers in 1941 could see a metaphor for an all-too-familiar political situation. The Abbé Calou, the well-meaning priest who is also Mauriac's most fully developed clerical character, and who will be rebuked and dismissed by his ecclesiastical superiors for having reluctantly given his blessing to Michèle and Jean's relationship (the alliance between the emerging French Resistance and England), helps to illustrate the divisions within the church itself. Like the ordinary French priest of the day, he is confused, but instinctively gives priority to the law of love over human law. Yet Brigitte (symbolizing the Vichy power structure) is able to gain access to church authorities (the hierarchy that generally supported the New Order in 1940), who in turn relieve him of his priestly functions. A reading such as this, which enriches and is not intended to replace what Mauriac was trying to achieve in this novel, helps us to understand why Maurice Schumann, who was with de Gaulle in London in 1941, could call *La Pharisienne* a "livre d'actualité" (Schumann, 606).

As mentioned above, each of the three geographic sites is a scene where the drama of love/desire and freedom/control is played out. In addition to the Brigitte Pian/M. Puybaraud/Octavie Tranche triad that I have already discussed, there is the Jean de Mirbel/Mme de Mirbel/Raoul triangle centered in Balauze, and the Jean de Mirbel/Abbé Calou/ Hortense Voyod grouping in Baluzac. The fact that Jean de Mirbel

occupies a position in two of the groupings illustrates his importance in
the overall economy of the novel.[14] Louis Pian, as narrator, is jealous of
him because of the power that he exerts over his sister as well as because
he is, quite simply, another one of Mauriac's *séducteurs*. In the triangle
with his mother, whom he watches making love to Raoul, both his feeling of abandonment and his carnal drives and instincts are stressed. He
is thus the polar opposite of Louis Pian who, so much like Mauriac himself, is an unloved *mal-aimé* and a pharisee.

The third cluster, that of Michèle and Jean de Mirbel/Abbé
Calou/Hortense Voyod, illustrates not only the importance of Jean to the
narrative, but also the central place that Mauriac accords to the Abbé
Calou. This character, a simple country priest who is content to devote
himself to the service of others, seems to be partly inspired by the example of Bernanos's Abbé d'Ambricourt of *Journal d'un curé de campagne*.[15]
Mauriac reviewed this novel when it first appeared in 1936 and correctly saw in it the portrayal of a true saint. To a certain extent he is trying
to achieve the same effect that Bernanos had in his novel: "Bernanos's
magnificent gift . . . is to make the supernatural natural, to introduce his
reader . . . into the hidden life of grace which for him is the only reality."[16] The Abbé Calou plays an important role here in giving the reader
a similar insight. Not surprisingly, he has many things in common with
Bernanos's country priest. They share, for instance, lowly social origins,
humility, and unquestioning love for those who do them wrong. But
better educated and more intelligent, the Abbé Calou is more lucid.
Nonetheless, his understanding of the hypocrisy of the Countess de
Mirbel as well as of the inner workings of the mind of Brigitte Pian still
do not keep him from being driven from his rectory. Mauriac later
reminded us of the importance of both Jean and the Abbé Calou to the
structure of the novel when he wrote that, despite the novel's title,
which highlights the role of Brigitte Pian, these two other characters are
at the heart of the work: *"La Pharisienne,"* he noted, "is to my mind the
story of a holy priest and of a tortured adolescent, before being the
drama of a proud and hard woman" (*ORTC*, 3:926).

As Jacques Monférier has put it, "With *La Pharisienne*, François
Mauriac is at the height of his form as an artist."[17] This novel not only is
his most complex and ambitious work, but also ranks with *Le Noeud de
vipères* as a truly great Catholic novel.

Chapter Six
The Last Novels

Le Sagouin (1951)

The final phase of Mauriac's career as a novelist began rather fortuitously. Since the end of World War II, he had devoted most of his time to the theater and journalism. After the production of *Les Mal-aimés* in 1945, *Passage du Malin* was produced in 1948 and *Le feu sur la terre* in 1951. Despite his high hopes for a new career as a dramatist, which in fact never did materialize, he still worked from time to time on sketches for possible future novels and, in 1948, had actually worked out a plan for what would eventually become *L'Agneau* (1954).

Le Sagouin (*The Weakling,* 1952) was written in its final form as a result of Mauriac's association with the literary and public affairs monthly *La Table ronde,* which was his most serious and time-consuming journalistic project in the immediate postwar years. Since the *NRF* had, in the eyes of many intellectuals, compromised itself by continuing to appear during the war years under German censorship constraints, its future was in doubt after the Liberation. From its creation in 1911, until 1940, it had been the preeminent showcase for the best writing in France, no matter what the ideological beliefs of its contributors. It had become a major cultural institution in France. *La Table ronde* was conceived by Mauriac and his friends as a replacement for the *NRF* and then, after the latter's reappearance, as a Christian alternative to it.

Since the editorial committee of *La Table ronde,* of which Mauriac was a member, had trouble locating an appropriate piece of short fiction to publish, he decided to provide one himself. But this decision was not taken lightly: "I had not written anything [in the realm of fiction] for ten years. The attitude of certain younger people led me to believe that I should no longer count on the understanding, even the complicity, of readers the way I had during the interwar years. Journalistic work took up the slack as I turned away from the novel" (*OC,* 12:1; *ORTC,* 4:994). Mauriac claimed that in going through his files from the war years, he came upon a 40-page typescript that he had completely forgotten. This first draft of what would become *Le Sagouin* had been written in 1941 but then abandoned for a number of reasons: he had gotten bogged down with the story for one thing, and then his wife (who was also his typist at the time) did not care for it. We should recall that wartime reality was such that Mauriac simply found it impossible to turn his attention to fiction in any sustained way. Current events absorbed him almost entirely during these years.

In *Le Sagouin* Mauriac places the unloved child, Guillaume, at the center of the story. The action is set in the years immediately following War World I. Guillaume, a child of the aristocracy, lives in the local château on the edge of a small town in the southwest of France. His grandmother, the Baroness (la baronne de Cernès), reigns over the household with the help of her Austrian-born domestic, who goes by the name of Fraulein (spelled without the umlaut over the a). A widow, the Baroness barely tolerates the presence of her son, Galéas, her daughter-in-law, Paule, and their seemingly backward son, Guillaume (whom they call Guillou so as not to have to pronouce the name that he shares with the German Kaiser). Her real affection is reserved for her daughter and grandchildren in Paris, whom she rarely sees and who hardly appear in the narrative.

Paule and the Baroness despise each other for several reasons. As the niece of the former mayor of Bordeaux, Paule has authentic upper-bourgeois credentials, but is an outsider to the aristocracy. Raised by her aunt and uncle, who no doubt wanted to marry her off, she had freely chosen to marry Galéas, even though she did not love him, in order to force her way into the aristocratic milieu. But once she had secured entry into this fabled domain, she realized that there was no means of escape. She was trapped. Like Thérèse Desqueyroux, she was caught in "la cage familiale." Her one offspring, the backward and slow-witted child Guillou, is a replica of his father. The latter, with no permanent employment and in fact psychologically unable to hold a job, is a self-appointed caretaker of the local cemetery. His pastime reinforces the dreadful effects of World War I, which had claimed the lives of so many Frenchmen. It also reflects Mauriac's rather dim view of the aristrocracy, for Galéas's obsession with his dead ancestors suggests the inablility of his class to adapt to new circumstances, just as Mme de Mirbel's behavior in *La Pharisienne* had displayed its moral corruption.

The action of this short but powerful novel, which Jacques Petit accurately evaluates as "one of the essential moments in Mauriac's fictional creation" (*ORTC,* 4:1213), is built around childhood (in the person of

Guillou) and the child's problematic relationship with his mother. The clash between the need for protection and the will to freedom is magnificently portrayed. Guillou is now about 12 years old and has never attended school. His parents had tried to put him in a boarding school, but the experiment proved unsuccessful: the boy was sent home for wetting his bed, the school unable to provide the attention he needed. The other alternative, schooling with the local parish priest (a solution that the Baroness would have preferred) also proved impossible because the curé had three parishes to watch over and lived too far away.

Thus, as the story begins, the education of this difficult child and the limited options open to those who are responsible for him take us to the heart of the crisis. The Baroness, on her own, has crossed over the invisible line that separates France's two major spiritual/intellectual groupings, or *familles d'esprit:* the traditional Catholics, for whom the French Revolution was a national disaster, and the local freethinking heirs to this same great event. In her desperation, she has gone so far as to contact the local atheistic and anticlerical schoolmaster in the hope that he will agree to take Guillou under his wing and serve as the boy's private tutor. She is able to make this gesture to Robert Bordas, who still walks with a limp because of a wartime injury, because she too has lost a son in the war. When Bordas refuses the Baroness's request, apparently because of a lack of time, Paule decides to visit him the next day. Although she imagines Bordas as a militant Communist, a true red, (*un rouge*), she wants to see if she can succeed where her mother-in-law has failed.

Their conversation, in which Bordas's wife, Léone, also takes part, leads to an agreement to let the boy visit the teacher and his wife to see if they can do anything with him. The visit, which takes place the following day, goes extremely well, and Guillou shows abilities that no one at home has ever noticed. Robert Bordas shows him some books belonging to his own son, Jean-Paul, who is by far the brightest student in the village, and Guillou is able to read aloud and discuss with ease various works of Jules Verne. The recurring contrast that we find in Mauriac's fiction between the *séducteur* (here it is Jean-Paul, the boy whom we never see but who is held in the highest esteem by everyone in the village), and the *mal-aimé* is played out once again. As usual the latter displays unsuspected qualities that are not readily apparent upon superficial inspection.

This initial visit leads to an argument between Robert Bordas and his wife, who has noticed that Paule has displayed more than a casual interest in her husband. Although Paule has not kept up her physical appearance and has allowed some facial hairs to grow unchecked (Robert derides her to his wife as a "bearded lady"), Léone knows that Paule would be a more redoubtable rival if she had a reason to care for herself. Thus, she urges her husband to write a letter to the château telling the de Cernès family that for purely ideological reasons he cannot become Guillou's tutor. Bordas follows his wife's counsel and informs them that as a leftist with a commitment to the working classes, he cannot in conscience come to the aid of an aristocratic family.

If this is a serious blow to the family as a whole, it is a catastrophe for Guillou, dashing his cherished dream of being perceived as "normal" and eventually fitting in with other youngsters. Bordas's letter also causes the Baroness and Paule to have another violent argument, which culminates in Paule's laying the blame for the backward and homely child at the feet of her mother-in-law: after all, doesn't the boy look just like his father?

The next day, Guillou and Galéas decide to go out walking, first to the cemetery, then down to the banks of the Ciron, a stream that flows nearby. Alone, in an isolated place, they will be far from any witnesses to their final act. They disappear, and the next day their drowned bodies are found in the water. Did the father push the boy into the water and then drown himself, or did he drown trying to save the boy? These are questions that remain unanswered at the end of this short novel.

As he had done with his short masterpieces of the 1920s, Mauriac maintains a great deal of ambiguity in the novel's denouement while stressing that those who destroy others often destroy themselves in the process. In other words, the assassin can in many cases also be a victim. Thus, Paule, chased from the Baroness's household, falls ill and does not have long to live. She despises the memory of her dead husband and his family, but in doing so she conveniently forgets that if she married Galéas and bore his child, it was in large part because of her desire to enter the ranks of the aristocracy.

The Baroness, happy that Paule has been banished and that her daughter in Paris will inherit her estate, is also swept up in the assassin/victim syndrome. She has finally won out over her daughter-in-law, but it is her own daughter who in turn banishes her (and Fraulein) from the château and places her in a nursing home. In a final scene Mauriac seems to "save" the Communist Robert Bordas, who recognizes his responsibility and vows to himself to make up in kindness to other little boys his rejection of this one. A tear on his black whiskers seems to symbolize this sense of guilt and repentance.

Le Sagouin is one of Mauriac's most powerful novels. It is no wonder that it is read widely by French secondary-school students, for it captures the essence of childhood (with its fears and insecurities), and of family life (with its conflicting allegiances), while using this microcosm of small-town life to reflect the larger picture of French history, social friction, and class antipathy.[1] Mauriac uses the color red as one of his organizing principles, for it symbolizes Robert Bordas and his political commitments as well as the hope that this man from an alien social caste holds out for Guillou.

The pacing of the story is also marvelously orchestrated, for the action takes place in four short days: Paule visits the schoolteacher's home on a Thursday, the day after her mother-in-law has been there. Guillou visits Bordas on Friday and sees what his life can become, but the next day, Saturday, he will disappear.

Like time, place is handled in a compressed and skillful manner. In addition, the six principal characters—the Baroness, Galéas, Paule, and Guillou on one side, and Bordas and his wife on the other—are portrayed with brief, but extremely deft brushstrokes. Mauriac's classical sense of economy is everywhere apparent as he makes each word count. Finally, three places dominate the action: the château, Bordas's home, and the cemetery. It is this temporal and spatial concentration, due in part to Mauriac's recent work in the theater, that helps to explain the novel's effect. This remarkable concentration of focus enables us to feel sympathy for Guillou, the principal victim in this tragedy, and to understand and accept his death.

Galigaï (1952)

The overwhelming success of *Le Sagouin* helped Mauriac to recover his self-confidence as a novelist. Any residual fears that he might have had because of Sartre's attack on his technique and method were now swept away. Also, while there was by now no afterthought about writing for the theater again, the awarding of the Nobel Prize was still several months away. It was in these circumstances that *Galigaï (The Loved and the Unloved,* 1953) was written. Since Mauriac realized that the title was misleading, he attempted to justify its use in the preface that he published in *La Table ronde.* "Yes, the title of *Galigaï* could have been *Desire and Disgust.* This is an aspect of the hatred between the sexes that is rarely studied, firstly because our thoughts turn away from it but also because requited love is a more pleasant subject."[2] He also explained the title in the text of the novel. It refers specifically to the book's principal character, Madame Agathe de Camblanes, who is called "Galigaï" by

Nicholas, the young man she loves. The name refers to a historical figure, one Leonora Galigaï, who, as a member of the French royal court in the seventeenth century, dominated the Italian-born Queen of France, Marie de Médicis. Nicholas states that she did so by using "no other potion than the one that strong personalities use on weak minds" (*ORTC*, 4:399). This explanation helps us to understand what Mauriac had in mind in creating a dominant female character like Madame Agathe: the mistaken belief that love and desire can be sparked in another person simply by an act of will. He knew that he was taking a risk with this novel, which contains some of his boldest prose and one of his most disturbing scenes. But at this point in his career he had little to lose. He seemed determined to swim against the literary tide of the day and to remain faithful to his traditional sources of inspiration. Even though the existentialist novel temporarily dominated the French literary landscape, just as the *roman fleuve* had in the 1930s (when his work also seemed out of fashion to some critics), he was not about to make any concessions.

Mme Agathe is a young woman in her twenties who traces her ancestry back to sixteenth-century Gascony. Several years earlier she had been married to the young Baron de Goth, the scion of an equally illustrious family. But their marriage was never consummated, for on their wedding night her husband ran off with the son of his father's gardener. Although an annulment has been arranged in Rome, leaving Agathe free to marry again, this legality does not solve her problem, for she is physically repugnant. Her young husband ran off in part because of his desire for another person, but also because of a lack of desire for Agathe. Agathe now lives in a small town that is once again a fictional representation of Bazas, one of the principal towns in the Gironde area, where Mauriac grew up. She is employed as the governess of Marie Dubernet, an attractive adolescent, and lives with her and her wealthy parents, Julia and Armand.

There are two love stories in the novel. The first concerns Marie Dubernet and her passion for the young Gilles Salone, the son of a wealthy doctor who is home from Paris for summer vacation. Marie and Gilles cannot meet without the help of Agathe, who is willing to look the other way if Gilles will help her gain the affections of Gilles's best friend, Nicholas Plessac. Nicholas and Gilles are very close friends indeed, so close in fact that Mauriac went out of his way in the preface of the book to point out that they are not to be considered lovers themselves. The action of the novel hinges on Gilles's convincing Nicholas to yield to the desires of Agathe. If he is successful in doing this, she in turn will help him overcome the roadblocks set in place by Marie's mother, Julia. His plan is that Nicholas should sacrifice himself on his friend's behalf for a few months, allowing Agathe to think that he loves her during their period of engagement. Nicholas will then break off with Agathe once Gilles becomes formally engaged to Marie. Despite serious misgivings, Nicholas agrees to go along with the plan in the name of friendship.

As a result of this accord, Agathe allows Gilles to see Marie more often. When Marie's mother suffers a stroke and has to go to a hospital in Bordeaux for treatment, Gilles is even allowed to spend long periods of time alone with Marie in a hotel room. In the meantime Agathe and Nicholas discuss their future, one in which he makes it clear that even after their marriage they will not be able to live as man and wife. Agathe, madly in love with this young man to whom she can give much in terms of wealth, for she is the sole heir to her father's vast landholdings, goes along with this arrangement.

Mauriac paints what is for him a bold scene when Agathe tries to seduce Nicholas, passing her hand inside his shirt. Such a scene, balancing as it does Agathe's carnal desire against Nicholas's disgust and revulsion, is a powerful one. It not only lays bare areas of the human psyche that are rarely explored, but also reverses the customary rules, placing the female in the role of unsuccessful initiator and would-be seducer. In this scene, as well as several others, Mauriac succeeds in making his reader experience the feeling of physical repulsion felt by Nicholas. It is also worth recalling that Mauriac had already explored this theme in *Les Anges noirs,* in which Catherine is willing to marry Andrès even though she knows he does not desire her. But in that case, the theme was not as fully explored and developed as it is here. Unaccustomed as we are to thinking of erotic "disgust" and "desire" in the terms proposed in this novel, many readers are disconcerted by the juxtaposition.[3]

We see the influence of Mauriac's experience of writing for the theater in the way that he reverses the apparent outcome at the end of the novel. Nicholas has been encouraged by his own mother to overcome his disgust and go along with the plan to marry Mme Agathe. After all, when the old Comte de Camblanes dies, Agathe will inherit his fortune, and as a result Nicholas and his mother will become wealthy overnight and enjoy the life of the idle rich. This is an enticing prospect for a woman who has lived in poverty her whole life. Her son, partly for her sake, is willing to go along. But after the death of Julia Dubernet, Armand, her widower, is suddenly alone. He is accustomed to having Agathe as a part of his household. He thus proposes marriage to Agathe, who, despite her disgust at the physically repulsive Armand, who is old enough to be her father and whose life seems dominated by the urgings and dictates of his stomach, agrees. Thus, the death of Julia completely reverses the assumed outcome: Nicholas will no longer marry the physically repulsive Agathe, but Agathe will marry the physically repulsive Armand.

At the denouement, Nicholas is alone with his mother. They agree now that the marriage of Armand and Agathe is an acceptable outcome for them, but they also foresee that Gilles will have a mortal enemy in the person of Agathe, who, as Marie's stepmother, will become his mother-in-law. Although Agathe cannot stop Gilles's marriage to Marie at this late date, time will be on her side when she sets out to destroy their union.

The summer has ended. Nicholas goes for a walk by himself along the river and sits on the parapet where he used to sit with Gilles, and later with Agathe. The denouement is a happy one in that Nicholas seems to be waiting for someone, and looking positively toward the future, for he has grown in moral stature as a result of his experience.

Galigaï is an interesting but flawed novel. It raises several intriguing questions about love and desire, as well as about the nature of friendship between men. At times, however, it seems to strain credibility.

L'Agneau (1954)

L'Agneau (The Lamb, 1956) was published in 1954, but the author's earliest plan for the book goes back to 1948. In terms of thematic construction, it can be considered a leftover from the interwar years, for it was begun before *Le Sagouin* and *Galigaï.* Mauriac's original intention seems to have been to write another Catholic novel like the ones he had composed before World War II. But since he was able to work on the novel only intermittently, the finished product was characterized by a lack of focus and concentration. For instance, Mauriac incorporates three characters from *La Pharisienne,* although *L'Agneau* is in no sense a continuation of the earlier novel. Also, as in *Les Anges noirs,* he wants to depict the interaction of a Satan figure who is also a *séducteur,* with a Christ figure who is also a *mal-aimé.* His intention to write another Catholic novel is reflected in the original title for the work, *La Griffe de Dieu* (God's claw), which suggests that he wanted to develop the theme of a man who, pursued by God, is called to a higher level of sacrifice and understanding of life's mysteries. This intention is still evident in the title that he finally chose for the novel, for *L'Agneau* evokes the common description of Christ as a sacrificial lamb.

The publication of this novel was fraught with difficulties almost from the beginning. The first chapter, under the title *La Griffe de Dieu,* was supposed to be published in 1953 in the glossy monthly magazine *Réalités,* but it shocked Mauriac's longtime friend Pierre Brisson, who had arranged to have it published, as well as the magazine's editors. After the project was quietly dropped, Mauriac lengthened and rewrote the text, turning it into a fully developed novel, and published it the following year. Nonetheless, the essential problems remained, including the would-be saint at the center of the novel. In addition, the opening sequence tests the reader's credulity.

As the novel begins, a man of 22, Xavier Dartigelongue, boards a train in Bordeaux to go to Paris, where he plans to begin his studies for the priesthood. He is scheduled to enter a seminary the next morning. Xavier feels that his life has already been spared in a very concrete way, since he did not have to serve in World War I. He is now ready to offer his life to God. Before the train leaves the station, he notices an attractive couple standing on the platform. They are 10 to 15 years older than he, and the man seems to be leaving the woman. Though they appear to be married, they are not on the best of terms.

The young man enters Xavier's compartment and takes a seat opposite him. A conversation ensues, in the course of which we learn that the stranger is Jean de Mirbel of *La Pharisienne,* that about 15 years have passed since the action recounted in the earlier novel, and that the woman on the platform is his wife, Michèle, the sister of Louis Pian and stepdaughter of Brigitte Pian. Xavier, Mauriac's "saint," and Jean, his "fallen angel," continue talking during the voyage to Paris. Jean ridicules the young man's religious beliefs and encourages him to give up his plan to enter the seminary. Instead, he asks that Xavier accompany him back to Bordeaux, but the reason for the invitation is kept deliberately vague by the narrative voice. Is it to force the would-be saint to confront the satanic Jean de Mirbel face-to-face, to save Jean's marriage, to keep Jean from committing suicide, or to reveal to Xavier that he really does not have a vocation for the priesthood? At this point, the reader cannot know for sure which of these factors is at play.

Xavier believes that anyone who comes into his life is sent by God, and that nothing happens purely by chance. His life is anchored in the Pascalian order of grace, far above the lower orders of mind and body, and he believes implicitly in the value of sacrifice. Thus, he takes his meeting Jean de Mirbel as nothing less than a heavenly sign. Xavier's important decisions are based on faith, not reason; in this he reflects Mauriac's conviction that true sanctity is obtained only with difficulty by the intellectual, who is inclined to attribute more importance to reason than to feeling. Thus, when Jean asks him about the reading material that he has brought along to help pass the time on the way to Paris, Xavier replies that he reads the dry clerical periodical *La Vie spirituelle* not because he derives any intellectual benefit from it, but because it is good for his soul to do something that gives him no satisfaction. Not unlike Brigitte Pian of *La Pharisienne,* he wants to accumulate merits for himself. But more important, he wants to share in the suffering of Christ by voluntarily introducing boredom into his own life. Mauriac's belief in the value of vicarious suffering in imitation of the suffering of Christ is at the heart of this novel. This doctrine indicates that all baptized believers are linked in a mystical union with one another and with Christ, and that it is through this union (sometimes referred to as the "communion of saints") that the sufferings of one person can redound to the benefit of another.[4] Xavier, who is anything but an intellectual, intuitively understands this doctrine and lives his life accordingly. From this perspective, there is the possibility of a strong attraction between people like Xavier and Jean, since the latter is someone who can be saved by the sacrifice of the former. Thus, Xavier makes the decision to turn his back on the seminary and to return to Larzujon because he sees in Jean (whose reputation he is already very much aware of) a person for whom he can sacrifice himself, and a soul whose salvation might require his own personal immolation.

    After the train arrives in Paris, Jean and Xavier go to a nearby café for a drink. There Jean continues to prod Xavier to follow him back to Bordeaux on the first train in the morning. They then separate, Xavier going off to a church where a perpetual adoration ceremony is taking place throughout the night, and Jean to a bordello, where he hopes to prove to himself that his impotence of the last few years can be cured. They meet later and return to Larzujon the next day. Here Michèle awaits them with Roland, the 10-year-old boy whom she and Jean have taken into their home, since they have been unable to have children of their own. But she has also invited her stepmother, Brigitte Pian. Because Michèle's life is so empty, and because she had no reason to believe that her departing husband would be back the next day, she had invited Brigitte to keep her company. Brigitte's presence and sudden departure will play a major role in the unfolding of the novel.

When Xavier arrives he learns that Brigitte, who is an acquaintance of his mother, has become involved in his life. Xavier's mother has already written to her asking that she closely supervise her son. But Brigitte has also brought along her personal secretary, Dominique. At this point the focus of the novel shifts, for Roland and Dominique now become the people for whom Xavier is willing to sacrifice himself, while Jean de Mirbel temporarily recedes into the background. This apparent lack of focus can probably be attributed to the six-year hiatus Mauriac took in composing the novel.

Roland becomes the primary focus of Xavier's concern, and his misfortune seems to kindle Xavier's desire for sacrifice. Roland has been living with Michèle and Jean for only a few months but already knows that he is unwanted and that his days are numbered in their household. Like Guillou in *Le Sagouin*, he has difficulty keeping himself clean. In addition, never having known the experience of being loved, he has so far been unable to play the expected role of a loving and submissive child. This is not the child the Mirbels would want if they could choose: they intend to send him back to the orphanage where they found him as soon as possible.

Xavier, however, immediately sees in this child someone who has come into his life by divine plan, and he wants to sacrifice himself for this boy. He pays attention to Roland, talks to him, and even seeks information about the games he plays. Most important, he reads him the Bible story about Joseph and his brothers, found in Genesis 37.

Mauriac clearly intends for the reader to see Xavier as a Christ figure. One particular scene makes this clear. After Jean locks Roland in the first-floor library to discipline him, Xavier is moved by the injustice of the act. After dark, he goes out to a shed in the woods where he knows there is a ladder. As he drags it back through the underbrush to the house, he stumbles and falls several times. He had removed his shoes when he left the house so as not to awaken Jean or Michèle, and now his bare feet and his shoulder begin to bleed. He is able to climb through the window and check on the boy: Roland is alive, but of course terribly afraid. And just to make sure that we do not misunderstand the symbolic intent here, the narrative voice assures us that if Dominique had seen his bloody feet, she would have washed them, like the woman of the Gospels who washes the feet of Jesus.

Xavier also undergoes several experiences in which he seems to lapse into a trance, apparently absorbed in prayer to such an extent that he loses contact with his surroundings. Each time it is a different female character who comes upon him in this state: in turn the maid, Michèle, and Brigette Pian. Michèle is ready to denounce Xavier to Jean only because he seems interested in Dominique. The sacrifice imposed on Xavier by Michèle's jealousy is a slightly different form of suffering, for Xavier has done nothing to promote it. Yet the novel makes it clear that this too must be endured if he is to save souls. Thus, thanks to Xavier's sacrifice, Jean de Mirbel is able to say: "I know now that love does exist in this world. But it is crucified in the world, and we with it" (*ORTC*, 4:527).

A little-noticed character in the novel is the curé de Baluzac, the friendly and unpretentious priest who has replaced the Abbé Calou in the local village. When Xavier confesses to him what he takes to be the sin that he committed in deciding at the last minute not to enter the seminary, the priest assures him that this is not a sin.

After a later visit with the curé de Baluzac, Xavier borrows a bicycle to return to Jean de Mirbel's home. Xavier and Dominique have made arrangements to extricate Roland from his unhappy situation, but as Xavier returns, he is run over and killed by an automobile driven by Jean de Mirbel. The sacrifices that Xavier has made until now seem small in comparison to the sacrifice of his life. But is the driver completely at fault, or did Xavier do nothing to avoid the oncoming car? Mauriac allows a certain amount of ambiguity to remain, but there is no doubt about the results achieved by Xavier's sacrifice. When, in the closing scene of the novel, we find Jean and Michèle about to live as husband and wife again, it is only because graces earned by Xavier have worked in Jean's soul and helped to reunite the couple.

As mentioned above, *L'Agneau* has a number of points in common with Mauriac's Catholic novels of the 1930s. It brings back three characters from *La Pharisienne* and deals specifically with questions that are directly related to the spiritual life. Furthermore, it seems to suggest at the denouement that Xavier's sacrifice will bring about a religious conversion in Jean de Mirbel. But lurking at the heart of this novel, which Mauriac wanted to be positive and uplifting, is the problem of credibility. The noted Mauriac scholar André Séailles expresses this problem when he refers to the novel as an "ambiguous work." It is not so much that Xavier himself is difficult to believe. There are many people in this world who are motivated by religious faith and who believe as he does that everyone who comes into his life is sent by God. But can we believe that Jean de Mirbel undergoes a change of heart because of his chance meeting with Xavier? It is in the transferring of the graces earned by

Xavier to the soul of Jean de Mirbel that the novel breaks down. The working of grace in the soul of Louis in *Le Noeud de vipères* had been developed gradually throughout the novel, but here it is implied rather abruptly in just this one scene. Although Mauriac was sufficiently obsessed with Jean de Mirbel to resurrect him for this novel, the character is never fully developed. Although, as an *ange noir,* he might indeed feel guilt and remorse for Xavier's death, the reader gets no clear indication of this and finds it difficult to believe that he will be fundamentally changed. In sum, despite Mauriac's good intentions, *L'Agneau* remains a flawed novel.[5]

Un Adolescent d'autrefois (1969)

Mauriac's last completed novel, *Un Adolescent d'autrefois (Maltaverne,* 1970), appeared about a year before his death. Rightly called, by Julian Moynihan, Mauriac's own personal "portrait of the artist as a young man," the book tries to show "how a young man of extrordinary imagination and religious endowment finds his way to an artistic vocation without renouncing a faith in God and a severe religious orientation that would seem utterly to deny the relevance of art to the central issues of human existence."[6]

The title of the novel can be translated literally as "An adolescent of days gone by." Its story is narrated by a young man, Alain Gajac, who is chronicling the seminal years between the ages of 17 and 22, when he made the transition from adolescence to manhood. The book takes the form of a diary written in four different installments of varying length. The first part, composed at the age of 17, is only about 15 pages long and can be read as an introduction to the novel. Part 2 is about twice as long and is written a little more than a year later. The third part, which contains the principal action of the novel, is about 100 pages in length. Here, two more years have passed and Alain, now 21, is a university student in Bordeaux. He has taken a first tentative step toward independence from his mother by living alone in the family apartment in the city during those periods when his mother is addressing business matters on their vast estates some 100 kilometers from Bordeaux. As was the case with Mauriac himself, as well as so many of his heroes, Alain's father has been deceased for a long time, although not completely forgotten.

It is here, at the beginning of this third section, that Alain tells us why he is writing. His first reason is that he wants to be able to provide a written report of his sentimental and intellectual development to his

friend André Donzac (the transposed version of the real-life André
Lacaze), who is studying for the priesthood in a seminary in Paris. He
decides at this time that this project is not really a diary, but what the
French call a *récit,* a fictional narrative in which the first-person narrator
is also the principal character. Like *Le Mystère Frontenac,* published more
than 40 years earlier, it will be "true" precisely because it is fiction: a
work in which "everything will be true . . . but everything will [also] be
imagined" (*ORTC,* 4:828).[7] What Mauriac meant by this is that the
relationships portrayed generally reflect his own experience, while fictional characters are invented to convey these realities.

The two principal subjects of the novel are Alain's relationship with
his mother and his emotional development after the death of his older
brother Laurent. By writing down his experiences, he hopes to see clearly into the essence of things and events. Finally, in the fourth and last
part of the novel, which amounts to only a half-dozen pages, the narrator brings closure to his story by letting us know that he is now in Paris.
He has made the symbolic and physical break with his mother and their
property, and has finally taken the first step toward independence. Here
it is a difference of place, more than of time, that is essential to the narration and that truly differentiates this last section from the others.

Underpinning the novel is the unmistakable impression that Mauriac
gives his reader that he and Alain Gajac have many things in common.
They were born and raised at about the same time, in the same social
milieu, and in the same region of France. They both struggled with
domineering mothers, and they both turned their backs on their ancestral roots by physically leaving their beloved pine forests in order to pursue careers as writers in Paris. But in so doing, they were both able
through literature to give a universal existence to their ancestral region
by re-creating and transforming its essence for millions of readers who
otherwise would have no knowledge of it. Each of these men, the aging
Mauriac, who is writing the novel, and the young man who represents
him, enters into and assumes through art a kind of religious vocation.
Like a priest who, through a vow of celibacy, seeks to serve a wider family than the one he would have had if he had married, Mauriac and Alain
Gajac serve the Catholic faith, the region from which they spring, and
their ancestors and families in a way that would never have been possible if they had stayed behind in the Landes cultivating their pine trees
and grape vines.

The novel is built on counterpoint of various kinds. The young Alain
Gajac is roughly the same age as Simon Duberc, whose parents are the

principal caretakers of the Gajac landholdings. To Simon, Alain is always "Monsieur Alain," his social superior. Simon's peasant origins are symbolized by a sixth finger on each hand and sixth toe on each foot. This oddity represents the influence of heredity (and of inbreeding, perhaps even incest, among his ancestors through the generations) in the Pascalian order of the body. But Simon also has intellectual qualities that set him apart and make him worthy of Alain's attention. Yet Alain is terribly aware, as he cultivates his friendship with Simon, that he is crossing class boundaries. Although Alain talks like someone who believes in social equality, the reader knows how important class stratifications are to him. We learn that the local priest had cultivated a religious vocation in Simon, that he entered a minor seminary at about age 13, and that the local population had assumed that he would become a priest. But the wife of an anticlerical politician, with whose son Simon used to play before his untimely death, persuaded him to leave the church and study for a university degree in Paris. These people offered to pay all his expenses in order to assure this small victory in the ongoing war against clerical influence over young people.

When Alain learns later that Simon has returned to the region and is now a *lycée* teacher, he reestablishes contact with his old friend, and they resume their friendship to the point where, at the denouement, Simon is ready to return to seminary studies. Simon, handicapped in the order of the body, later attains genuine distinction in the order of the mind. Now he is about to rise even higher in the Pascalian order of grace. Mauriac portrays this ascent against the backdrop of the recurring clash between France's traditional Catholics and the freethinking anticlericals. This battle for men's hearts and minds, which in contemporary times is only a vestige of what it was in the first half of this century, included pettiness and wrongheadedness on both sides, as Alain readily admits, even though he is irrevocably committed to the Catholic side.

Another important contrast exists between the girl whom Alain's mother would like him to marry and the girl whom he meets in Bordeaux and who temporarily replaces her. After the death of his brother, Alain is the sole heir to his mother's vast estates. Likewise, the 10-year-old Jeannette Séris is the sole heir to 3,000 hectares of adjoining land. Both families are committed to a union between Alain and Jeannette, but Alain is violently opposed for two reasons: he finds her physically repulsive and he is wary of the responsibility of ownership. Alain's rejection of marriage to Jeannette is a way of expressing his disapproval of his mother's lust for land and wealth. He and his friend refer to the young Jeannette as "the Louse" (*le Pou*), and Alain Gajac's description of her still-infantile appearance is merciless. Alain will learn later, and much to his displeasure, that he has been wrong in his evaluation of Jeannette, but since he now associates her unconsciously with his mother and the venal aspect of his mother's personality that he is not quite ready to recognize in himself, he can only reject Jeannette out of hand. In addition, there is perhaps a third reason for Alain's resistance to the marriage: he suspects that he has a poetic vocation. Poetry is a calling that requires freedom, openness, and flexibility: an arranged marriage would stand in the way.

In addition to discovering his artistic vocation and friendship with other men (not only Simon but also Donzac, whom we never see, but for whom this whole *récit* is presumably written), Alain also discovers love and sexual passion. As a student in Bordeaux, he takes to haunting one particular bookstore, la librairie Bard. There he meets Marie, who manages the store in place of the aging and ailing M. Bard. She shows an interest in Alain, or at least he thinks she does, after his first few visits to the store. Only 20 years old and uninitiated in sexual experience, Alain is unsure of what is happening. He tries to compare the feelings he has for Marie (who, he will later learn, is 28 years old), with the usual reactions that he has among girls of his own social milieu. He admits that he has always been shy with girls, preferring to hide in the corner rather than dance with them at approved and arranged social functions, but this is only because he considers himself homely and does not believe that girls can be attracted to him. Thus, their interest in him at such functions can be explained only by the fact that he is heir to thousands of acres of timberland. This is one of the appealing aspects of his flirtation with Marie: since she has seen him only in his shabby overcoat and student attire, and not in a tuxedo, she has no way of knowing about his wealth.

Over the next few months Alain and Marie become friends. The discovery of emotional ties to a woman other than his mother is accompanied by sexual exploration. The first touches, then caresses, are duly noted by Alain. Finally, he is able to spend a night with Marie (while his mother is away on a pilgrimage to Lourdes), and it is now that he thinks he has found perfect happiness. Perhaps predictably, like so many boys raised as he was, he thinks that sex must of necessity go with marriage. Thus, he announces to his mother that he intends to marry Marie in the name of love. Shocked, his mother sets about examining Marie's character. Alain had known she would do this in an attempt to sabotage their union, but he had presumed that because Marie had already told him about her past, its importance and relevance had been neutralized.

Mme Gajac goes directly to the shop where Marie works. Such behavior is perfectly logical for this woman, who, so much like Brigitte Pian, is described by her son as a *pharisienne*. Like Brigitte, she lives "in the knowledge that she is right about everything" (*ORTC*, 4:770). We learn about this confrontation through a later conversation between Marie and Alain. Of course the conversation is filtered through Alain's memory as he writes down what occurred in a scene that he did not actually witness. It is apparent that the search for truth is difficult at best and that what really happened depends in large part on the viewpoint of the observer. Thus, according to Marie, she recognized Alain's mother immediately and did not need an introduction because the mother is so much like her son. They withdraw to Marie's cubicle in the rear of the shop, where a frank discussion reveals to Marie how much the mother and the son truly do resemble each other. Irritated by this discovery, Marie tells Mme Gajac that they plan after their marriage to share with their sharecroppers a part of the profits generated by their holdings.

When Marie recounts to Alain the details of her meeting with Mme. Gajac, he is aghast that she could have said such a thing to his mother. Although Marie's words are technically a lie, since she and Alain had never formally made such a decision, the statement was nonetheless a logical extrapolation based on Alain's assurances to Marie that he felt guilty about owning so much property and detested the fact that his mother seemed to love her property before everything else, even her son. But Marie has touched a raw nerve here. In a flash Alain instinctively defends his mother and his family's right of ownership: how, he argues, could anyone really dream of sharing profits with social inferiors who are happier and better off the way they are?

The affair with Marie is effectively over at this point, and Alain has become a man in more ways than one. Through his sexual initation, his obsessive guilt about erotic love has been dealt with; and by thinking through the implications of marriage to someone from outside his own social sphere, he has come to recognize that, like his mother, he is enamored of the land and the wealth that it brings.

When he formally reconciles with his mother, she gives him an altogether different version of her meeting with Marie, prompting Alain to come to the realization that "nothing had happened the way Marie had described it. She had in fact relived in front of me a scene that was half imaginary" (*ORTC*, 4:784).

Alain, like Marie and Simon, is in search of himself. In such a quest one often recounts and reconsiders events in a purely imaginary way, one that is more in accordance with the way we would have liked things to be than the way they really were. Mauriac's omniscient narrator of the great novels of the interwar years has given way here to one whose perspective is limited in every way. Ambiguity abounds; nothing is certain. We can only agree when Alain's mother tells him near the end of the novel that "we have been wrong about everything" (ORTC, 4:807).

The central drama of the novel unfolds after the breakup with Marie, who will now marry the aging M. Bard and presumably take over the bookstore after his death. Upon learning of her plans from Simon, Alain self-consciously flirts with the idea of suicide and then returns home to Maltaverne to recover from his emotional trauma. During a walk through the forest on a lovely summer afternoon, he comes across a beautiful girl bathing nude in the river. He fails to recognize that it is Jeannette Séris, who has now reached puberty. He watches her sunbathing and then follows from a distance when she leaves. But then a branch cracks under his foot, causing her to turn around. She looks in his direction and then suddenly runs off.

This experience is a veritable epiphany for Alain, in which he perceives, however fleetingly, a reality that usually remains hidden beneath the surface of daily life. Feminine beauty, innocence, and purity have been revealed to him, even though he has no idea who the girl is. But the scene takes on a new meaning when he learns the next day that Jeannette has disappeared. Did she run because she recognized him and knew that he had made fun of her for so many years? When her dead body is discovered the next day—she has been strangled, and her murderer has already admitted his crime—Alain is racked by guilt. If he had not frightened her off, would she still be alive? Would the girl, whose adolescent beauty so moved him in the forest, have become his wife if she had not been murdered? Would he then have been able to reconcile his yearning for sexual pleasure with his love of the land? Alain asks himself all these questions, but it is unclear whether he is truly sorry for what has happened to "le Pou" or is simply using her tragedy as a pretext for self-absorption.

It is amid all these questions that the third part of the novel ends. In part 4, the last section and only five pages in length, Alain is in Paris. He has clearly accepted that he can be happy only if he tries to become a writer, and he realizes that his inner life will be the subject matter of his first book. On his daily walks through the streets of Paris, one of his favorite stops is the great Saint-Sulpice Church, which is near his flat on the Left Bank. There he stops before the famous Delacroix painting entitled *Jacob Wrestling with the Angel,* since it reminds him of his own interior struggle. He tells himself: "I am both Jacob and the angel: it's me fighting with myself" (*ORTC,* 4:821). The modern artist, he is telling us, has no choice but to portray himself in some way or another as the principal subject of his fictional universe. Alain Gajac, like Mauriac, had to leave Bordeaux for Paris in order to gain the perspective he needed to look deeply into himself and to unlock the secrets hidden there. This novel clearly is Mauriac's "portrait of the artist as a young man." Although it is a "fiction," it tells us as much about Mauriac the man as do any of his autobiographical works.

Maltaverne (1972)

Even while writing *Un Adolescent d'autrefois,* Mauriac was thinking of a sequel to the work. The young Alain Gajac, visiting the old man called "Le Vieux de Lassus," a neighboring landowner who holds within himself a vast collective memory, imagines himself many years later as "Le Vieux de Maltaverne." This is the name by which the narrator of *Maltaverne* calls himself. Seated on the front steps of his house, he writes letters to the young writer Jean de Cernès, modeled probably on Roger Nimier, one of the young writers who had contributed regularly to *La Table ronde* in the late 1940s and early 1950s. This brief text of some 25 pages is really no more than a patchwork of fragments that would have eventually been included in the novel. Mauriac knew while writing that time was running out for him, but he pressed on nonetheless.

We should not attribute too much importance to *Maltaverne* because, after all, it is only a fragment. But as Mauriac's last written text, it is worth commenting on. Like Yves Frontenac in *Le Mystère Frontenac,* Alain Gajac has been the author of only one book, presumably *Un Adolescent d'autrefois.* Now he plans to continue the story of his intellectual and emotional development by chronicling what has happened to him since his arrival in Paris. The principal scenes depict for us his experiences in Parisian literary salons before World War I and the death of his mother, both told with brutal honesty, humor, and irony. Gajac is trying desperately to tell his young reader what it was like to have been a young man making a career for himself in Paris more than a half century earlier. In so doing, he is also attempting to overcome the ignorance of the new generation of writers, who know nothing of the writers who meant so much to Gajac as a young man and whose contemporary sense of literature is so different from his own. In this continuation of *Un Adolescent d'autrefois,* time lurks in the background as the major force in life, eroding, leveling, and erasing all that stands in its way.

Mauriac's health declined to such an extent in the weeks and months before his death that he could no longer write. But he pressed on with this final project by dictating the last few pages to his wife.

At the end of the text, Jean de Cernès comes to visit the Old Man of Maltaverne at his country estate. He comes by car and brings along his girlfriend, Isabelle. Every word of this brief scene resounds with the clash of the old and the new. The old man looks at the handsome youth of 19 and realizes that his own days are numbered. Jean and Isabelle plan to publish an anthology of his old newspaper columns, so that the new generation will see what a great writer he was. But as these young people speak, he realizes that for him life is over. Now past 80, he tells himself that "it's over, it's over for good," and that the end is near. If he is to live on, it will be through the interest that successive generations of young people take in his work, and he is grateful for that. The text ends with the realization, juxtaposed against the youth and energy of Jean de Cernès and Isabelle, that "It's over, over forever" (*ORTC,* 4:851).

Chapter Seven
Theater and Poetry

Theater

Mauriac's four plays were summed up quite well by François Durand when he wrote that "Mauriac's theater seems like a poor relation or an unwanted child in comparison to its successful brothers: the novel, essay and journalism."[1] Mauriac would later claim, when publishing his *Oeuvres complètes* in the 1950s, that he had never really been overcome by the experience of the theater until he attended the Mozart Festival in Salzburg in August 1934. When he saw *Don Giovanni* on stage for the first time, he received a special "illumination" (*OC,* 9:iii; *ORTC,* 3:928).[2] We should probably take this assertion with a grain of salt, for it is difficult to understand how a traditionally presented eighteenth-century opera could inspire him to write for the modern theater. On the other hand, Mauriac during his whole adult life had been a fervent admirer of Mozart's music.

In reality, Mauriac was tempted by the theater when the director of the Comédie-Française, Edouard Bourdet, invited him to write a play for the company. A stronger motivation may have been the uncertainty that Mauriac was then experiencing about the longer novels he was trying to write, which would presumably be more in keeping with the then current literary vogue of the cycle novel.[3] As Mauriac was undergoing his spiritual crisis of the late 1920s, one of the places to which he turned for consolation was the theater of his spiritual cousin, Jean Racine, especially his play *Phèdre,* which depicts the passionate attachment of an older, mature person, to a younger one—even in the face of social taboos. French classicism, as expressed in Racine's work, is based on Greek tragedy and gives special emphasis to the inherent conflict between the passions and human reason. As Mauriac wrote his biography of Racine, he came to identify with both the spiritual itinerary and the *ars poetica* of his subject. Thus, just as he saw Racine's struggle to overcome carnal temptation as an emblem of his own experience, so he considered Racine's depiction of the struggle between reason and desire to be a useful and appropriate model for his own work in the theater.

As André Séailles has pointed out, "Mauriac's theater owes much to the concept of classical restraint, which is based in turn on psychological consistency and coherence."[4] The classicism of Mauriac's plays lies in the realism of both character and plot—that is, the psychological consistency and credibility of the action. Interestingly, the greatest difference between Racine's theater and Mauriac's lies in the latter's refusal to end his plays with murder and/or suicide. This structural difference might in fact be one of the most realistic elements in Mauriac's theater, at least as far as modern audiences are concerned, for it reminds us that life continues after the crisis depicted on the stage.

Asmodée (1937)

Mauriac had been interested in writing for the theater as early as 1917. He even wrote a play at the time (he later called it a "farce") with his friend Jacques-Emile Blanche, but it was never produced.[5] Mauriac seems to have believed that the way to write a play was to develop characters first and develop the plot later. Thus, when Edouard Bourdet, in the late 1930s, asked him to consider writing a play, Mauriac told him that he would like to try his hand at it, but that all he had were characters and no plot. This roadblock, a temporary one as it turned out, did not discourage Bourdet, who was determined to produce a Mauriac play. Undaunted, he offered his advice to Mauriac as the play was being written and, as the surviving manuscripts clearly demonstrate, the play went through three different versions with six different denouements. Asmodée opened at the Comédie-Français on 22 November 1937.

The principal character in the play is Blaise Coûture, a former seminarian who is now between 35 and 40 years of age. He lives with a wealthy family in the Landes pine forest region, where so many of Mauriac's novels are set. He has been living in the home of Mme de Barthas, a striking widow and mother of four, whose husband died seven years earlier in a riding accident. With some 3,000 hectares of land, a vast and thriving domain as the basis of her wealth, Mme de Barthas has decided to hire teachers to instruct her children at home rather than move to the city to be near a school. Thus, for the past eight years M. Coûture has been an authoritarian figure in the de Barthas household, where he does more than oversee the education of the oldest son, Bertrand, now 15 years old. Like Gradère of Les Anges noirs and Thérèse of La Fin de la nuit, he is also able to see into people's souls, instinctively understanding their inner turmoil.

As the play opens, three of the de Barthas children are highly excited as they await the imminent arrival of Harry Fanning, an English boy from a proper family who is scheduled to spend two months in their home in exchange for Bertrand, who has already left for England. The oldest of the three, Emmanuele, is 17 (she too has her own preceptor, Mademoiselle) and the younger ones, Anne and Jean, are 13 and 12. In the midst of their agitation in act 1, scene 2, Blaise Coûture appears on stage, and with his arrival a shudder seems to run through the children. Mademoiselle chases them off to play, leaving her alone with Coûture. In the ensuing dialogue we learn that she is hopelessly in love with him, while Coûture himself is obsessed with his duties toward Mme de Barthas. Although he could have gone off on vacation during Bertrand's stay in England, he tells us that he has decided to remain behind in order to serve as Mme de Barthas's spiritual mentor. The real reason, we suspect, is that he wants to maintain control over her emotions, for she has already told him some of the intimate details of her married life. Like Georges Filhot, who confesses certain details of his past to Thérèse in *La Fin de la nuit* and then falls under her spell, we now find Mme de Barthas giving M. Coûture more and more responsibility over the management of her business affairs as well. It is he who tells her what is going on in the outside world, for she no longer even tries to read the daily newspapers. He is the moral equivalent of her confessor, even though he is not a priest.

Seven years after the first staging of the play, upon its revival during the Occupation in 1944, Mauriac claimed to have finally come to understand this complex character. *Asmodée,* he wrote, is "the drama of an aborted vocation: The frightening M. Coûture would have been a good priest, an excellent spiritual director, if pride had not misdirected him, if he had used his genius to win souls for God instead of chasing them, tracking them down for his own ends" (*ORTC,* 3:1117).

This would-be priest has attached himself to the still beautiful Mme de Barthas; his desire to save her soul is mixed with a strong feeling of jealousy if another man comes near her. Thus, when young Harry Fanning arrives and turns out to be 20 years old and not 15, and indeed looks a few years older than his age, Blaise is overcome with jealousy: he must do everything in his power to force the young man out of the house and away from his spiritual charge. Not long after Harry's arrival, he and Mme de Barthas go for a walk together in the moonlight amid the mighty pine trees. When they return, Blaise hides behind a door to overhear their conversation. Mademoiselle, who will seemingly do what-

ever he asks, is with him. As we listen to Mme de Barthas talking to
Harry about M. Coûture, it is not difficult to imagine the reaction of the
frustrated (and hidden) spiritual director. When Harry tells his hostess
that it is obvious that one particular member of the household wants
him to leave immediately, she knows without his even mentioning a
name that he is talking about Coûture. She tells Harry that seven years
earlier her husband's sudden death and Bertrand's precarious health (he
was just recovering from pleurisy when her husband died) necessitated
that he remain at home instead of attending school in Bordeaux. This is
why she has hired M. Coûture and has been willing to tolerate his idio-
syncrasies all these years.

Meanwhile, M. Coûture and Mademoiselle continue to listen to the
conversation. Finally, when Mme de Barthas tells Harry that her children's preceptor is an unfortunate fellow who had been allowed to go to
minor seminary even though his parents did not have the means to pay,
that he had been expelled because of his *mauvais esprit,* and that she had
taken him in because his superiors did not know what to do with him,
Coûture faints. The noise of his fall curtails the conversation, and Harry
and Mme de Barthas immediately come running to his aid.

By the end of the second act the principal conflict has been made
clear: Blaise Coûture is jealous of anyone who challenges, even unconsciously, his domination of Mme de Barthas, and he sees Harry as a serious rival. But Harry, of course, is not interested in Mme de Barthas in
this way. As a young man, his natural instincts are directed toward
Emmanuele, but here too, there is a problem. Emmanuele, who attends
mass every morning at seven o'clock, has always thought that hers was a
religious vocation. Thus, there are two major conflicts that must be
resolved in the remaining acts. Mauriac directs the action with a master-
ful hand (although it is impossible to say how much credit should be
given to Edouard Bourdet or director Jacques Copeau for this achievement), with several plot reversals before the denouement.

At play's end, Emmanuele has decided that she is in love with Harry
and will marry him, while her mother and Blaise appear, more than ever,
to be condemned to live with each other indefinitely in their physically
chaste, yet psychologically intimate relationship. Mme de Barthas
resigns herself to living a life imposed on her by someone else because
she is unable to face up to the reality of the situation.

Asmodée was an overwhelming success for Mauriac. It was translated
into English, produced in both London and New York (briefly), and successfully revived on the Paris stage in 1944 and 1953. Mauriac lament-

ed at the time how difficult it had been to have his initial vision constantly reworked and modified by Bourdet and Copeau; but as he continued to write for the theater it would become evident that this type of support was critical to his success. Their support not only helped him to focus on a single character in each play, but also was critical in creating on stage the atmosphere of the Landes, with which many theatergoers were already familiar from the novels.

The title of the play is derived from the long dialogue between Harry Fanning and Marcelle de Barthas in the second act when he tells her that, living in her house and observing from the inside the conduct of each member of her household, he feels like the legendary devil Asmodée. This character, taken from Lesage's eighteenth-century novel *Le Diable boiteux,* evokes the image of the literary devil who is capable of lifting the roof off houses and watching the actions of the people living inside.[6] The choice of a proper name as a title was also fairly common in the seventeenth-century classical French theater, especially in the works of Racine, which Mauriac admired so much. But if the title seems archaic, it is important to remember that Mauriac deliberately sets the action of the play in the contemporary world and not in some ersatz antiquity. In fact, he would give a contemporary setting to each of his four plays, and in so doing was reacting against one of the important trends in the French theater of the 1930s and 1940s: the attempt to give a timeless essence to a play by situating the action in ancient Greece. When reproached by a critic for not following this convention, Mauriac rejected what he took to be the artificiality of such a strategy: "If I had wanted to, I could have easily transposed the subject of *Les Mal-aimés* into legend and even given a part to the Atrides, like all my contemporaries, from Cocteau to Giraudoux, and from Anouilh to Sartre, have done" (*ORTC,* 4:981–82).[7] If Mauriac chose not to do so, it was to prove both to his critics and to himself that his characters had enough substance to stand alone without such props. Just as he had rejected the cycle novel as inappropriate for the expression of his particular genius as a fiction writer, he also rejected this contemporary trend in the theater.

Les Mal-aimés (1945)

Mauriac's second play, *Les Mal-aimés (The Egoists),* was written before the war but did not debut (at the Comédie-Française) until 1 March 1945. It was in the first afterglow of the success of *Asmodée* in 1937 that Mauriac decided to write again for the theater. Once he finished *Les*

Chemins de la mer, the novel to which he devoted a good part of the first
half of 1938, he then went on during his summer vacation to work on
what would become *Les Mal-aimés.*

Whereas *Asmodée* is based on an idea that Mauriac had for a character,
this second play is based on an idea for a plot. He wanted to write a play
in the Racinian mode, a tragedy of modern life in which all subplots and
distractions from the principal conflict would be eliminated. In *Asmodée* he
had used the children as a form of comic relief. Likewise, a character like
Mademoiselle (hopelessly in love with Coûture) added yet another element
to a play that dealt principally with the love conflicts between Coûture
and Mme de Barthas on the one hand and Emmanuele and Harry Fanning
on the other. *Les Mal-aimés,* with only four main characters and little if any
action, tries to go in an entirely different direction. It consists only of dialogue (with no comic relief or action on the stage), and each time a character attempts to escape from the sick family circle, he is forced to return,
less able than ever to function as an independent person. The feelings and
passions of the characters must propel the plot by themselves. The only
deviations from the Racinian formula that Mauriac allowed himself were
to have the action take place in two days (with a year in between) instead
of 24 hours and to eliminate suicide in the last act.

At the heart of the play is the rivalry between two sisters for the love
of Alain, a young doctor who has just completed his studies and
returned to the Landes region to begin practicing medicine. Alain, now
23 years old, is secretly engaged to Elisabeth, the older Virelade sister,
who is 30. But the younger sister, 17-year-old Marianne, also loves him.
When, at the midpoint of the first act, she learns of the wedding plans,
the conflict begins to come clearly into focus. Marianne, young, ener-
getic, and outspoken, is set against Elisabeth, who, in the name of family solidarity, has in the past always been willing to sacrifice herself for
others. In his notes for the play Mauriac even talks of the "Antigone
aspect" of Elisabeth's character, a reminder that Anouilh's play of the
same title had been a major success in 1944. This character was still in
the back of his mind as he wrote.

Caught between the two competing sisters is the weak Alain. Easily
influenced, he is incapable of living without the moral support that he
derives from the older Elisabeth, but also incapable of resisting the
charm and attraction of Marianne. Balancing Alain is another male character, the girls' father, M. de Virelade. A former army officer, he is an
agnostic who has retired to his country estate to live out the rest of his
life. A slave to his appetites, he drinks whiskey all day, incessantly

smokes his pipe, and keeps a mistress in Bordeaux, whom he visits regularly. We learn early in the play that his wife left him 15 years earlier because of these bad habits, which she could not tolerate. She had fled in the name of love for someone else. Years later, on the day before she died, she sent a message asking Elisabeth to visit her, but M. de Virelade had forbidden Elisabeth to go—and she obeyed. She is the dutiful daughter who has devoted her life to taking care of her aging father in a spirit of self-renunciation. Marianne, on the other hand, physically resembles her mother. She is more independent and unpredictable, and she also craves love and recognition.

When Marianne learns that Elisabeth will marry Alain, she is shocked by the news. Left alone, she goes to her father's desk and opens the drawer in which he keeps his revolver. She seems to be contemplating suicide when her father comes into the room and sees what she is doing. Once Marianne explains what is going on, he announces his intention to impede Elisabeth's marriage plans, for he wants his older daughter to himself. Most of act 2 is devoted to his talking Elisabeth (successfully) out of her marriage plans in order to avoid having Marianne commit suicide. It is a brilliant scene of psychological analysis.

When the third and final act begins, Marianne and Alain have been married for a year, but unsuccessfully, for Alain still loves Elisabeth. While Marianne, on a return visit to the house, goes upstairs to see her father, Alain describes to Elisabeth the chilling reality of his barren life with Marianne. Quickly, he and Elisabeth decide to run away once and for all, but Marianne sees them drive off. When she tells her father what has happened he makes clear his intent to leave in search of them the next morning. Elisabeth must return, no matter what, to wait on him. Possessive, domineering, selfish, he is one of Mauriac's great monsters. But then, in the last plot reversal of the play, the two lovers reappear. They have given up and are resigned to their fate. The last lines of the play, spoken by Elisabeth, "And yet we love each other," are a final ironic reminder of Mauriac's convictions about how destructive a family can be for some or all of its members (*ORTC,* 4:100). The *cage familiale* that entrapped Thérèse Desqueyroux has been evoked once again.

The play was a solid critical success for Mauriac. Following closely upon the revival of *Asmodée* in Paris in November 1944, it seemed to confirm Mauriac's late vocation as a playwright. Jean-Louis Barrault's brilliant direction (with his wife Madeleine Renaud playing the role of Elizabeth), also helped to assure its success. Pol Gaillard, for instance, found the play even superior to *Asmodée,* chiefly because the character of M. Coûture had seemed unbelievable to him.[8] Here, however, he found a riveting drama of love and possession, albeit written from a Jansenistic point of view. Although Gaillard generally hailed the play, he thought it also revealed Mauriac's basic weakness as a dramatist, since he was more adept at psychological analysis than at moving the action of the play along. He points out that in the last act it is the psychological development of the characters more than their actions that is of most importance, and he holds this against Mauriac; yet this is precisely the effect that Mauriac was trying to achieve in imitating Racine. Mauriac was pleased with the result of *Les Mal-aimés,* for he wanted to project on the stage in a contemporary setting what André Séailles has called "the somber Jansenistic universe of guilt and sin, the universe of those condemned by God."[9]

Passage du Malin (1947)

Of the four plays that Mauriac was to write before finally turning his back on the theater, *Passage du Malin* (Visit of the evil one) received the most hostile reception from Parisian critics. The play opened on 9 December 1947 at the Théâtre de la Madeleine and was bitterly attacked for a variety of reasons: too many subplots, a heroine who strains credibility, and a comical element that is more grotesque than humorous. This last element, the desire to inject comedy into what is supposedly a modern tragic setting, reveals Mauriac's lack of judgment about the stage when left to work essentially on his own.[10]

At the center of *Passage du Malin* is Emilie Tavernas, the founder of a successful private girls' school. Due in part to her forceful personality, she has built the institution from scratch. Her husband, Fernand, a widower 15 years her senior, is the school's business manager, without whom the institution's financial affairs would not be as firm as they are. Their Ecole Swetchine is truly a family business, for it supports Fernand and Emilie, their two aging mothers, and Fernand's two children by his first wife—Raymond, who is physically attracted to his stepmother, and Irène, who shares her stepmother's religious beliefs. It is not difficult to see that Mauriac has only slightly altered some of the basic elements of his fiction: the school, as a family business, complicates family relationships in the same way that landownership does in the novels, and the possible *Phèdre*-like relationship between Raymond and Emilie has also been used elsewhere (e.g., *La Fin de la nuit* and *Destins*.) Finally, Irène reminds us in certain respects of Octavie Puybaraud in *La Pharisienne* and Emmanuele in *Asmodée.*

As the play opens, the two mothers-in-law are involved in discussion. Fernand's mother, Irma, domineering, possessive, and emasculating of her son (much like Félicité Casenave in *Genitrix*), has never allowed him to have a life of his own, though she insists that all she does is in his best interests. Now she is speculating as to why his wife, Emilie, is locked away in her room with another woman. Clotilde, blind to her daughter's faults, has always doted on Emilie, and is still available to make her bed and serve her breakfast. Despite her weak attempts to defend her daughter, the audience gets a clear impression that Emilie is a lesbian. This impression is reinforced by the fact that Emilie and her husband have had a platonic relationship for years. Such cheap bedroom allusions unfortunately lower the level of intended comedy to that of Parisian "boulevard" theater. The carping between the two mothers-in-law, spiced with sexual innuendo, is crude and humorless. What Mauriac had seemingly intended to be funny, comes across as vulgar.

At the close of the first act, the first reversal takes place with the arrival of an outsider, Bernard. He is a *séducteur* in the Mauriac mold, eternally in quest of female victims. He has come precisely to carry off the woman, Agnès, who is in seclusion in Emilie's bedroom. A former student of Emilie's and her most brilliant graduate, Agnès has gone on to pass the competitive *agrégation* exam and is fleeing Bernard to avoid becoming his sexual victim. Thus, she and Emilie are not lovers, after all. In fact, Emilie herself is sexually repressed. Although Agnès is willing to be psychologically dominated by Emilie, she fears the inevitable physical domination that a meeting with a Don Juan figure like Bernard would provoke, for she considers herself defenseless against him.

Thus, the stage is set for the meeting between Emilie and Bernard. It will contrast a frigid woman with a thirst to dominate people's minds and hearts and a man who seeks to possess women's bodies. This is an interesting conflict, one that is in fact consistent with Mauriac's literary obsessions over the previous 30 years, but since it taxes the spectator's credulity, it comes across awkwardly on the stage. Fernand's mother, hoping to get rid of Agnès (whom she sees as her son's rival for Emilie's affections), gives Bernard a skeleton key, hoping that he will seduce Agnès and carry her off. But now that Bernard has met Emilie, he has forgotten Agnès. In this he reminds us of Georges Filhot of *La Fin de la nuit,* who loses interest in Marie Desqueyroux after he meets her mother, Thérèse. Thus, he uses his key instead to enter Emilie's room, where he seduces her and spends the night. The whole of the second act is devoted to the bedroom encounter between these two self-centered and strong-willed characters.

In the last act, set a week later, Emilie has decided to leave her school with its many responsibilities and to flee with Bernard. While she waits for him, she resists entreaties by various family members that she remain. She is determined to leave and not have to face the perpetual scorn of those who know about the night spent with Bernard. When he finally comes and they begin to discuss that night and its meaning, a somewhat predictable plot reversal takes place: by the end of the play Bernard is going off by himself, for Emilie has finally decided to remain faithful to her many personal and professional responsibilities. She has resisted the temptation to seek happiness in mere sexual pleasure, for she knows that this is impossible. As the play ends, Bernard assures her that he will be forever ready to drop everything the moment she changes her mind.

Although Mauriac clearly intends Bernard's statement to be sincere, the Don Juan figure is forever making such promises and it is difficult for a spectator to take him seriously. When Emilie responds: "I'll never call you again. One doesn't escape twice from the jail cell that I am returning to," the fallen pharisee seems to recognize that freedom is not absolute and that one is always influenced by one's past. (*ORTC,* 4:200). Before the curtain falls, her husband, the two mothers-in-law, her stepchildren, and Agnès all come back into the room. Finally, she proclaims: "And here come my guards." (*ORTC,* 4:200). The clash of the two domineering personalities has ended in a draw. Bernard has briefly possessed Emilie's body but not her soul, while Emilie has won Bernard's love, previously denied to any woman. Each has suffered injury, but each has also returned to a previous state—Emilie to the family cage (much like that of Thérèse Desqueyroux) and Bernard to the eternal wandering of the Don Juan figure.

A little more than a month after the play opened, Mauriac gave a lecture to journalists and theater critics in which he tried to explain what he was attempting to do in *Passage du Malin:* create for the stage a kind of "pharisienne," like Brigitte Pian, who is tempted, falls, but immediately recovers and returns to her former ways. In his justification and explanation of Bernard's character, he stated that Emilie is "the first woman under whose power he falls to the point of suffering," and what makes it worse is that she is a frigid, unbending "enemy of the flesh."[11]

Mauriac was hurt and somewhat indignant at the reception the play received and could not understand that in this case the criticism was quite justified. He wanted to portray Emilie as a tragic figure forced back into *la cage familiale,* but Bernard is such a superficial character that one can easily get the impression that she is doing the right thing in sending him away. Her work as an educator is far more important and fulfilling than a liaison with Bernard could ever be. Mauriac meant the work to be a modern tragedy with a comic element, but the characters never come alive, making it difficult for us to empathize with them, while the intended comical element comes quite close to the level of bedroom farce. To put this failure in perspective, it should be recalled that the play was written during the immediate postwar years, when most of Mauriac's energies were devoted to politics and journalism. In addition, he had to do without the constructive criticism of the staff of the Comédie-Française. The effects of these handicaps are all too apparent.

Le Feu sur la terre (1950)

Mauriac's last play, *Le Feu sur la terre* (Fire covers the land), was written during the summer of 1949 and presented on stage for the first time on 12 October 1950. It opened in Lyons rather than Paris, which can be interpreted as another step down for Mauriac as a dramatist. He was so anxious for it to succeed that he even introduced the play at its Lyons premiere, explaining its genesis to the audience and critics. The Paris opening took place on 7 November 1950 at the experimental Théâtre Hébertot, where it was performed by the resident repertory company.

The play owes its title to a verse from the Gospel of Saint Luke (12:49), in which Jesus states that he has come to bring fire to the earth. The massive pine forests of the Landes were also ravaged by forest fires during the summer of 1949. To Mauriac, "the fire, which, before my eyes, devoured the pines of my childhood became Laure's devastating tenderness" (*ORTC*, 4:1142). It should also be recalled that the image of fire that jumps from treetop to treetop recurs a number of times in Mauriac's fiction and connotes passion and desire. The subtitle, *Le Pays sans chemin* (The land without roads), evokes Mauriac's native region of Jouanhaut, which he calls in *Nouveaux Mémoires Intérieurs* a wilderness, or "a land without roads" (*OA*, 666). Of Mauriac's four plays, this one has by far the strongest sense of place.

As the play begins, the wealthy Du Prat de la Sesque family, consisting of mother, father, and two daughters living at home (Laure, 37, and Lucile, 17), awaits the triumphant return of their son and brother, who has been studying law in Paris for the last 10 years. Maurice's father has just sent off a large check to his son to pay for the printing of his doctoral thesis, a work that must be published no matter the cost because Maurice's family has planned a marriage for him with Caroline Lahure, the daughter of wealthy neighbors. Since one of the La Sesque children, Raymond, died in childhood of tubercular meningitis, the Lahure family is concerned about the health of the La Sesques and will not go through with the wedding unless he obtains his doctorate and has his thesis published. It will soon be learned that Maurice is unable to meet these requirements. Of course, the motif of checking on the health of the whole family before allowing a marriage to take place recurs a number of times in Mauriac's fiction, most notably in *Thérèse Desqueyroux* and *Le Noeud de vipères.*

When Maurice arrives home in act 2, he is accompanied by his wife, Andrée, and their five-year-old son, Eric. Here it is revealed that all the sacrifices made by the family (and about which Maurice's father never misses an opportunity to complain) have gone for naught. Maurice has never even studied law, and the money sent to him over the years was used to cover other expenses. Like Gradère of *Les Anges noirs,* who leads a similar double life, Maurice has deceived those who have paid his bills.

Despite his willful deception, Maurice's mother seems ready to accept him, for she sees in her grandson Eric a replica of the deceased Raymond. Even his father, the miserly Osmin, finally agrees. His sister Laure, however, is unable to accept this new situation. She had been expecting him to marry Caroline Lahure, whom she considers stupid and easily dominated, and who, because of her ties to the land, would never dream of living anywhere but in their small, isolated world. Having preserved Maurice's room like a blessed site during the many years of his absence, Laure must now adapt her strategy to new circumstances. The existence of the child indicates to her a carnal relationship between husband and wife that is beyond her control. Andrée, an outsider who is of humble social origins, loves her husband and is loved in return.

This is the essence of the problem for Laure. As in *Asmodée,* in which Coûture, the former seminarian swollen with pride, is a monster placed at the center of the action, here Laure, who is unduly interested in—indeed even obsessed by—the private and personal life of her brother Maurice, is also a "monster." In the final act, after Maurice has cut all his ties to Caroline, and thus to his sister, Laure goes off walking by herself. The family members are afraid that she is planning to commit suicide by throwing herself into an abandoned well. To have her take such drastic action would have perhaps been a preferred solution for Racine, but Mauriac, as usual, could not bring himself to use such a denouement. All except Andrée go running off in search of Laure. When she suddenly returns, there is a powerful final scene between her and her sister-in-law, in which Laure recognizes that she has been defeated and implores Maurice and Andrée to leave immediately.

Critical reaction to the play was mixed, and it had only a short run. By the usual standards of the Paris stage, it could not be considered successful. In fairness to Mauriac, it should also be said that the theater is arguably the most difficult genre in which to succeed, and by 1950 the play was quite out of step with the prevailing fare on the Paris stage. In addition, the quality of the actors, as well as of the production in general, was below that of the Comédie-Française. In later years, Mauriac wrote wistfully that Laure de la Sesque was one of his greatest creations: "People will realize some day that I haven't written anything better than the role of the sister in *Le Feu sur la terre*" (*OA,* 817).

In recent years, the eminent Mauriac scholar François Durand has voiced agreement with this assessment, even going so far as to call *Le Feu sur la terre* one of Mauriac's greatest works: "In my view, it is Mauriac's theatrical masterpiece and one of his greatest successes in any genre. It is the play that achieves a perfect balance of all its elements. It is the most rooted in its social context, the most focused on the passion of one individual, the most nostalgic, the most passionate, [and] the one with the most lively and diverse characters."[12] Since characters with a personal obsession are somewhat more difficult to present on the stage than they are in fiction, Laure, Mauriac's last theatrical "monster," would have probably been a more successful creation if she had been portrayed in a novel.

Mauriac attained little real success with his last two plays. This fact, combined with the effects of age (by 1950 he was 65 years old) and his increased commitment to journalism and politics, convinced him that what creative powers he still had should be devoted to the novel. Thus, by 1960, he could write to Jean Cocteau: "I have become a complete stranger to the theater and that's not the whole story. I stay away from it as much as I can."[13] None of Mauriac's plays has been revived in recent years, although *Asmodée* and *Les Mal-aimés* still officially belong to the repertory of the Comédie-Française.

Mauriac's two most important achievements in the theater are *Asmodée* and *Le Feu sur la terre.* The former will probably be revived from time to time by the Comédie-Française, while the latter will be produced only if a small theater group decides to launch a revival. In any event, Mauriac's theater will always remain a marginal part of his total oeuvre. It is perhaps Jean Lacouture who has best summed up Mauriac's career as a dramatist: "Despite the Racinian aspect of Mauriac's art, easily transposable within the structures of classical tragedy, and his lively enthusiasm and concentration as a spectator, his relationship with the theater was always a bit awkward, frustrating and frustrated. This is an astonishing disequilibrium, quite difficult to explain."[14]

Poetry

Mauriac published four principal collections of poetry during his lifetime. The first, *Les Mains jointes* (1909; Joined hands), was hailed by Maurice Barrès in a newspaper article that helped to launch Mauriac's career. Two years later *L'Adieu à l'adolescence* (Farewell to adolescence) had a similar reception. These works contain pious and sentimental poems written by a young man who admired Rimbaud but had been unable to escape from the grip of his overbearing mother and the clerics who shaped the early years of his life. The third collection, *Orages* (Storms), appeared in 1925, just before the crisis that led to Mauriac's "conversion" of 1928. The fourth collection, *Le Sang d'Atys* (The blood of Atys), was published in 1940 and brings a closure to his efforts in this domain. Mauriac's poetry has been used by critics on occasion to illuminate certain aspects of his life, but it has received relatively little attention on its own merits.[15]

When the two early collections appeared in volume 4 of his *Oeuvres complètes* in 1951, Mauriac claimed that these works bear the hallmark of what he calls their *facilité (OC*, 4:323), adding that both the technique and the spirit of the poems were to be rejected. He did not go so far as to renounce the content of the Catholic faith that he professed at the time, but rather his manner of belief. He felt in retrospect that because he had not yet been truly tested by life, these poems (which speak of friendship, family, simple faith, and the beauty of the traditional Catholic liturgy), had been too easy for him to write and did not reflect true personal suffering, while the later poems, written during and after the spiritual crisis of the late 1920s, did reflect that anguish. His point is well taken, but this does not mean that the early poems have little or no value for us. On the contrary, they belong to the Catholic Renaissance in French literature of the first quarter of the twentieth century and are linked thematically in a number of important ways to the works of Huysmans, Francis Jammes, Péguy, and Claudel. Written in the wake of the Dreyfus Affair, which culminated so disastrously (it seemed) for bourgeois Catholics when the church and state were formally separated in 1906, they portray tenderly that other, traditional, Catholic non-Republican vision of French life. For Mauriac to want to turn his back on these works in the 1950s is understandable: times had changed, and he had written much more serious and important things in the intervening years. But these poems are a minor treasure today, for they offer an exquisite and faithful reflection of the Catholic worldview of an era whose remaining vestiges were completely swept away by Vatican II.

Orages and *Le Sang d'Atys* come at the beginning and the end of the most tormented and productive years of Mauriac's life, 1925–40. Mauriac reprinted them in volume 6 of the *Oeuvres complètes,* but to date no critical edition of any of his books of poetry has been published. The romantic title of *Orages,* evoking the storms that rage within the heart and soul of a young man awakened to the realities of sexual desire, is intensely personal. Whereas the earlier collections may be seen as a faithful reflection of the heartfelt pieties offically endorsed by the French Catholicism of the day, *Orages* reflects the poet's interior crisis. These poems portray a young man obsessed by sexual temptations. He finds himself in a desert from which there is no escape, and in which religion can offer no succor. The *souffrance amoureuse* (*OC,* 6:ii) of this period, to which Mauriac would later allude obliquely and discreetly, is violently portrayed in these poems. The pantheistic images are worthy of a pagan writer of antiquity and, from a Pascalian point of view, reflect Mauriac's nature uninformed by divine grace.

Le Sang d'Atys follows *Orages* and uses much of the same imagery. The 19 separate and titled poems of the collection are intended to be read as one long work. Cybèle, the great earth mother, lusts after Atys, the innocent shepherd of classical antiquity.[16] Mauriac had worked on this collection of poems for many years and finally published them in the January 1940 issue of the *NRF* without a title, notes, or commentary. Strangely, they did not receive a formal title until they were republished in the *Oeuvres complètes* in 1951. These poems recount the same suffering found in *Orages,* but here the poet attempts a reconciliation between the flesh and the spirit through an imagined mystical union of bodies rising from the dead.

Mauriac had begun writing these poems in 1927, while still very much immersed in his religious crisis, and continued working on them through 1938. Fragments of *Le Sang d'Atys* surface in the novel *Destins* (1928), to which they seem to have been written as an adjunct. Later, extensive excerpts from the poem would appear in *Les Chemins de la mer* (1939), where they assume such importance in the fates of the various characters that they sometimes give the impression that the novel and its poetic young protagonist, Pierre Costadot, have both been inspired by the poem. Various characters in the novel hear Pierre read passages of his poem, and the reader is able to establish links between them and the characters in the poem. The two works play off each other in a subtle manner and in the process give to the novel an interest, and perhaps even an importance, that it is not able to sustain on its own.

The poem follows a simple narrative line. Cybèle, the earth mother, sings of her love for the handsome young shepherd Atys, whose liaison with the nymph Sangaris has caused her sorrow. She takes her vengeance by turning Atys into a pine tree. But he still manages to escape by transforming himself into a Christ figure and then castrating himself, thus achieving liberation from temptations of the flesh. The image of the pine tree is essential to the poem, for it signifies that Atys is rooted in the earth and therefore still attached to Cybèle. At the same time, by his very nature as a tree, he is able to reach mystical heights. Thus Mauriac, like Atys, does not deny his carnal roots, but simply adds to them another element that comes from a mystical source. The poem completes *Orages* and demonstrates that, by the conclusion of the work, the poet has finally achieved stasis. He is at rest and sure of victory over both his own flesh and the domineering mother figure who reappears so often in his fiction, from *Genitrix* to *La Pharisienne*. As the poem ends, the troubled waters and hidden sources that spring from the center of the earth in the early part of the poem, representing Cybèle's power, are replaced by the healing waters of baptism.

In 1929 Mauriac offered an important key to understanding this poem, and indeed all his work, when he mentioned the poem (under the tentative title he had in mind at the time) in his essay "Bonheur du chrétien": "For years now, I have been devoting free time to a poem, 'Les Larmes d'Atys' [The tears of Atys]. . . . I have lived with this poem, constantly assembling and disassembling it. The pagan roots of my personality are here laid bare to the point of horror" (*OA,* 142; *ORTC,* 3:1418–20). This contrast between what can be called, in the Pascalian scheme of things, the order of the body and the order of grace is at the heart of Mauriac's whole creative oeuvre. The chasm between them is infinite, for grace is not a part of nature, but can be added onto it by an act of God. In his novels, theater, and poetry, Mauriac transposed endlessly this basic conflict, but it is in the poetry that it receives its most powerful expression.

Chapter Eight
Conclusion

Mauriac's greatest strength as a writer is his style. His power as a stylist is due to both his imagery and the concentration of his prose. Mauriac could say a great deal in relatively few words, and no translation, however well done, can ever completely convey the rich and evocative complexity of his language. This is one of the reasons that his novels, despite their brevity, were almost always so successful: he did not need four or five hundred pages to express himself. Indeed, even what I refer to above as his longer novels were seldom longer than two hundred pages. Thus, if Mauriac endures as a writer, and if works like *Thérèse Desqueyroux* and *Le Sagouin* are widely read in school curricula in France today, I would argue that this fact owes as much to their magnificent style as it does to their overall structure, the psychological analysis of the characters, or the portrait of French society that they offer.

Mauriac's contributions to French literature as a poet and dramatist await further evaluation. While it is doubtful that his plays will ever be considered of the first rank, his poetry, not yet studied in any systematic way, may be evaluated in a more positive manner in the future. Owing to space limitations, I have not treated his hagiographic or biographical writings. His essays and autobiographical writings have also been neglected for the same reason. Unfortunately, these dimensions of Mauriac's oeuvre have been understudied until now; scholars should look at these works more closely in the years ahead.

Jean Touzot's recently published critical edition of Mauriac's *Bloc-Notes* will no doubt enable us to appreciate Mauriac further as a literary critic, political and social commentator, and overall "man of letters" in the French tradition. There is barely a subject that he did not touch on in these newspaper columns of the last 20 or so years of his life, and there are few important contemporaries who escape mention therein. Future generations might very well turn to the *Bloc-Notes* to rediscover the essence of the years marked by the Cold War, the rise and fall of existentialism and the new novel, the Second Vatican Council, and General de Gaulle's reign (1958–69) as first president of the Fifth Republic. Mauriac in the *Bloc-Notes* is anything but an objective chronicler of these years. On the contrary, he is a committed combatant, who never hesitates to express his opinion. Once made more accessible, the *Bloc-Notes* could very well emerge in the eyes of future readers as an achievement to rival that of the novels.

Since the focus in these pages has been on Mauriac's creative writing more than on his life per se, it is important to recall that he was politically active and committed as a journalist from 1938 until his death in 1970. In this capacity, he played an important role in forming political opinion at a critical juncture in French history. As we evaluate these years with more objectivity, (and here the new edition of the *Bloc-Notes* can only add to Mauriac's glory), he emerges as one of the heroes of the political center, committed to the parliamentary system despite its shortcomings, yet always supporting man against the system. Firmly committed at great personal risk to the Allied side during World War II, he remained faithful in the postwar years to what he called *la démocratie chrétienne,* or what we would simply call liberal democracy. Throughout these decades, when so many intellectuals followed the herd and adopted Marxist or pseudo-Marxist positions, Mauriac held firm. Often ridiculed, he had the courage of his convictions, and is now seen to have been right at nearly every turn.

Mauriac's career as a novelist evolved in time and can be seen to have had a beginning, a middle, and an end. The early novels, written prior to about 1922, are works that belong to what we can call Mauriac's period of apprenticeship. Then, beginning with *Le Baiser au lépreux,* other masterpieces, like *Genitrix* and *Thérèse Desqueyroux* (and, for some readers, even *Le Désert de l'amour*), followed in the 1920s. After the religious crisis that lasted for about three years, 1927–30, a new phase, in which Mauriac strives to write Catholic novels, begins. I have tried to be flexible in defining the Catholic novel, stipulating that in the strictest sense of the term, it should refer to a work in which the salvation of a soul is at stake, but conceding that it can also be used to describe novels in which the overall atmosphere of the work makes use of the Catholic world of sign and symbol simply to achieve its effects. Thus, *Ce qui était perdu* represents Mauriac's first attempt to write a Catholic novel, followed immediately by two other important novels of the same type, *Le Noeud de vipères,* (a Catholic novel in the fullest sense of the term, for it depicts the faith journey of its protagonist and hints at the salvation of his soul), and *Le Mystère Frontenac,* (which re-creates and transforms Mauriac's own family experiences as a boy and in so doing gives particular emphasis to the worldview that permeated his Catholic family). These novels culminate in the creation of *La Pharisienne,* which I consider Mauriac's most complex and important novel, a work that deserves to be rediscovered. Underrated at present, it should be ranked, in my view, among Mauriac's highest achievements.

Finally, in the postwar years, *Le Sagouin* is a final jewel in Mauriac's crown. Like *Thérèse Desqueyroux,* it portrays the inner workings of a well-to-do family and delineates the relationship of a fragile and sensitive individual with both the family and the larger society. The world that it creates is a microcosm of French society before World War II, with special emphasis on the struggle between France's two great modern *"familles d'esprit,"* the conservative Catholic tradition and the anticlerical forces that have been so antagonistic to it since the Revolution. Mauriac was always able to portray characters from these two traditions in a credible and engaging manner, and the tension between them is depicted in some way in each of his novels.

It is important to remember in this regard that neither *Thérèse Desqueyroux* nor *Le Sagouin,* the two novels that continue to be the most widely read and appreciated in France, and which for many readers are his true and enduring masterpieces, is a Catholic novel. I underscore this fact to make it clear that if Mauriac tried to work in the genre of the Catholic novel off and on during his long career, this was only one area of endeavor for him and should not be considered the exclusive focus of his work. Mauriac's principal concern as a novelist was the human condition as seen from his personal perspective. That this perspective was influenced by his regional background from the southwest of France, by his Catholic upbringing in a wealthy and politically conservative family, and by his lifelong commitment to Catholicism, can in no way detract from or restrict the universal reach and validity of what he depicted. In sum, the Nobel committee was right when it stated that Mauriac belongs to world literature, and that what he has to say is valid for all mankind.

Notes and References

Chapter One

1. "Un Sondage IPSOS–*Le Monde*–Europe 1: La Littérature française jugée par les professeurs de lycée," *Le Monde,* 19 May 1989, 17.

2. "Livre de Poche," *Journal Français d'Amérique* 15, no. 6 (5–18 March 1993): 11.

3. Harriet Tillson, "Images of Malagar: Claude and François Mauriac," in *François Mauriac: Visions and Appraisals,* ed. John E. Flower and Bernard C. Swift (Oxford: Berg, 1989), 165–79. See also J. Montférier, "Préface," *Cahiers de Malagar* 1 (1987): 7–10.

4. Mauriac was obsessed by the Dreyfus case during his whole lifetime. See Malcolm Scott, "Mauriac and the Raising of Dreyfus," in Flower and Swift, eds., 133–46; and Bernard Cocula, "Mauriac et l'affaire Dreyfus," *Cahiers François Mauriac* 7 (1980): 11–30. This journal is hereafter cited in text as *CFM.*

5. The extracts from Mauriac's grandfather's diary appeared in Claude Mauriac, *Le Temps immobile,* vol. 1 (Paris: Grasset, 1974). Claude, François Mauriac's oldest son, has been an important man of letters in France since the end of World War II. After trying his hand at the *nouveau roman* in the 1950s and early 1960s, he has devoted his energy to his diary, which has been published in 10 volumes (1974–1988).

6. *Oeuvres romanesques et théâtrales complètes,* 4 vols., ed. Jacques Petit (Paris: Gallimard, Editions de la Pléiade 1978–1985), 4:661. This work, hereafter cited in text as *ORTC,* has become the standard reference work for Mauriac's novels, short stories, and theater. In addition to providing critical editions of Mauriac's texts, these four volumes offer an abundance of background information. The opening sentence of the novel, "Je ne suis pas un garçon comme les autres" ("I'm not like other boys"), sets the tone of the work. It is also a key to understanding Mauriac's life and career.

7. Pierre Mauriac, "Une amitié fraternelle," quoted in Jean Lacouture, *François Mauriac* (Paris: Seuil, 1984), 31.

8. *Oeuvres autobiographiques,* ed. François Durand (Paris: Gallimard, Editions de la Pléiade, 1990), 679; hereafter cited in text as *OA.*

9. Jansenius (Cornelius Jansen) (1585–1638) was bishop of Ypres in Flanders. His doctrine, which he drew from the works of Saint Augustine, was expressed most completely in the posthumously published treatise *Augustinus* (1640). Jansenism was introduced into the Abbey of Port-Royal, a convent of Cistercian nuns, in 1634, and by the end of the century it permeated the royal court. Jean Racine, the classical playwright, was imbued with the spirit of Jansenism while writing his greatest plays. Jansenism was strongly opposed by

the Jesuits, who took exception to its extremely negative view of the human condition. It was condemned by Pope Innocent X in 1653 and by Pope Clement XI in his papal bull *Unigenitus* in 1713. Its most famous and skillful exponent was Blaise Pascal, the mathematician and philosopher. With Racine, he is perhaps the writer who influenced Mauriac the most. This is another paradox of Mauriac's work: his undisguised admiration for the two most famous Jansenist writers, despite his personal aversion for Jansenism. This subject is explored by Yves Leroux, "Mauriac et la tentation du jansénisme," *CFM* 14 (1987): 105–10.

10.   For further reading on the positive and negative aspects of Jansenism, see Jean-Pierre Landry, "Mauriac, lecteur de Pascal," *CFM* 14 (1987): 111–31; and Margaret Mein, "François Mauriac and Jansenism," in Flower and Swift, eds., 147–64.

11.   In the encyclical *Pascendi Dominici Gregis*, Pope Pius X condemned the new, liberal ideas under the generic term of *modernism*. Many of the ideas to be proscribed, like liberty of conscience, later became dear to Mauriac. Maurice Blondel (1861–1949) was one of the "modernist" philosophers to be condemned. In his work he had attempted to stake out a middle ground between modern philosophical and scientific ideas and Catholic doctrine. The Abbé Alfred-Firmin Loisy (1857–1940), a modernist theologian who specialized in biblical exegesis, and whom Mauriac read extensively as a youth, was also condemned. Loisy attempted to apply modern notions of textual criticism to the four Gospels, and questioned in particular the authenticity of Saint John's Gospel. It is important to note that although André Lacaze introduced Mauriac to the world of philosophical and theological speculation, Mauriac never took an active interest in this field. His faith, like that of Pascal, was based on a direct experience of God. Mauriac deals with this subject in the first chapter of his autobiographical essay *Ce que je crois* (*What I Believe*). See *OA*, 567–73. Regarding the now defunct *Index of Forbidden Books*, see "Index of Forbidden Books," *The New Catholic Encyclopedia* (New York: McGraw Hill, 1967), 7:434–35.

12.   See the section devoted to "Le Démon de la connaissance," in chapter 2, for further discussion of this subject.

13.   Mauriac left the *Sillon* movement at about the same time that the French hierarchy was becoming concerned about it. The movement had originated in 1899 and sought to take up the challenge enunciated by Pope Leo XIII in his encyclical *Rerum Novarum* (1891), in which he had reaffirmed the rights of workers and attacked the excesses of capitalism. The encyclical had stopped short of rejecting the capitalist system outright and discouraged workers from revolting against their condition. But Sangnier's task was exceedingly difficult because the Dreyfus Affair had brought about a radical transformation in French society between 1891 and 1899. Marc Sangnier supported the principle of social justice while remaining both a Catholic and a citizen in good standing of the Republic. But given the fact that the church and the state were practical-

ly at war during these years, it was almost impossible for Sangnier to realize his goal. The *Sillon* was eventually condemned by Pope Pius X in 1910 and disbanded shortly thereafter.

14. See Lacouture, 80–81. One factor that seems to have helped Claire Mauriac to accept her son's decision to embark on a career as a writer was the fact that her second son, Jean, had recently decided to study for the priesthood. She perhaps took consolation in the belief that Jean, henceforth living in Paris, would be able to keep a discreet eye on his little brother.

15. *Oeuvres complètes*, 12 vols., (Paris: Arthème Fayard, 1950–56), 10:ii; hereafter cited in text as *OC*. The prefaces written for this edition of the complete works are reprinted in the Pléiade edition of the *ORTC*. This citation is found in 1:1988.

16. *Bloc-Notes* (vols. 1–3, Paris: Flammarion, 1958–1965; vols. 4–5, Paris: Grasset, 1970–71), 3:412; hereafter cited in text as *BN*. The new, critical edition of the *Bloc-Notes* appeared in late 1993, after this study had gone to press.

17. The unpublished texts in question in the Bibliothèque Jacques Doucet are entitled "Gens de l'arrière" and "L'Oiseau bleu" and are cataloged under number MRC 84.

18. F. Mauriac, "Roman-fleuve et roman-ruisseau," *L'Echo de Paris,* 17 December 1932. This article has been reprinted in *ORTC,* 2:895–98.

19. See *OC,* 1:i–ii, 4:iii, and 10:i–iii for Mauriac's disparaging remarks about the early years of his career. These prefaces are reprinted in *ORTC,* 1:988–95.

20. Jean Touzot, *Mauriac avant Mauriac* (Paris: Flammarion, 1977), 6. See also Jean Touzot, "L'après-guerre de François Mauriac chroniqueur au *Gaulois* de 1919 à 1921," *CFM* 10 (1983): 61–79.

21. See Bernard Roussel, "Marcel Proust, 1871–1922," in *François Mauriac et les grands esprits de ce temps* (Paris: Bibliothèque Historique de la Ville de Paris, 1990), 35–40. Also of interest is Jacques Bersani, "Mauriac du côté de chez Proust," *CFM* 4 (1976): 98–111. These articles offer useful commentary on Mauriac's essay on Proust, *Du côté de chez Proust* (Paris: La Table ronde, 1947), reprinted in *OA,* 271–317. The Mauriac/Rivière correspondence is of great interest in elucidating this period of Mauriac's life. See John E. Flower, ed., *François Mauriac et Jacques Rivière: Correspondance 1911–1925* (Exeter: University of Exeter Press, 1988). See also Alain Rivière, "François Mauriac et Jacques Rivière," *CFM* 4 (1976): 137–60.

22. Jean Calvet, *Le Renouveau catholique dans la littérature contemporaine* (Paris: Lanore, 1927), 332. Calvet was referring here to several writers, including Mauriac. Of course, Mauriac was also condemned by Catholic critics because of the negative portrait that he painted of the bourgeoisie. This subject is developed by Jean Touzot, "Quand Mauriac était scandaleux," *Oeuvres et Critiques* 2, no.1 (1977): 133–44. Mauriac's reception by Communist critics in the 1930s has been studied by Philippe Baudorre, "Un Romancier catholique devant la critique de gauche: François Mauriac et *Monde*," Travaux du Centre d'Etudes et de

Recherches sur François Mauriac, no. 21 (June 1987): 29–44. This journal is hereafter cited as *TCERFM*.

23. *La Vie de Jean Racine* (Paris: Plon, 1928). This work is also found in *OC*, 8:55–150.

24. For a copy of the letter that Gide sent to Mauriac in May 1928 and which appeared as an "open letter" in the June 1928 issue of the *NRF*, see *ORTC*, 3:832–5.

25. See Simon Jeune, "Charles Du Bos et François Mauriac," *CFM* 4 (1976): 161–74.

26. Mauriac commented on his detractors in his *Mémoires intérieurs*. See, for example, *OA*, 742–43, 924.

27. *Mémoires politiques* (Paris: Grasset, 1967), 63.

28. See David O'Connell, "François Mauriac's *Le Cahier noir*," *Commonweal*, 23 April 1993, 22–23.

29. See Tony Judt, *Past Imperfect: French Intellectuals, 1944–1956* (Berkeley: University of California Press, 1992). This most interesting study of French intellectuals and their political allegiances between 1944 and 1956 begins to restore to Mauriac the recognition that he deserves for standing up for broadly human and humane values in the face of the leftist intellectuals who turned their backs on such values in order to justify the excesses of communism. Mauriac's bittersweet experience with *La Table ronde* is studied in Michel Bressolette, "Mauriac et *La Table ronde*," *CFM* 7 (1980): 67–78.

30. François Durand has called into question the widely perceived image of Mauriac always being subservient to de Gaulle and never criticizing him. Although he concedes that the positive comments far outweighed the negative ones, he reminds us that Mauriac criticized de Gaulle much more often than we have been led to believe. See François Durand, "Mauriac et de Gaulle," in *De Gaulle et les écrivains* (Grenoble: Presses Universitaires de Grenoble, 1991), 39–53.

Chapter Two

1. In recent years there has been a renewed interest in these early novels. See, for example, Betty Tew, "Chute et crucifixion dans *L'Enfant chargé de chaînes* et *La Robe prétexte*," *TCERFM*, no. 30 (December 1991): 13–26; and Olivier Maison, "Sens et signification du thème du double dans les premiers romans de Mauriac," *TCERFM*, no. 32 (December 1992): 47–63.

2. See Richard Griffiths, *The Reactionary Revolution: The Catholic Revival in French Literature* (New York: Ungar, 1965), which describes the use of this theme by several of Mauriac's predecessors. The theme recurs often in the novels of Dostoevsky, who exerted a powerful influence over Catholic writers in the closing decades of the nineteenth century. The first French novel in which this theme was developed was *Le Désespéré*, by Léon Bloy (1886). For further investigation of this topic, consult the following articles in *The New Catholic Encyclopedia* (New York: McGraw-Hill, 1967): "Grace and Nature," 6:683–85; "Merit," 9:683–86; and "Suffering," 13:775–777. Under "Merit," one reads: "theologians hold that a man in grace can congruently

merit special graces for himself. They also maintain that such a man can congruently merit a grace (even the grace of justification itself) for another man." (9:686); under "Suffering," one reads: "The suffering of Christ is presented in the New Testament as a wholly vicarious suffering, necessary for effecting man's Redemption; the Christian, in turn, as a redeemed member of Christ's Mystical Body, must share in his Lord's suffering if he wishes to particpate in His glory." (13:776).

3. Arthur Rimbaud (1845–1891), who as a teenager abandoned his home and family in Charleville, in the north of France, in order to run off to Paris, exerted a great power of attraction over the young Mauriac. Wanting to seek a reality of some kind beyond the level of the senses, he experimented in self-induced delirium. In the summer of 1871 he composed his greatest and most famous poem, "Le Bateau ivre." This was followed a few years later by the collection of poems entitled *Une Saison en enfer*. These poems are remarkable for their language, imagery, and unbridled spirit of self-examination, and seem to suggest a longing to return to the world of his religious upbringing. By the age of 21 Rimbaud took up a life of travel and adventure—mostly in Africa—which occupied the rest of his life. In so doing, he turned his back on his poetic calling.

4. With the exception of "Insomnie," Mauriac's stories have been generally overlooked by critics. See Marie-Françoise Canérot, "La Nouvelle, lieu du meilleur théâtre mauriacien," *La Licorne* 7 (1983): 53–65; Helena Shillony, "'Insomnie,' ou le sommeil de la raison," *CFM* 15 (1988): 210–16.

5. This fragment was originally entitled by Mauriac *Conscience, instinct divin* and can be found in ORTC, 2:3–13.

6. For further reading on Mauriac's changing attitudes with respect to Freudianism, consult Paul Croc, "Mauriac et Freud," in *François Mauriac*, ed. Jean Touzot (Paris: Editions de l'Herne, 1985), 219–29; and Mireille Lhomme, "La Querelle de l'ancien et des cadets à travers *Les Mémoires intérieurs* et *Les Nouveuax Mémoires intérieurs*," *TCERFM*, no. 26 (December 1989): 21–39. A useful critical analysis of Mauriac's hostility to Freud is found in Robert Stuart Thomson, "Mauriac and Psychoanalysis," *Literature and Psychology* 34 (1988): 41–51.

7. Jacques Petit argues that "Le Rang" must have been written in 1936, since Mauriac usually published his work without delay. *(ORTC*, 3:1097). While this observation is correct, "Le Rang" bears a number of points in common with both *Le Baiser au lépreux* and *Genitrix*, and might very well have been written in the 1920s and not the 1930s. It also seems to evoke the essence of *Préséances*, a novel that is also an *étude de moeurs*, a genre that tempted Mauriac before he finally settled on his own style and atmosphere. It concentrates on one theme—the power of the domineering mother—but it does so from the social point of view: the need to keep up appearances even when one does not have the income to do so.

Chapter Three

1. This novel has tempted three different translators in the English language. James Whitall translated it as *The Kiss to the Leper* (London: Heinemann, 1923), while Louis Galantière translated it along with *Genitrix* and

published the two together under the title *The Family* (New York: Covici-Friede, 1930). Gerard Hopkins brought out his own translation under the title *A Kiss for the Leper* (London: Eyre and Spottiswoode, 1950).

2.   In the 1920s Paul Souday was a regular contributor to the *New York Times*, reporting on the Parisian literary scene. His articles on Mauriac's novels still make for interesting reading. He never reviewed *Kiss to the Leper* for the *Times*, but he wrote on *Desert of Love* (31 May 1925, 19), *Thérèse Desqueyroux* (27 March 1927, 7) and *Destinies* (29 April 1928, 6). In the last review he said of Mauriac's art, which mixed faith and carnal instinct: "Nothing could be more impure, in every sense of the word, than the novel as composed by M. François Mauriac."

3.   Friedrich Wilhelm Nietzsche (1844–1900), the son of a Lutheran minister, was trained in philosophy and philology in Bonn and Leipzig, and became a professor of classical languages at the University of Basel in 1869. Because of ill health he had to resign his position in 1879. The idea of the will to power is developed in his later writings, such as *Also sprach Zarathustra* (1883–92), and *Der Antichrist* (1888). There are conflicting interpretations of the meaning of Nietzsche's writings. A still useful general introduction to his thought is Walter Kaufmann, *Nietzsche: Philosopher, Psychologist, Antichrist* (Princeton: Princeton University Press, 1950).

4.   Extended analysis of *Le Baiser au lépreux* can be found in Michel Bonte, *Images et spiritualité dans l'oeuvre romanesque de François Mauriac* (Paris: La Pensée Universelle, 1981).

5.   This story remained unpublished during Mauriac's lifetime. It can be found in *ORTC*, 1:973–80.

6.   André Séailles, *Mauriac* (Paris: Bordas, 1972), 31.

7.   This novel has been studied recently by Maurice Maucuer, "Un Territoire féminin: Le Royaume de Félicité dans *Genitrix*," *CFM* 13 (1986): 232–38; and Arlette Lafay, "Réflexions sur la fonction cathartique dans *Genitrix*," *CFM* 13 (1986): 248–58.

8.   Conor Cruise O'Brien, *Maria Cross: Imaginative Patterns in a Group of Catholic Writers* (London: Burns and Oates, 1963).

9.   Cited in Josette Sainte-Marie, *Grands écrivains choisis par l'Académie Goncourt*, vol. 21 (Paris: E.P.I., 1987).

10.   It should be noted that Stendhal's *Le Rouge et le noir* (1830) is also based on the account of a celebrated murder trial, while Emma, the heroine of Gustave Flaubert's *Madame Bovary* (1857), obtains poison through a subterfuge in order to take her own life.

11.   Denis and Pierre in *Les Chemins de la mer* and Nicholas and Gilles of *Galigaï* are close friends whose relationships resemble that of Anne and Thérèse in certain respects.

12.   Variations on the same formula are repeated three more times: *ORTC*, 2:31, 37, and 105.

13.   This novel has generated more critical commentary than any other

book by Mauriac. Many worthwhile articles could be cited. Space limitations permit reference to only four articles, of which two focus on the relationship between Thérèse and Phèdre, a topic not touched upon in my discussion. See Geneviève Sutton, "Phèdre et Thérèse Desqueyroux, une communauté du destin," *French Review* 43 (1970): 559–70; and Jacques Monférier, "Thérèse Desqueyroux, Phèdre et le destin," *Revue des lettres modernes* 516–17 (1977): 109–18. For an appreciation of the richness, density and complexity of the novel, see Arthur Holmberg, "Thérèse Desqueyroux: L'Impossibilité du moi," *CFM* 13 (1986): 125–37. Also of interest is Edward J. Gallagher, "Sexual Ambiguity in Mauriac's *Thérèse Desqueyroux*," *Romance Notes* 26 (1985): 215–21.

Chapter Four

1. J. C. Whitehouse, "Catholic Writing: Some Basic Notions, Some Criticisms, and a Tentative Reply," *French Studies* 83 (1978): 241–49.

2. John Cruickshank, "The Novel and Christian Belief," in *French Literature and Its Background,*, ed. John Cruickshank, vol. 6 (Oxford: Oxford University Press, 1970), 185–204.

3. Maurice Bruézière, *Histoire descriptive de la littérature contemporaine,* vol. 1 (Paris: Berger-Levrault, 1975), 155.

4. Albert Sonnenfeld, *Crossroads: Essays on the Catholic Novelists* (York, S.C.: French Literature Publishing Co., 1982), 11.

5. See chapter 2 for a discussion of the stories written at this time, especially "Un Homme de lettres," "Coups de couteau," and "Insomnie," which also reflect the effects of this crisis on Mauriac.

6. Hugh M. Davidson, *Blaise Pascal* (Boston: Twayne, 1983), 88.

7. He wrote about this subject in an important article entitled "Roman-fleuve et roman-ruisseau," *L'Echo de Paris,* 17 December 1932. It is reprinted in *ORTC,* 2:895–98. We should also recall that the principal characters of *Ce qui était perdu* reappear a few years later in *Les Anges noirs.* Likewise, Mauriac brings back Thérèse Desqueyroux for a cameo apperance in *Ce qui était perdu* as well as devoting two stories, "Thérèse à l'hôtel" and "Thérèse chez le docteur," and another novel, *La Fin de la nuit,* to her later on in the 1930s. Vast *roman-fleuve* cycles by other novelists include: *Jean Christophe* (1906–12) and *L'Ame enchantée* (1922–33) by Romain Rolland; *Les Hommes de bonne volonté* (1932–47) by Jules Romains; *Les Thibault* (1922–40) by Roger Martin du Gard; *Hauts-Ponts* (1932–35) by Jacques de Lacretelle; and *Vie et aventures de Salavin* (1920–32) and *Chronique des Pasquier* (1933–45) by Georges Duhamel. Of course, Proust's *A la recherche de temps perdu* can also be seen as a *roman-fleuve.*

8. Jacques Monférier, *François Mauriac du "Noeud de vipères" à "La Pharisienne"* (Paris: Champion, 1985). The most complete discussion of the novel in English is John Flower's *A Critical Commentary on Mauriac's "Le Noeud de vipères"* (London: Macmillan, 1969). See also Robert Denommé, *"The Vipers' Tangle:* Relative and Absolute Values," *Renascence* 17, no. 1 (1963): 32–39.

9. Jean Lacouture also provides further information on this subject in his biography of Mauriac, 267.

10. See Roger Pons, "*Le Mystère Frontenac* ou le rayonnement d'une mère," in his *Procès de l'amour: études littéraires* (Paris: Casterman, 1955), 183–93, for a detailed study of the mother–son love relationship. Of more recent interest is Claude Dirick, "Une Approche plurielle du *Mystère Frontenac*," TCERFM, 27 (1990), 31–50.

Chapter Five

1. See Kenneth L. Woodward, *Making Saints: How the Catholic Church Determines Who Becomes a Saint, Who Doesn't, and Why* (New York: Simon and Schuster, 1990).

2. Georges Bernanos, *Oeuvres romanesques* (Paris: Gallimard, 1961), 221.

3. In this respect, he reminds us of Louis in *Noeud de vipères*, who finds it convenient to blame his less edifying character traits on heredity.

4. For further reading on this novel, see J. E. Flower, *"Les Anges noirs" de François Mauriac: esquisse critique* (Paris: Archives des Lettres Modernes, 1969). A perceptive analysis of the theme of freedom is found in Laurence M. Porter, "Demonic Possession and the Problem of Freedom in Mauriac's *Les Anges noirs*," *Claudel Studies* 13, no. 2 (1986): 57–65. See also Liliane Fenech, *"Les Anges noirs:* Le Mensonge à la source du mal," *TCERFM* 28 (1990): 37–50.

5. A copy of Gide's open letter to Mauriac can be found in *ORTC*, 2:832–35.

6. See, for example, his article entitled "Le Romancier peut se renouveler par le théâtre et le cinéma," *Paris-Soir*, 25 November 1937, reprinted in *ORTC*, 3:962–63. After 25 years of writing novels, creating a play like *Asmodeé* made Mauriac feel "young" again.

7. Information about the commercial success of *La Pharisienne* is found in Jean Touzot's excellent study, *Mauriac sous l'Occupation* (Paris: La Manufacture, 1990), 13. Claude Mauriac's diary records under the date of 30 July 1941 that the authorities had banned the publication of any articles and reviews about *La Pharisienne*. See Claude Mauriac, *Le Temps immobile 2: Les Espaces imaginaires* (Paris: Grasset, 1975), 229–30. Thus, the only written commentary on the novel was the lengthy article by Pierre Drieu La Rochelle, the editor of the collaborationist *NRF*. It typifies the reaction of those who saw Mauriac as an enemy, and his novel as a threat to the regime in power. See Pierre Drieu La Rochelle, "Mauriac," *NRF* 331 (September 1941): 343–50.

8. Maurice Schumann, "Trois Journées chez Mauriac," *Revue des deux mondes*, June 1982, 606. Hereafter cited in text. Jean Lacouture mentions in passing the possibility of a political interpretation of *La Pharisienne*, but does not develop the idea (*Mauriac*, 369).

9. See also Jean-Paul Sartre, "M. François Mauriac et la liberté," *NRF*,

February 1939, 212–32. The article appeared later in *Situations,* vol. 1 (Paris: Gallimard, 1951), 36–57. Further commentary on this controversy can be found in Paul Croc, "François Mauriac et la technique du point de vue," *CFM* 2 (1975): 26–43; and Philip Thody, "J.-P. Sartre as a Literary Critic," *London Magazine* 7 (1960): 61–64.

10.   The relationship between the two writers is described and analyzed by Bernard Chochon, "Le Diable et le Bon Dieu: Sartre et Mauriac," in *François Mauriac 3: Mauriac et son temps* (Paris: Les Lettres Modernes, 1980), 97–111. Chochon points out that Sartre never responded directly to Mauriac's many barbs in the postwar years. It is also worth noting that Madeleine Chapsal asked Sartre in a newspaper interview in 1960 if he still thought that Mauriac was not a novelist. He answered: "I think that I would be more flexible today, since the essential quality of the novel must be to provoke involvement and interest, and I would be much less finicky about the methods employed. . . . You always find a way to say what you want, and the author is always present." Quoted in Chochon, 109.

11.   Mauriac, reminiscing about Sartre's attack on his work in 1939, wrote in *Mémoires intérieurs (OA,* 527): "I belong to that group of people who, on death's door, are brought back to life by Extreme Unction. Because of this childish attack, I was much more careful with the book that I was working on at the time and *La Pharisienne,* of all my books, is the one in which the signs of haste are the least evident. And since it was understood best by Protestants, especially in Sweden, I am perhaps indebted to a certain extent to the author of *La Putain respectueuse* for my Nobel Prize."

12.   M. Puybaraud joins a long list of Mauriac's characters who are former seminarians. Among them are Blaise Coûture of *Asmodée,* Gabriel Gradère of *Les Anges noirs,* and Claude Favereau of *La Chair et le sang.*

13.   It is interesting to note that the relationship between Brigitte and Dr. Gellis, in which there seems to be so much mutual understanding, replicates the many theological positions shared by Jansenism and Calvinism.

14.   It should also be recalled that he continued to haunt Mauriac for many years to come. For this reason he reappears again as one of the principal characters in *L'Agneau* (1954).

15.   Georges Bernanos, *Journal d'un curé de campagne* (Paris: Plon, 1936). There is a curious parallel between the fictional portrayal of the priest by Mauriac and Bernanos at this time. As mentioned in chapter 4, Bernanos's Abbé Donissan of *Sous le soleil de Satan* had helped to inspire the portrait of Alain Forcas in *Les Anges noirs.* But could Mauriac have also influenced Bernanos? For example, could *Le Noeud de vipères* (1932) have served as a model for Bernanos's *Journal d'un curé de campagne,* since the diary technique, which chronicles the saving of a soul, is essential to both?

16.   "A propos du *Journal d'un curé de campagne,*" *Gringoire,* 24 April 1936.

17.   Jacques Monférier, "Absence et présence de François Mauriac dans *La Pharisienne,*" *Australian Journal of French Studies,* 22, no. 2 (1985): 167–74.

Monférier's longer study of Mauriac's novels is also illuminating for our understanding of this novel.

Chapter Six

1. Because the novel is so widely read in secondary school classrooms, quite a bit of scholarly attention has been paid to it. Of significant interest is the volume edited by Roland Desné, *Lectures du "Sagouin"* (Reims: Presses Universtaires de Reims, 1987). See also Henri Laru, "Points de vue et modalités du discours dans *Le Sagouin* de François Mauriac," *Ecole des lettres* 83 (1991): 41–47; and Jacques Monférier, "Les Eléments pathétiques dans *Le Sagouin* de François Mauriac," in *Cent ans de littérature française 1850–1950: Mélanges offerts à Jacques Robichon,* ed. Martine Bercot et al. (Paris: Sedes, 1982), 243–48.

2. See "Postface à *Galigaï,*" *ORTC,* 4:450.

3. In two other novels, it is the male who causes revulsion: in *La Chair et le sang,* the unattractive Augustin is led along by May, who cannot take his love seriously, in part because he is so physically repulsive; and in *Le Baiser au lépreux* Jean inspires feelings of disgust in his wife, Noémi.

4. See "Communion of Saints," in *The New Catholic Encyclopedia,* 4:41–43. This doctrine reflects an ancient Catholic belief and is expressed in the Apostles' Creed in the expression "credo in sanctorum communionem." This doctrine emphasizes the "solidarity and vital interdependence of all members of the church" and is based on the notion that among baptized believers there is a "horizontal sharing of goods and life."

5. André Séailles, "La Problématique de la grâce dans *L'Agneau,*" *Revue des lettres modernes* 516–522 (1977): 25–42. See also Liliane Fenech, "Approche christique dans *L'Agneau,*" *TCERFM* 26 (1989): 7–20.

6. Julian Moynihan, "Maltaverne," *New York Times Book Review,* 28 June 1970, sec. 7, 3.

7. In *Le Mystere Frontenac,* he had written: "Everything is true in it, but it is a novel" (*ORTC,* 2:885).

Chapter Seven

1. François Durand, "Le Théâtre de Mauriac," *La Licorne* 11 (1986): 17.

2. Mauriac grudgingly admits that he might be dramatizing the influence of the opera on his work when he tells us that "the opera is the most artificial and most false of all the genres," and then goes on to wonder if it might actually have been "Mozart's adorable music" that enthralled him.

3. Mauriac expressed this hope to start a new career in the theater in the article entitled "Le Romancier peut se renouveler par le théâtre et par le cinéma," *Paris-Soir,* 25 November 1937. It is reprinted in *ORTC,* 3:962–63.

4. André Séailles, "François Mauriac et Jean Racine, ou l'enfer des mal-aimés," in *François Mauriac,* ed. Jean Touzot (Paris: L'Herne, 1985), 299.

5.   See *ORTC*, 3:1108–9, for Jacques Petit's discussion of this subject. See also Caroline Mauriac, ed., *Lettres d'une vie* (Paris: Grasset, 1981), 97, 396.

6.   No link of any other kind has been established between Mauriac and Alain-René Lesage (1668–1747), who is best known for his satirical comedy *Turcaret* (1709) and for his picaresque romance in four volumes, *Gil Blas* (1715–1735). *Le Diable boiteux* (1707) was written in imitation of an earlier Spanish novel, Guevara's *El Diablo cojuelo*, also in the picaresque mode. After Asmodée, the "limping devil" of the title, is released from a bottle where he has been held captive, he diverts his benefactor by lifting the roofs off the houses of some of Madrid's finest families to show what is going on within. Lesage's intent was to satirize the Parisian society of the day.

7.   Cocteau's plays set in Greek antiquity are *Orphée* (1926), *Antigone* (1928), and *La Machine infernale* (1934). Giraudoux's major works set in antiquity are *La Guerre de Troie n'aura pas lieu* (1935) and *Electre* (1937). Sartre's play *Les Mouches* (1943) is set in antiquity, as are Anouilh's *Eurydice* (1941), *Antigone* (1944), and *Médée* (1953).

8.   Pol Gaillard, "Chronique Théâtrale: *Les Mal-Aimés* de François Mauriac," *La Pensée*, March 1945, 110–14.

9.   André Séailles, *Mauriac* (Paris: Bordas, 1972), 139. Mauriac also received sympathetic reviews from his friend Robert Brisson, in *Le Figaro* (1 March 1945), and from Robert Kemp in *Le Monde* (10 March 1945). Of interest is the reproach made a few years later by the philosopher/playwright Gabriel Marcel, who questioned the setting of the play in the Landes region. Since Mauriac was writing in the Racinian mode and presumably wanted to make a generally valid statement about human nature, Marcel wondered why he did not use an Athenian setting, suggesting that Mauriac was perhaps afraid of competing directly with the playwrights of the day. See Gabriel Marcel, "Notes sur le théâtre de François Mauriac," *La Table ronde*, January 1953, 126.

10.   See "Le Théâtre et l'idée que je m'en fais," *Conferencia*, 15 January 1947. Most of this lecture was reprinted in the preface to volume 11 of *OC*. The complete text appears in *ORTC*, 4:975–85. This quote can be found in *ORTC*, 4:983.

11.   "Pourquoi j'ai écrit *Passage du Malin*" was delivered orally on 29 January 1948 and published in *Conferencia* on 15 June 1948. In this lecture there is a strong note of bitterness and disillisionment with the theater. It marks one of Mauriac's low points during the existentialist era, when his work seemed to be so terribly out of step with the times.

12.   François Durand, "Le Théâtre de Mauriac," *La Licorne* 11 (1986): 17.

13.   Caroline Mauriac, *Lettres d'une vie* (Paris: Grasset, 1982), 349.

14.   Lacouture, *Mauriac*, 205. It should be noted that scholarly interest in Mauriac's theater continues unabated. See André Séailles, ed., *Mauriac et le théâtre* (Paris: Klincksieck, 1993). This collection of more than 20 articles on Mauriac's theater from a wide variety of points of view will perhaps lead to a revival of one or more of his plays.

15. See Jacques Monférier, ed., *La Poésie de François Mauriac* (Paris: Minard, 1975). Selections from Mauriac's poetry have been published most recently in an anthology entitled *Le Feu secret,* ed. Jean-Louis Curtis (Paris: Orphée/La Différence, 1992).

16. See the "Notice" to *Le Sang d'Atys (ORTC,* 3:1418–20).

Selected Bibliography

PRIMARY WORKS

The following list of Mauriac's writings provides a selected bibliography of his published works. With the exception of the Collected Writings, primary works are listed chronologically within each genre.

Collected Writings

Oeuvres complètes. 12 vols. Paris: Arthème Fayard, 1950–56.
Oeuvres romanesques et théâtrales complètes. Edited by Jacques Petit. 4 vols. Paris: Gallimard, Editions de la Pléiade, 1978–85.
Oeuvres autobiographiques. Edited by François Durand. Paris: Gallimard, Editions de la Pléiade, 1990.

Bloc-Notes I: Bloc-Notes 1952–1957. Paris: Flammarion, 1958.
Bloc-Notes II: Le Nouveau Bloc-Notes 1958–1960. Paris: Flammarion, 1961.
Bloc-Notes III: Le Nouveau Bloc-Notes 1961–1964. Paris Flammarion, 1965.
Bloc-Notes IV: Le Nouveau Bloc-Notes 1965–1967. Paris: Grasset, 1970.
Bloc-Notes V: Le Dernier Bloc-Notes 1968–1970. Paris: Grasset, 1971.
Bloc-Notes 1952–1970. Edited by Jean Touzot. 5 vols. Paris: Seuil/Points, 1993.

Journal I. Paris: Grasset, 1934.
Journal II. Paris: Grasset, 1937.
Journal III. Paris: Grasset, 1939.
Journal IV. Paris: Flammarion, 1950.
Journal V. Paris: Flammarion, 1956. Excerpts from vols. 1–3 translated as *Second Thoughts: Reflections on Literature and Life.* Cleveland: World, 1961.

Mémoires politiques. Paris: Grasset, 1967.

D'autres et moi. Edited by Keith Goesch. Paris: Grasset, 1966. Prefaces to books by others.
Les Paroles restent. Edited by Keith Goesch. Paris: Grasset, 1985. Interviews.
Paroles perdues et retrouvées. Edited by Keith Goesch. Paris: Grasset, 1986. Lectures and other formal public statements.

Fiction

L'Enfant chargé de chaînes. Paris: Grasset, 1913. Translated by Gerard Hopkins as *Young Man in Chains.* London: Eyre and Spottiswoode, 1961. New York: Farrar, Straus and Cudahy, 1963.

La Robe prétexte. Paris: Grasset, 1914. Translated by Gerard Hopkins as *The Stuff of Youth.* London: Eyre and Spottiswoode, 1960.

La Chair et le sang. Paris: Emile Paul, 1920. Translated by Gerard Hopkins as *Flesh and Blood.* London: Eyre and Spottiswoode, 1954. New York: Farrar, Straus, 1955.

Préséances. Paris: Emile Paul, 1921. Translated by Gerard Hopkins as *Questions of Precedence.* London: Eyre and Spottiswoode, 1958. New York: Farrar, Straus, 1959.

Le Baiser au lépreux. Paris: Grasset, 1922. Translated by James Whitall as *The Kiss to the Leper.* London: Heinemann, 1923. Translated by Lewis Galantière with *Genitrix* as *The Family.* New York: Covici-Friede, 1930. Translated by Gerard Hopkins as *A Kiss for the Leper* and published with *Genitrix* under the title *A Kiss for the Leper and Genitrix.* London: Eyre and Spottiswoode, 1950.

Le Fleuve de feu. Paris: Grasset, 1923. Translated by Gerard Hopkins as *The River of Fire.* London: Eyre and Spottiswoode, 1954.

Genitrix. Paris: Grasset, 1923. Translated by Lewis Galantière with *Le Baiser au lépreux* as *The Family.* New York: Covici-Friede, 1930. Translated by Gerard Hopkins with *Le Baiser au lépreux* as *A Kiss for the Leper and Genitrix.* London: Eyre and Spottiswoode, 1950.

Le Désert de l'amour. Paris: Grasset, 1925. Translated by Samuel Putnam as *The Desert of Love.* New York: Covici-Friede, 1929. Translated by Gerard Hopkins with *Le Mal* as *The Desert of Love.* London: Eyre and Spottiswoode, 1949 and New York: Pellegrini and Cudahy, 1951.

Un Homme de lettres. Paris: Lapina, 1926.

Thérèse Desqueyroux. Paris: Grasset, 1927. Translated by Eric Sutton as *Thérèse.* New York: Boni and Liveright, 1928. Translated by Gerard Hopkins with *La Fin de la Nuit,* "Thérèse chez le docteur," and "Thérèse à l'hôtel" as *Thérèse: A Portrait in Four Parts.* London: Eyre and Spottiswoode, 1947. New York: Henry Holt, 1947. New York: Farrar, Straus, 1951.

Destins. Paris: Grasset, 1928. Translated by Eric Sutton as *Destinies.* New York: Covici-Friede, 1929. Translated by Gerard Hopkins as *Lines of Life.* London: Eyre and Spottiswoode, 1949. New York: Farrar, Straus, 1957.

Le Démon de la connaissance. Paris: Trémois, 1928.

La Nuit du bourreau de soi-même. Paris: Flammarion, 1929.

Trois récits. Paris: Grasset, 1929.

Ce qui était perdu. Paris: Grasset, 1930. Translated by Harold F. Kynaston-Snell as *Suspicion.* London: Burns, Oates and Washbourne, 1931. Translated by J. H. F. McEwen as *That Which Was Lost* and published with the Gerard Hopkins translation of *Les Anges noirs* under the title *That Which Was Lost.* London: Eyre and Spottiswoode, 1951.

Le Noeud de vipères. Paris: Grasset, 1932. Translated by Warre B. Wells as *Vipers' Tangle.* London: Golancz, 1933. New York: Sheed and Ward, 1933. Translated by Gerard Hopkins as *The Knot of Vipers.* London: Eyre and Spottiswoode, 1951.

Le Drôle. Paris: Hartmann, 1933. Translated by Anne Carter as *The Holy Terror.* London: Jonathan Cape, 1964. New York: Funk and Wagnalls, 1967.

Le Mystère Frontenac. Paris: Grasset, 1933. Translated by Gerard Hopkins as *The Frontenac Mystery.* London: Eyre and Spottiswoode, 1952. Translated by Gerard Hopkins as *The Frontenacs.* New York: Farrar, Straus, 1961.

Le Mal. Paris: Grasset, 1935. Translated by Gerard Hopkins with *Le Désert de l'amour* as *The Desert of Love.* London: Eyre and Spottiswoode, 1949. New York: Pellegrini and Cudahy, 1951. The same translation was published with *Le Sagouin* as *The Weakling and the Enemy.* New York: Pellegrini and Cudahy, 1952.

La Fin de la nuit. Paris: Grasset, 1935. Translated by Gerard Hopkins with *Thérèse Desqueyroux* as *The End of the Night* and published with two stories as *Thérèse: A Portrait in Four Parts.* London: Eyre and Spottiswoode, 1947. New York: Henry Holt, 1947. New York: Farrar, Straus, 1951.

Les Anges noirs. Paris: Grasset, 1936. Translated by Gerard Hopkins as *The Mask of Innocence.* New York: Farrar, Straus and Young, 1953. Translated by Gerard Hopkins as *The Dark Angels* and published with J. H. F. McEwen's translation of *Ce qui était perdu* under the title *That Which Was Lost.* London: Eyre and Spottiswoode, 1951.

Plongées. Paris: Grasset, 1938. Translation by Gerard Hopkins of two of the five stories,"Thérèse chez le docteur" and "Thérèse à l'hôtel," was published with *Thérèse Desqueyroux* as *Thérèse.* London: Eyre and Spottiswoode, 1947. New York: Henry Holt, 1947. New York: Farrar, Straus, 1951.

Les Chemins de la mer. Paris: Grasset 1939. Translated by Gerard Hopkins as *The Unknown Sea.* London: Eyre and Spottiswoode, 1948. New York: Farrar, Straus, 1948.

La Pharisienne. Paris: Grasset, 1941. Translated by Gerard Hopkins as *A Woman of the Pharisees.* London: Eyre and Spottiswoode, 1946. New York: Farrar, Straus, 1946.

Le Sagouin. Paris-Geneva: La Palatine-Plon, 1951. Translated by Gerard Hopkins as *The Little Misery.* London: Eyre and Spottiswoode, 1952. Translated by Gerard Hopkins with *Le Mal* as *The Weakling and the Enemy.* New York: Pellegrini and Cudahy, 1952.

Galigaï. Paris: Flammarion, 1952. Translated by Gerard Hopkins as *The Loved and the Unloved.* London: Eyre and Spottiswoode, 1953. New York: Pellegrini and Cudahy, 1953.

L'Agneau. Paris: Flammarion, 1954. Translated by Gerard Hopkins as *The Lamb.* London: Eyre and Spottiswoode, 1955; and New York: Farrar, Straus and Cudahy, 1956.

Un Adolescent d'autrefois. Paris: Flammarion, 1969. Translated by Jean Stewart as *Maltaverne.* London: Eyre and Spottiswoode, 1970. New York: Farrar, Straus and Giroux, 1970.

Maltaverne. Paris: Flammarion 1972.

Plays

Asmodée. Paris: Grasset, 1938. Translated by Basil Bartlett as *The Intruder*. London: Secker and Warburg, 1939.
Les Mal-aimés. Paris: Grasset, 1945.
Passage du malin. Paris: Grasset, 1948.
Le Feu sur la terre. Paris: Grasset, 1951.

Poetry

Les Mains jointes. Paris: Falque, 1909.
L'Adieu à l'adolescence. Paris: Stock, 1911.
Orages. Paris: Champion, 1925.
Le Sang d'Atys. Paris: Grasset, 1940.

Biographies

La Vie de Jean Racine. Paris: Plon, 1928.
Blaise Pascal et sa soeur Jacqueline. Paris: Hachette, 1931.
La Vie de Jésus. Paris: Flammarion, 1936. Translated by Julie Kernam as *The Life of Jesus*. London: Hodder and Stoughton, 1937. New York: David McKay, 1937.
Sainte Marguerite de Cortone. Paris: Flammarion, 1945. Translated by Barbara Wall as *Margaret of Cortona*. London: Burns, Oates and Washbourne, 1948. Translated by Bernard Frechtman as *Saint Margaret of Cortona*. New York: Philosophical Library, 1948.
Le Fils de l'homme. Paris: Grasset, 1958. Translated by Bernard Murchland as *The Son of Man*. Cleveland: World, 1960.
De Gaulle. Paris: Grasset, 1964. Translated by Richard Howard as *De Gaulle*. Garden City: Doubleday, 1966.

Autobiographical Writing

Dieu et Mammon. Paris: Capitole, 1929. Translated by Bernard and Barbara Wall as *God and Mammon*. London and New York: Sheed and Ward, 1936.
Souffrances et bonheur du chrétien. Paris: Grasset, 1931. Translated by Harold Evans as *Anguish and Joy of the Christian Life*. Wilkes-Barre, Pa.: Dimension, 1964.
Commencements d'une vie. Paris: Grasset, 1932.
La Rencontre avec Barrès. Paris: La Table ronde, 1945.
Du côté de chez Proust. Paris: La Table ronde, 1947. Translated by Elsie Pell as *Proust's Way*. New York: Philosophical Library, 1950.
Journal d'un homme de trente ans. Fribourg: L.U.F., 1948.
Mes Grands Hommes. Monaco: Rocher, 1949. Translated by Elsie Pell as *Great Men*. London: Rockliff, 1949. Also translated by Elsie Pell as *Men I Hold Great*. New York: Philosophical Library, 1951.

La Pierre d'achoppement. Monaco: Rocher, 1951. Translated by Elsie Pell as *The Stumbling Block*. New York: Philosophical Library, 1952.
Mémoires intérieurs. Paris: Flammarion, 1959. Translated by Gerard Hopkins as *Mémoires intérieurs*. New York: Farrar, Straus and Cudahy, 1960.
Ce que je crois. Paris: Grasset, 1962. Translated by Wallace Fowlie as *What I Believe*. New York: Farrar, Straus, 1963.
Nouveaux Mémoires intérieurs. Paris: Flammarion, 1965. Translated by Herma Briffault as *The Inner Presence: Recollections of My Spiritual Life*. Indianapolis, Ind.: Bobbs-Merrill, 1968.

Literary Criticism

Proust. Paris: Lesage, 1926.
Voltaire contre Pascal. Paris: La Belle Page, 1930.
Trois grands hommes devant Dieu. Paris: Capitole, 1930. A study of Molière, Rousseau, and Flaubert.
René Bazin. Paris: Alcan, 1931.
Le Romancier et ses personnages. Paris: Corrêa, 1933.
Lettres ouvertes. Monaco: Rocher, 1952. Translated by Mario A. Pei as *Letters on Art and Literature*. New York: Philosophical Library, 1953.

Works of Piety and Apologetics

De quelques coeurs inquiéts: Petits Essais de psychologie religieuse. Paris: Société Littéraire, 1920. Contains discussions of Henri Lacordaire, Maurice de Guérin, Charles Baudelaire, Henri-Frédéric Amiel, and Henri Beyle.
Divagations sur Saint-Sulpice. Paris: Champion, 1928.
Supplément au traité de la concupisence de Bossuet. Paris: Trianon, 1928.
Paroles en Espagne. Paris: Hartmann, 1930.
Le Jeudi Saint. Paris: Flammarion, 1931. Translated by Harold F. Kynaston-Snell as *Maundy Thursday*. London: Burns, Oates and Washbourne, 1932. Translated by Marie-Louise Dufrénoy as *The Eucharist: The Mystery of Holy Thursday*. New York: Sheed and Ward, 1933. Translated by Marie-Louise Dufrénoy as *Holy Thursday: An Intimate Remembrance*. Manchester, N.H.: Sophia Institute, 1989.
Pèlerins de Lourdes. Paris: Plon, 1933.
Terres franciscaines. Paris: Plon, 1950.
Paroles catholiques. Paris: Plon, 1954. Translated by Edward H. Flannery as *Words of Faith*. New York: Philosophical Library, 1955.

SECONDARY SOURCES

Alyn, Marc. *François Mauriac*. Paris: Seghers, 1960. Published in the "Poètes d'aujourd'hui" series, this is still the best and most comprehensive introduction to Mauriac's poetry.

Anglard, Véronique. *François Mauriac: "Thérèse Desqueyroux".* Paris: PUF, 1992. This useful paperback is published in the "Etudes littéraires" series. Any serious attempt to unlock the many possible meanings of this novel should take advantage of the keys offered by Anglard's study.

Canérot, Marie-Françoise. *Mauriac après 1930: Le Roman dénoué.* Paris: Sedes, 1985. Argues convincingly that Mauriac's novels become richer and more complex after 1930.

Cormeau, Nelly, *L'Art de François Mauriac.* Paris: Grasset, 1951. Reliable, scholarly, but generally uncritical study of Mauriac, in which he is defended against Sartre's attacks.

Fabrègues, Jean de. *Mauriac.* Paris: Plon, 1971. This early biography of Mauriac illuminates beautifully the "Catholic" aspect of his life and work.

Flower, J[ohn] E[rnest]. *Intention and Achievement: A Study of the Novels of François Mauriac.* Oxford: Clarendon, 1969. Argues the now largely rejected thesis that Mauriac reaches the pinnacle of his artistic achievement with Le Noeud de vipères, and that what follows is of less importance.

Glénisson, Emile. *L'Amour dans les romans de François Mauriac: Essai de critique psychologique.* Paris: Editions Universitaires, 1970. An unsympathetic study that reproaches Mauriac for repeating the same basic problems over and over again in each novel, avoiding monotony only by varying the circumstances slightly in each book.

Jarrett-Kerr, Martin. *François Mauriac.* London: Bowes and Bowes, 1954. New Haven: Yale University Press, 1954. This brief study offers a succinct and dependable introduction to Mauriac's work, especially to the novels through the mid-1930s.

Jenkins, Cecil. *Mauriac.* London: Oliver and Boyd, 1965. Argues in vain that Mauriac's greatest works date from the 1920s and that after his conversion he lost his spontaneity and freedom as a novelist.

Kushnir, Slava. M. *Mauriac journaliste.* Paris: Lettres Modernes, 1979. This ground-breaking study of what for many readers is the most important aspect of Mauriac's total oeuvre is still quite valuable.

Lacouture, Jean. *Mauriac.* Paris: Seuil, 1980. Comprehensive, critical, and fair-minded biography of Mauriac.

Majault, Joseph. *Mauriac et l'art du roman.* Paris: Laffont, 1946. Analysis by a young Catholic critic, novelist, and poet, of the style and structure of Mauriac's novels through the late 1930s. A long chapter treats Sartre's attack on Mauriac's novels.

Maloney, Michael F. *Francois Mauriac: A Critical Study.* Denver: Swallow, 1958. This is still one of the better short introductions to Mauriac in English.

Monférier, Jacques. *François Mauriac du "Noeud de vipères" à "La Pharisienne."* Paris: Champion, 1985. A seminal study that has helped to refocus critical attention on the novels of the 1930s.

Paine, Ruth Benson. *Thematic Analysis of François Mauriac's "Genitrix," "Le Désert de l'amour" and "Le Noeud de vipères."* University, Miss.: Romance Monographs, 1976. Clear and useful analysis of the principal themes in three novels published during the creative decade (1923–33).

Pell, Elsie. *François Mauriac: In Search of the Future.* New York: Philosophical Library, 1947. Dated but moving testimony to Mauriac by one of his American translators, written at a time when his reputation in the United States was at its apogee.

Prou, Suzanne. *Mauriac et la jeune fille.* Paris: Ramsay, 1982. A novelist and essayist offers an original and at times heartwarming account of her reading of Mauriac's novels.

Quoniam, Théodore. *François Mauriac: Du péché à la rédemption.* Paris: Téqui, 1984. A subjective and nonscholarly, though rich and intriguing, evaluation of Mauriac's oeuvre.

Robichon, Jacques. *François Mauriac, écrivain français.* Paris and Brussels: Editions Universitaires, 1953. This is still one of the best introductions to Mauriac's work through the end of World War II. Sees Mauriac as one of a handful of France's naturally born novelists, who succeeded in his day in creating a fictional universe as unique and recognizable as Balzac's in the nineteenth century.

Smith, Maxwell A. *François Mauriac.* New York: Twayne, 1970. A somewhat dated but clear and authoritative study of Mauriac's career.

Speaight, Robert. *François Mauriac: A Study of the Writer and the Man.* London: Chatto and Windus, 1976. This was the first Mauriac biography to be published and is still the only one in English. Although outdated on several minor points, it remains one of the best entry points for an English-speaking student of Mauriac.

Touzot, Jean. *Mauriac avant Mauriac, 1913–1922.* Paris: Flammarion, 1977. Important study of the early years of Mauriac's career, including a number of hitherto unpublished or long neglected pieces.

———. *La Planète Mauriac: Figure d'analogie et roman.* Paris: Klincksieck, 1985. Study of rhetorical structures and largely unconscious mental imagery in Mauriac's fiction.

———. *François Mauriac: Une Configuration romanesque.* Paris: Lettres Modernes, 1985. Shows the hidden and deeply embedded mental structures that lie at the heart of Mauriac's fiction.

Index

The Author

David O'Connell is Professor of French at Georgia State University and has been named by the French Ministry of Culture as a *Chevalier* in the *Ordre des Palmes Académiques*. He received his Ph.D. in 1966 from Princeton University, where he was a National Woodrow Wilson Fellow, the Bergen Fellow in Romance Languages, and a National Woodrow Wilson Dissertation Fellow. He is the author of *The Teachings of Saint Louis: A Critical Text* (1972), *Les Propres de Saint Louis* (1974), *Louis-Ferdinand Céline* (1976), *The Instructions of Saint Louis: A Critical Text* (1979), and *Michel de Saint Pierre: A Catholic Novelist at the Crossroads* (1990). He is the editor of *Catholic Writers in France since 1945* (1983) and has served as review editor (1977–79) and managing editor (1987–90) of the *French Review*. He has edited more than 50 books in Twayne's World Authors series.

Gramley Library
Salem College
Winston-Salem, NC 27108